A COURSE IN PHONETICS AND SPOKEN ENGLISH

SECOND EDITION

J. SETHI

Formerly Professor of English
Central Institute of English and Foreign Languages
Hyderabad

P.V. DHAMIJA

Formerly Professor
Department of Phonetics and Spoken English
Central Institute of English and Foreign Languages
Hyderabad

PHI Learning Private Limited

Delhi-110092
2025

In fond memory of ***Shri Asoke K. Ghosh*** *(October 1942 – February 2024), Founder Chairman and Managing Director of PHI Learning, whose vision endlessly inspires.*

The Legacy Continues....

Published by Pushpita Ghosh, PHI Learning Private Limited, Rimjhim House, 111, Patparganj Industrial Estate, Delhi-110092 and Printed by Glorious Printer, Delhi-110092.

₹495.00

A COURSE IN PHONETICS AND SPOKEN ENGLISH, Second Edition
by J. Sethi and P.V. Dhamija

ISBN-978-81-203-1495-5 (Print Book)
ISBN-978-93-90669-90-5 (e-Book)

The export rights of the book are vested solely with the publisher.

Contents

Preface

In the preface to the first edition, while acknowledging that there was always scope for further improvement of this course, we invited constructive comments and tangible suggestions. The response to that has been quite encouraging, and we express our sincere gratitude to all those who have given us suggestions, which, more than any other single factor, has motivated us to bring out this revised edition.

Other factors which encouraged us to revise the book include: a better appreciation now of students' needs as reflected in the demands of universities, and a need for updating the subject-matter. In recognition of the former, we have now included a new chapter on Assimilation (Chapter 14). Besides, we have replaced the Appendix to the chapter on Intonation with a section on Tones in Relation to Attitudes (Section 15.4). While updating the subject-matter, we have made quite a few refinements in the description of certain phonetic terms such as 'flaps', 'taps', 'semi-vowels', and 'hard palate', to mention but a few. Also updated in this edition are the IPA chart and the Bibliography.

Ever since its publication, the book has been in great demand. This fact, while duly encouraging us, lays upon us, at the same time, a greater responsibility to give the students the very best we can. We have endeavoured to do so and, therefore, hope that the book will be found very useful. As before, we invite valuable suggestions, which we will gratefully acknowledge.

J. Sethi
P.V. Dhamija

Preface to the First Edition

The need for learning spoken English has, over the last few decades, grown enormously all over the world. Time was when most learners of English in India, for example, could do reasonably well even without adequate proficiency in speaking the language. But this is no longer true. With the tremendous increase in the volume of international tourism, travel, and trade, and a bigger-than-ever exchange of experts in various fields and professions now, the demand for acquiring the spoken form of English has gone up considerably. People are no longer content with acquiring only the reading and writing skills of the language; they want to be able to speak it too—and speak it in a way that they are understood not only by their next-door neighbour (with whom they can use the local language anyway), but also by the English-knowing inhabitant of a distant continent. Such desire to be able to speak English intelligibly and acceptably is clearly seen in the rapid rise of the number of English-medium schools in recent years.

Such increase in the number of English-medium schools notwithstanding, a stage will perhaps never be reached when all our pupils pass out of schools with good spoken English. (The point becomes self-evident when one realizes that the large majority of our secondary-level school teachers cannot themselves speak English.) Many learners will therefore have to learn spoken English as a special subject at a later stage. In any case, the strong urge and motivation for learning spoken English also appear in later life—at a time when children grow into adults and look for attractive careers or advancement in their chosen professions. But adults cannot learn spoken English by sheer imitation; they learn it by undergoing a regular course in it. And that is what the present book offers.

There exists no language the spoken form of which can be learnt directly from its written form. This is so because no language is written exactly as it is spoken. In other words, in no language is the relationship between the sound and the spelling perfect. And in a language like English such relationship does not even begin to be satisfactory. This makes the need for a special course in spoken English all the stronger.

A course in spoken English can take the form of either a course in 'what to say' or a course in 'how to say'. The former is usually a course in English conversation, and the latter a course in English pronunciation. The former is a situationally-governed course, which aims at training the learner in how to express greetings, farewells, thanks, apologies, regrets, and so on. The latter is a course in how to say English words, phrases, and sentences. Both these courses are important, and useful. The present course is one of the latter kind—a course in English pronunciation.

On a subject like English pronunciation, there is no dearth of books.

Nevertheless, this book is not simply 'yet another' in the series. It differs from others in a number of ways. *First,* it takes into prominent account the learner of English in India (and similar other countries), and provides for him examples from certain Indian languages, and exercises and practice material specially suited to his needs. *Second,* it makes a judicious selection of the subject-matter, leaving out much of what is of no great consequence to such a learner. *Third,* it gives a summary of each chapter to facilitate recapitulation. *Fourth,* it provides numerous exercises at the end of every chapter, which not only impart practice and test what has been learnt already, but also, in several cases, stimulate fresh information. *Fifth,* it offers several conversational passages related to useful everyday situations in phonemic transcription, along with their orthographic texts, for practice by learners. *Finally,* it gives a fairly exhaustive bibliography, not so much for the student as for the teacher who would like to sharpen and update his knowledge.

The book starts with general phonetics (Chapters 1–5), then gives a brief account of general phonology (Chapters 6 and 7), after which it deals in detail with the phonetics and phonology of English (Chapters 8–14), and finally provides a few conversational passages, in phonetic script as well as ordinary spelling, for practice in reading aloud (Chapter 15). In its detailed treatment of the phonetics and phonology of English, the book provides an in-depth coverage of the sounds of English, the phonotactic (i e combinatorial) possibilities of English, and the suprasegmental features of word accent, accent and rhythm in connected speech, and intonation. Under the sounds of English, it gives not only a description of how each sound is made, but also the following: (i) sound-spelling relationship, (ii) occurrence of each sound in different positions in the word, (iii) occurrence, and even the tendencies of occurrence, of each vowel in accented or unaccented syllables, and (iv) comparison and contrast of a sound with other 'similar' sounds with which it can be confused—all with numerous examples and considerable amount of practice material, most of which are drawn from the authors' knowledge and experience of Indian learners' problems. (Many of the examples given in all chapters also constitute sizable practice material.) Under word accent are given not only a number of 'rules' of accentuation, but also a large number of accentual patterns to practise. Under accent and rhythm in connected speech, are given, besides the general rules, the tendencies of accentuation and the overriding influence of rhythm, which accounts for the emergence of weak forms and contracted forms. Under intonation, while a beginner studies the grammatical, attitudinal, and accentual functions of some selected tones, an advanced student can go beyond and learn some of the highly sophisticated uses of tones to convey finer nuances of meaning and subtler attitudes.

For a meaningful phonological description of a language like English, which has several distinct accents (i e speech forms), one has to, first of all, choose a particular accent. In this book, we have chosen RP, the Received Pronunciation of England. This choice is based not so much on the prestige that RP still enjoys in several countries, as on certain practical considerations: wider intelligibility; availability of books, dictionaries, and practice materials; availability of 'models' or 'near-models'; and the special orientation of the teacher-trainers themselves (see Chapter 8). In making this choice, it is not our expectation that every learner will turn out to be an RP speaker. This is generally not possible, and is not perhaps necessary either. All that is expected instead is that a good and motivated learner will achieve, after sustained effort for a few years, a fair degree of *approximation to RP*, so that he is easily understood all over the English-speaking world and at the same time his pronunciation is regarded as widely acceptable.

Taking these factors into account, it is hoped that this book will prove useful for all professional and non-professional courses in phonetics and spoken English. It is intended to serve the needs of the training programmes for tertiary- and secondary-level teachers, including such pre-service training as the B.Ed. programme. It will at he same time adequately meet the needs of all new postgraduate courses in English, in which English phonetics and phonology may very soon find their due place.

Throughout, we have endeavoured to ensure that the course meets the requirements of the different groups of readers already mentioned. Nevertheless, we lay no claim to perfection, and there must ever be scope for improvement in a course of this kind. Constructive comments on the book and tangible suggestions for its possible improvement will therefore be most gratefully welcome.

J. Sethi
P.V. Dhamija

1
The Organs of Speech

1.1 Introduction

For the production of speech sounds, as indeed for the production of any sounds, there must be some disturbance in the air. Such disturbance, in the case of speech sounds, is provided by the movement of certain organs of the body such as the muscles of the chest, the *vocal cords* (described later), the tongue, the lips, and so on. This disturbance, in the form of sound waves, travels to the ear of the listener, who interprets the waves as sounds.

The organs of the human body which produce speech sounds (some of which are named above) are together called *organs of speech*. Speech, according to one view, is only the secondary function of these organs, their primary functions being breathing, chewing, eating, smelling, tasting, and so on. According to another view, speech is as essential a function of these organs as are the other functions. This controversy notwithstanding, we can use the phrase *organs of speech* to refer to these organs, for this is a well-established phrase in all writings on phonetics.

The organs of speech, and their speech functions, can best be described under three systems: the *respiratory system*, the *phonatory system*, and the *articulatory system*. We now discuss these systems.

1.2 The Respiratory System

The respiratory system comprises the lungs, the muscles of the chest, and the windpipe (also called the *trachea*). The lungs, as we know, perform the function of breathing, or respiration, under the action of the muscles of the chest. Under such action, when the lungs are compressed, they throw the air out; and when they expand, they draw the outside air in. The former process is breathing *out*, or exhalation, and the latter, breathing *in*, or inhalation. In both cases, the air passes through the trachea.

1.21

The role of the respiratory system in relation to the production of speech sounds is as follows: Through the process of breathing, the system provides an airstream that acts as a source of energy. Without an airstream no amount of activity on the part of the speech organs can produce a sound. Now, it is not that only the lungs can provide an airstream for the production of speech sounds; certain other organs can do so too. But, it is the airstream provided by the lungs that *all* languages of the world use—some do so exclusively, and others mainly. Further, it is the airstream initiated by the air *exhaled* from the lungs that is chiefly used for speech production. This airstream mechanism is called *pulmonic egressive airstream mechanism*. (*Pulmonic* is the adjective from *lungs*, and *egressive airstream* means the stream of air going *out of* the lungs.) English and all other European languages, as also all Indian languages except Sindhi, use only the pulmonic egressive airstream mechanism.

1.3 The Phonatory System

The airstream released by the lungs undergoes several modifications before it goes out into the atmosphere. The first such modification is effected in the trachea. If you try to produce the sounds at the beginning of the English words *seal* and *zeal*, that is, the **s**-sound and the **z**-sound, one after the other, you will notice that there is a certain 'hum' in the **z**-sound, which is not heard in the **s**-sound. This 'hum' is the result of some modifications in the trachea, which we shall discuss in section 1.33.

1.31 The Larynx

In the upper part of the trachea is a structure called the *larynx* (see Fig. 1). Formed of cartilage and muscle, its primary function is to act as a valve: when necessary, it closes off the air from and to the lungs and also prevents food etc. from entering the trachea. Its front part is prominent in the neck, and is commonly known as the

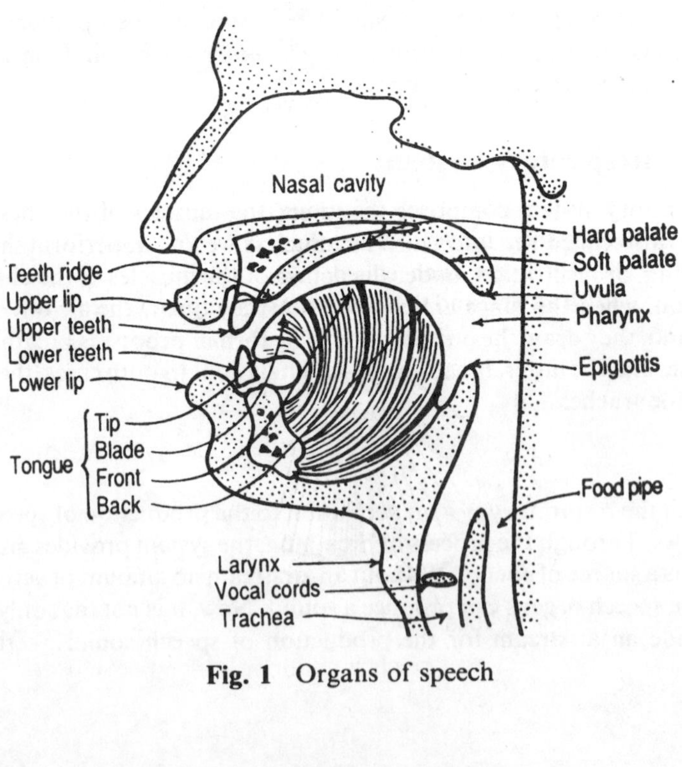

Fig. 1 Organs of speech

'Adam's apple'. Situated inside the larynx is a pair of lip-like structures, called the *vocal cords*. These are placed horizontally from front to back, joined at the front, but separated at the back. As they are separated at one end, they can assume a large number of positions. Important from among these are three positions, which are now described.

1.32 Vocal Cords Drawn Wide Apart

When the vocal cords are drawn wide apart, there is a wide opening between them. called the *glottis* (see Fig. 2). Through this opening, the air can pass freely without setting the vocal cords into vibration. This is the normal position of the

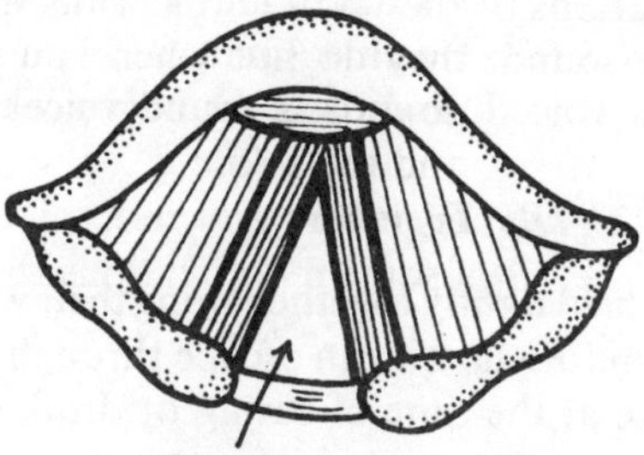

Fig. 2 Vocal cords drawn wide apart

vocal cords during the process of breathing. The speech sounds produced when the vocal cords are in this position do not have the 'hum' we spoke of earlier. They are called *voiceless* sounds. Examples of such sounds are the initial sounds in the English words *pot, ten, cot, chair, film, thin, sin, sheet, hot* and in the Hindi words फल [phəl] 'fruit', थैला ['ṭhæla] 'bag', खेल [khe:l] 'play'. (In the English words given here, some other consonants are also voiceless.)

1.33 Vocal Cords Held Loosely Together

When the vocal cords are held loosely together (Fig. 3), the air from the lungs can escape only by setting them into vibration. Such vibration imparts a 'hum' to the sounds produced, which are then called *voiced* sounds. Examples of voiced sounds are all English vowels and the initial consonants in the English words *bed,*

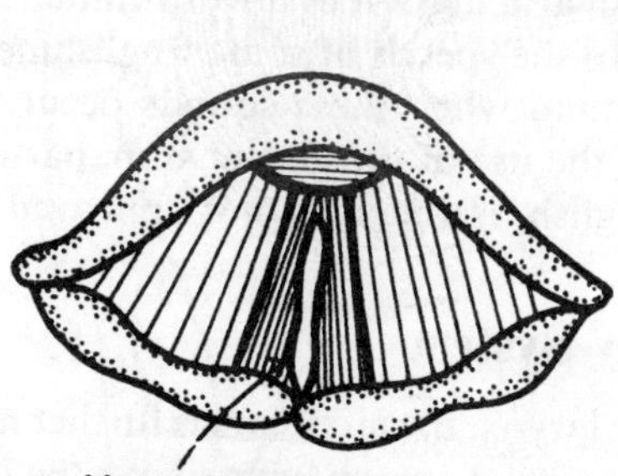

Fig. 3 Vocal cords held loosely together

dead, get, jug, men, nest, red, late, very, then, zinc, well. (In these words, some other consonants are also voiced.) All languages have voiced as well as voiceless sounds. Ordinarily, all vowels are voiced sounds; as for consonants, some are voiced, others are voiceless.

The distinction between voiceless and voiced sounds can easily be felt in the case of the sounds that can be lengthened. The **s**-sound and the **z**-sound constitute one such pair. Put your finger on your Adam's apple, and produce a prolonged **s**-sound. You will feel no vibrations on your finger. Now, perform the same experiment with the **z**-sound. This time you will feel vibrations on the finger. (A similar experiment can be performed by plugging your ears with your little fingers while producing the two sounds.) The vibrations felt on the fingers are the result of the vibrations of the vocal cords. Thus the vocal cords vibrate when you produce the **z**-sound; they do not when you produce the **s**-sound. Therefore, the **z**-sound is voiced, and the **s**-sound voiceless.

1.34 Vocal Cords Held Tightly Together

When the vocal cords are held tightly together along their whole length, the glottis is closed (Fig. 4), and therefore no air can escape through it. This is the position the vocal cords must take at the time of eating or drinking so that no food or

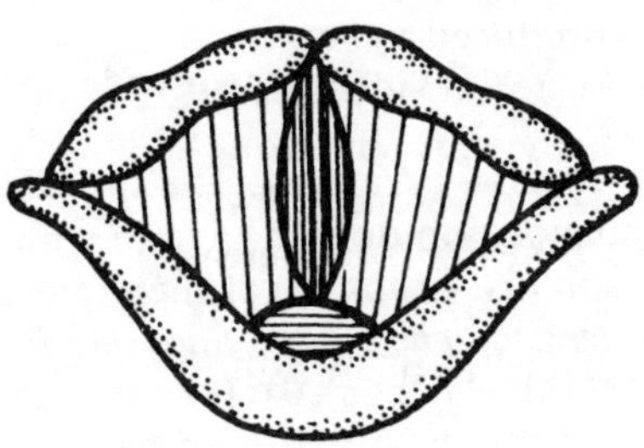

Fig. 4 Vocal cords held tightly together

liquid enters the windpipe. Proceeding from this position, when the vocal cords are suddenly drawn apart, an explosive sound called the *glottal stop* is produced. Such a glottal stop, which resembles the sound of a mild cough, may be found to occur in front of a forceful articulation of a word-initial vowel as in the English words *act, empty, uncle*. In the speech of some Englishmen, it can also occur in place of the **p**, **t**, or **k** sound when these sounds occur finally in words as in *lip, shut, sick*. (However, the use of the glottal stop, particularly in place of the **p**, **t**, and **k** sounds in English, is generally not approved of.)

1.4 The Articulatory System

After passing through the larynx, the airstream is further modified by the various shapes assumed by the organs of speech lying above the larynx, before it passes out into the atmosphere; and every such modification affects the quality of the sound produced. These organs of speech, together constituting the *articulatory system*, are now described.

1.41 The Pharynx

Extending from the top of the larynx to the hindermost part of the tongue is the *pharynx* (see Fig. 1). The shape and size of the *pharyngeal cavity* (the cavity of the pharynx) can be greatly modified by the contraction or expansion of the muscles of the pharynx, by the movement of the back of the tongue, by the position of the soft palate, and by the raising or lowering of the larynx, each such modification affecting the quality of the sound produced.

1.42

Let us now describe those parts of the articulatory system which can be seen in a mirror. This we shall do from front to back, starting with the lips.

1.43 The Lips

The lips play an important part in the production of certain speech sounds. The initial sounds in the English words *pot* and *boat*, for example, are made by first closing the lips together, and then releasing the closure abruptly. The initial sound in the word *men* is produced by keeping the lips shut and allowing the air to escape through the nose. Many vowels, and the initial sound in the word *wet*, are produced by protruding the lips and rounding them, such protrusion and rounding being an important difference between the vowel sound in the word *pot* and that in the word *part*, for example: whereas for the vowel in the word *pot*, the lips are protruded and rounded, for the vowel in the word *part*, they are not. The lip position is an important factor in the production of vowels; we shall therefore discuss this in Chapter 4 in some detail.

1.44 The Teeth

Certain consonants are produced with the help of the teeth. Such are the initial sounds in the English words *think, that, fan* and *van*. So also are the Hindi sounds त*[t̪], थ[t̪h], द[d̪], ध[d̪h], and न[n̪].

Beyond the teeth, in the upper jaw, is a whole area called the *roof of the mouth*, comprising the *teeth ridge*, the *hard palate*, the *soft palate*, and the *uvula* These are described in sections 1.45–1.48.

1.45 The Teeth Ridge

The *teeth ridge* (also called the *alveolar ridge*) is the convex part of the roof of the mouth lying immediately behind the upper teeth. It can be easily felt by placing the tongue behind the upper teeth. Many consonant sounds are produced at the teeth ridge. By making a complete closure at the teeth ridge, followed by a sudden

* The diacritic 'halant' [्] has not been used in this book with the Devanagari letters representing consonant sounds.

release of the closure, one can produce the **t** and **d** sounds as in the English words *ten* and *day*. Or, by narrowing the passage of air at the teeth ridge and forcing the air out of the narrow passage, one can produce the **s** and **z** sounds that occur at the beginning of the English words *sue* and *zoo*.

1.46 The Hard Palate

Lying immediately behind the teeth ridge is a hard, bony surface, called the *hard palate* (Fig. 1). It is a curved surface leading to the highest point of the roof of the mouth. At the beginning of the curve are small corrugations that facilitate the movement of food. They also provide obstacles to the outgoing air, thus causing a hissing noise that characterizes the [s] and [ʃ] sounds as in *so* and *show*. An example of the sounds produced at the hard palate is the initial sound in the English word *yes* or the Hindi word याद [jaːd̪] 'memory'.

1.47 The Soft Palate

If you move your tongue backwards along the roof of the mouth, starting from the teeth ridge, first you will feel the bony, hard palate described above, and then, after the tongue has travelled some distance, you will feel the roof becoming suddenly soft. This soft portion of the roof is called the *soft palate* or the *velum*. It is responsible for the production of a large number of sounds such as the initial sounds in the English words *king* and *go*, and the Urdu words ख़राब[xə'raːb] 'bad' and ग़लत['ɣələt̪] 'wrong'.

In the production of the sounds mentioned above, two simultaneous actions of the soft palate are involved: one, its articulation with, or against, the back of the tongue; and two, its raising itself to make a contact with the back wall of the pharynx (see Fig. 5). When you produce the **k**-sound, under the first action, the back of the tongue makes a closure with the soft palate; under the second action, the soft palate itself is raised to make a closure with the back wall of the pharynx. The former closure is called *velar* closure, and the latter *velic* closure, both *velar*

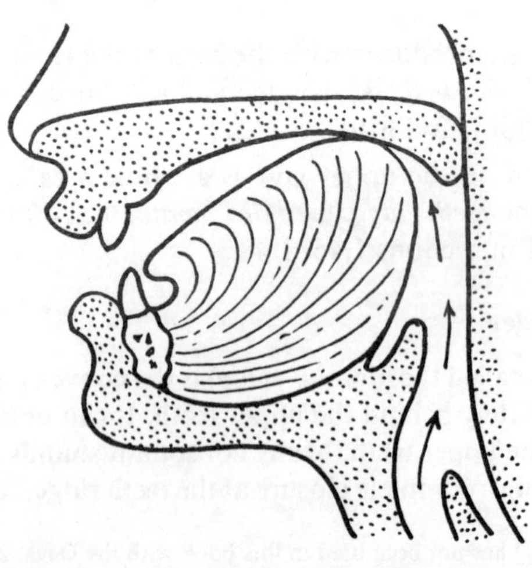

Fig. 5 Velar closure and velic closure

and *velic* being adjectives from the word *velum*. The second action of the soft palate needs to be described in some detail, which follows.

The soft palate can either be raised to make a velic closure (Fig. 5) or lowered to remove such closure (Figs. 6a, 6b). When raised, no air can escape through the nose; it can escape only through the mouth, and therefore the sounds produced in this state of the soft palate are called *oral* sounds. Examples of oral sounds are all the sounds contained in the English words *take*, *play*, *radio*, *lecture*. When lowered, the air can escape through the nose. Here two further possibilities arise: One, if there is a closure at some point in the oral passage, the air can escape through the nose *only* (see Fig. 6a); two, if there is no closure at any point in the oral passage, the air can escape through the mouth *as well as* the nose (see

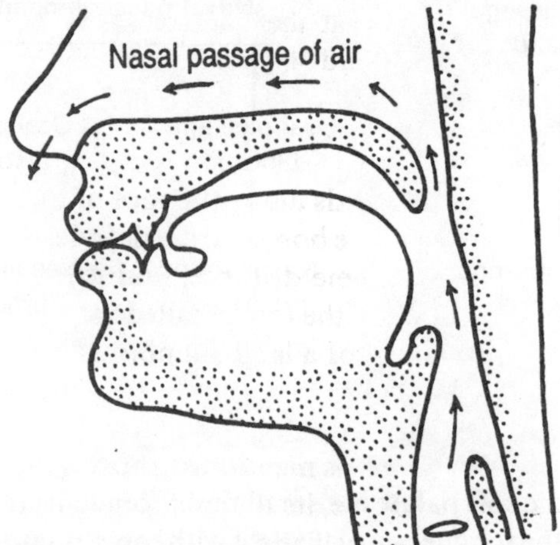

Fig. 6a Nasal passage open; oral passage closed

Fig. 6b). The sounds produced in the former position are called *nasal* sounds, and those produced in the latter position are called *nasalized* sounds. Examples

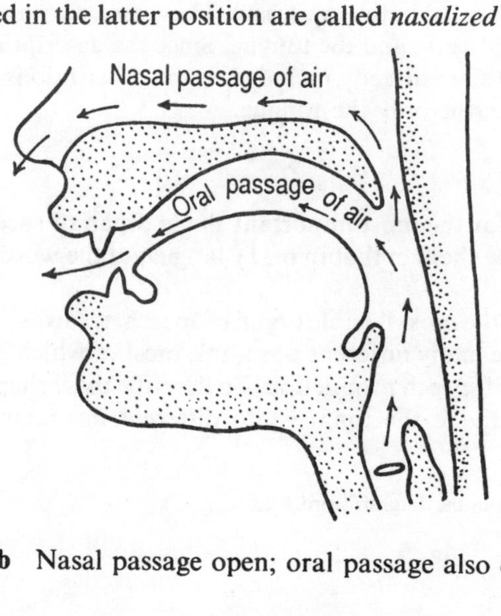

Fig. 6b Nasal passage open; oral passage also open

of the former are the final sounds in the English words *him*, *hen*, and *hang**; those of the latter are the vowel sounds in the Hindi words ईंट [ĩ:t] 'brick', सांस [sã:s] 'breath', and हैं [hæ̃] 'are'.

All the three foregoing possibilities are represented in a schematic form in Fig. 7.

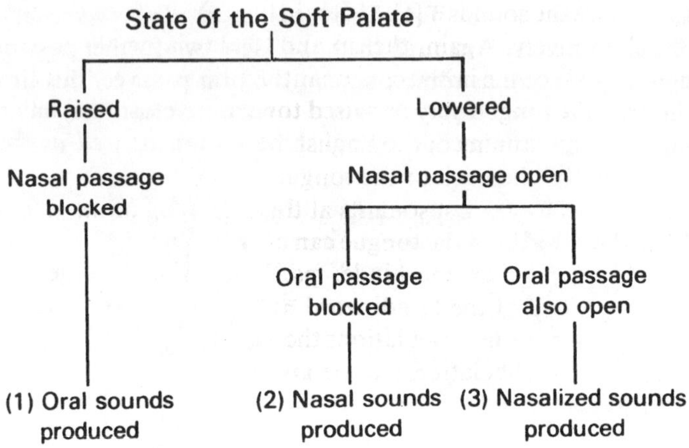

Fig. 7

1.48 The Uvula

At the very end of the soft palate is a small fleshy pendent structure known as the *uvula*. The back of the tongue can articulate with this structure to produce sounds such as the **q**-sound in the Urdu words क़रीब [qə'ri:b] 'near', क़ौम [qɔom] 'community'.

With this, the description of the roof of the mouth ends. We now describe the organs of speech located in the lower jaw. These are, starting from the front, the lower lip, the lower teeth, and the tongue. Since the descriptions of the lower lip and the lower teeth are already included in the descriptions of the lips and the teeth, we here describe only the tongue.

1.49 The Tongue

The tongue is by far the most important single organ of speech. Its importance can be judged from the fact that in many languages the word *tongue* also means 'language'.

The tongue is the most flexible organ of speech: it can assume a large number of shapes and take many different positions, most of which are significant from the point of view of speech production. To describe these shapes and positions, it is customary to divide the tongue into different imaginary parts: When the

* There is no g-sound in the English word *hang*.

tongue is in the state of rest, the part of it lying behind the lower teeth is called the *tip*, and that lying against the teeth ridge, the *blade*; the part against the hard palate is called the *front*, and that against the soft palate, the *back* (see Fig. 1). The edges of the tongue are called the *rims*.

Any part of the tongue can be raised to any height or be made to touch the roof of the mouth. Thus, the tip of the tongue and the rims may touch the upper teeth and produce the sounds त [t̪], द [d̪] as in the Hindi words तुम [t̪um] 'you' and दो [d̪o] 'two', respectively. Again, the tip and blade may make a contact with the teeth ridge to produce the initial consonants in the English words *ten*, *do*, and *no*. Or, the front of the tongue may be raised towards the hard palate to produce the consonants at the beginning of the English words *yet* and *unit*, or the vowel in the word *sea*. Similarly, the back of the tongue may be brought in contact with the soft palate to produce the consonants at the beginning of the English words *kill* and *girl*. Further, the tip of the tongue can even be curled back and the underside of it made to tap against the hinder part of the teeth ridge to produce the consonant at the end of the Hindi word तोड़ [t̪oːɽ] 'break'. These are but a few examples of the numerous articulations the tongue can make. A fuller description of each significant articulation will be given under the detailed description of vowels and consonants.

1.5 Active and Passive Articulators

Before we conclude this chapter, we must introduce an important distinction—the distinction between *active articulators* and *passive articulators*. Active articulators are those organs of speech which move from their position of rest to articulate against other organs of speech that do not (or cannot) move. The latter are called passive articulators. Thus, in the production of the **t**, **d**, **n**, **s** sounds, for example, the tip and blade of the tongue move from their position of rest to articulate against the teeth ridge. The tip and blade of the tongue are therefore the active articulator, and the teeth ridge the passive articulator. Again, in the production of the **f**-sound as in the English word *fat*, the lower lip is the active articulator and the upper teeth are the passive articulator.

As the lower jaw is movable while the upper jaw is not, the active articulators are mostly located in the lower jaw and the passive articulators in the upper jaw. A notable exception, however, is the soft palate, which is both an active and passive articulator. It is an active articulator in that it can be raised to shut the nasal passage of air to produce oral sounds. It is a passive articulator in relation to the back of the tongue (active articulator), which articulates against it to produce sounds such as the initial consonants in the English words *come* and *go*. Indeed, in the production of these (and some other) oral sounds, it is both an active articulator and passive articulator at once.

1.6 Summary

An outline of the organs of speech is given in Fig. 8.

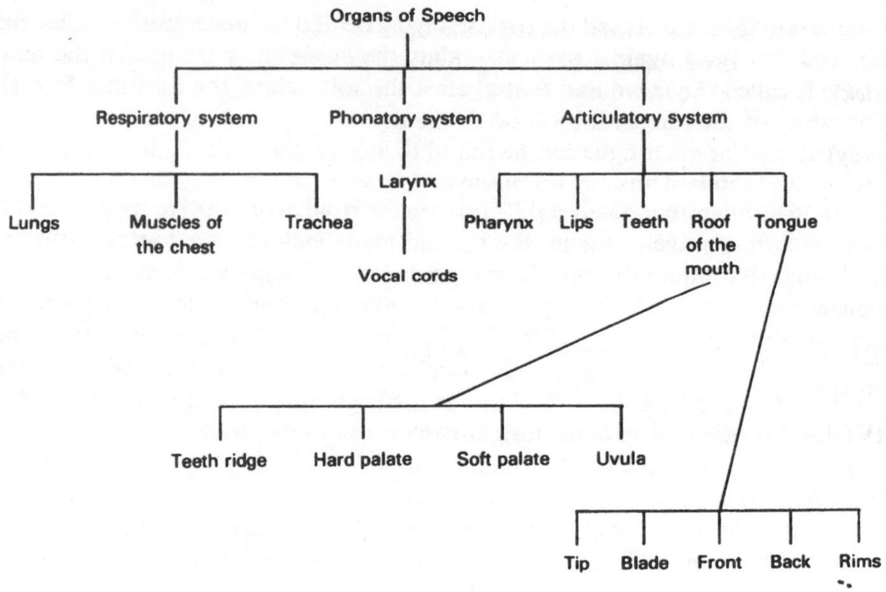

Fig. 8

EXERCISES

I Complete the following statements:

1 For the production of speech sounds, it is necessary to cause disturbance in the air. Such disturbance is caused by _________.

2 The organs of speech can be described under three systems: ______, _________, and _________.

3 It is mainly the process of _________ which produces the air required for the production of sounds.

4 Voiced sounds are produced when the vocal cords _________.

5 When we breathe normally, the vocal cords _________.

6 The soft palate is _________ when we produce the initial sound in the English word *know*.

7 To produce nasalized sounds, the soft palate must _________ and at the same time _________.

8 The initial sound in the English word *you* is articulated by _________ and _________. The former is _________ articulator and the latter _________.

9 The bony portion of the roof of the mouth immediately behind the teeth ridge is called _________.

10 The initial sound of the English word *will* is produced by _________ and by raising the back of the tongue towards the soft palate.

II Say whether the following statements are true or false:

1 Sounds are produced by causing some disturbance in the air.

2 The sounds of English are produced by inhaling air into the lungs.

3 The air escapes out of the lungs through the nose only.

4 The vocal cords remain wide apart during normal breathing.

5 To produce a voiceless sound (like the initial sound in the English word *sick*), the vocal cords must vibrate.

6 To produce an oral sound (like the initial sound in the English word *play*), the soft palate must be raised.

7 Nasalized sounds are produced through the nose only.

8 In a mirror, you can clearly see the divisions of the tongue.

9 English does not have any sounds produced at the uvula.

10 The lips are kept wide apart in the production of all English consonants.

III Go back to Exercise II above, and give reasons in support of your answers to statements 4, 5, 6, and 10.

IV Look at Fig. 9 carefully, and answer each of the questions that follow:

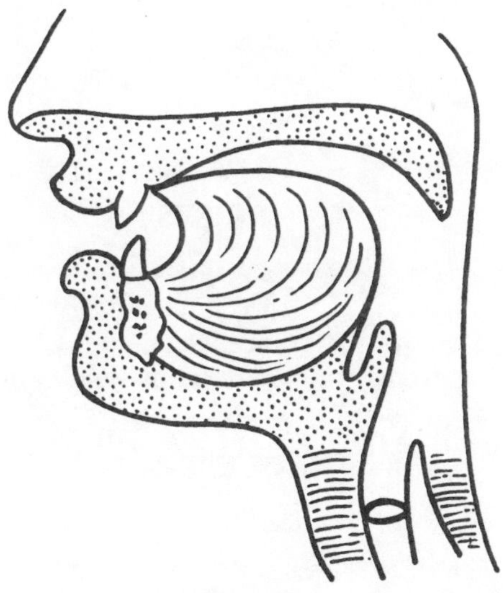

Fig. 9

1 Are the vocal cords vibrating or not?

2 Is the nasal passage open or shut?

3 Is the sound produced oral, nasal, or nasalized?

4 Name the articulators involved, and identify the active and passive articulators.

5 Can you guess what sound the diagram represents?

V Produce the initial sounds in the following English words, and, by performing the experiment mentioned in section 1.33, state whether they are voiced or voiceless:

1 stick	6 zoo
2 father	7 on

3 shine	8 thin
4 very	9 that
5 eat	10 hat

VI From the following list of English words, choose those which contain a nasal sound. Then say which letters in the spelling of such words represent the nasal sound:

1 lamb	6 brother
2 father	7 nephew
3 uncle	8 cousin
4 niece	9 knight
5 king	10 finger

2
The Description and Classification of Speech Sounds

2.1 Introduction

In Chapter 1, we considered how speech sounds are produced. In this chapter, and in Chapters 3 and 4, we shall discuss how they can be described and classified. (It should be remembered that in these three chapters we are concerned with speech sounds in general, and not those of any particular language. The examples given are, however, from particular languages.)

We speak in order generally to be heard. The use of speech for any other purpose, for example, in loud thinking, is rare. Normally, therefore, when we produce a speech sound, we intend it to be transmitted and heard. As this is the case, there are clearly three stages at which a speech sound can be studied: the production stage, the transmission stage, and the reception (hearing) stage. Correspondingly, the speech sound can be described and classified in *articulatory* terms, *acoustic* terms, and *auditory* terms, respectively. In other words, we can describe how the speech organs act in order to produce a given sound (articulatory terms); what physical properties it has (acoustic terms); and what features of it are perceived by the listener (auditory terms).

It is clear from the above discussion that a complete description of a sound must include its description in articulatory, acoustic, and auditory terms. Such an exhaustive description, however, is neither easy nor necessary. As the purpose of description in books like the present one is to aid the teaching of pronunciation of a language, it should generally suffice to give a description of sounds mainly in articulatory terms and partly in auditory terms. The sounds regarded as 'consonants' are best described in terms of their articulation, and those regarded as 'vowels' in terms of both their articulation and auditory impressions.

2.2 Vowels and Consonants

2.21

Speech sounds of all languages are classified, first and foremost, into *vowels* and *consonants*, the two categories mentioned in the foregoing section. These two categories are defined differently in different descriptions. The most popular, and at the same time the most misleading, way of defining them is in terms of the letters of an alphabet. Thus, in some 'grammar' books of English, the letters *a*, *e*, *i*, *o*, *u*, of the Roman alphabet are labelled as 'vowels', and the rest as 'consonants'. Now, this is most misleading and confusing because vowels and consonants are, essentially, categories of *speech sounds*. When we label some letters of an alphabet as 'vowels' and others as 'consonants', we assume a perfect correspondence between the letters and the sounds they stand for in a given language. Such correspondence, unfortunately, is not perfect in any language; indeed in a language like English, it is far from being even barely satisfactory (see Introduction). We therefore at once reject such definition of vowels and consonants.

2.22

There are two other ways in which 'vowels' and 'consonants' are defined: in *phonetic* terms and in *linguistic* terms, i e in terms of the production of sounds and their function in a given language, respectively. In phonetic terms, a speech sound is defined as a 'vowel' if, in the production of it, there is, in the pharynx and the mouth, no obstruction, and no narrowing of a degree that would cause audible friction. All other sounds are taken as 'consonants'. To illustrate this, take the English word *bee*. The word clearly consists of two sounds—the sound represented by the letter *b* and that represented by the letters *ee*. To take the second sound first, i e the sound represented by the letters *ee*, the speaker produces it by raising the front of the tongue fairly high. This process results in an appreciable degree of narrowing in the mouth, but even this degree of narrowing is not enough to cause any audible friction in the resultant sound. The sound is therefore regarded as a vowel. Now take the sound represented by the letter *b*. To produce it, the speaker first makes a complete closure of the mouth by bringing the two lips together, and then suddenly releases the air held behind the lips. There is thus an obstruction, at least for a while, to the flow of the air issuing from the lungs. Because of this, the resultant sound is regarded as a consonant. Similarly, the **s**-sound as in the English word *see* is a consonant; for, in the production of this sound, the tip and blade of the tongue rise so high towards the teeth ridge, and thereby create such a degree of narrowing, that the air passes out only with audible friction, the hissing noise so characteristic of the **s**-sound.

We have seen above that it is not just a narrowing in the mouth that results in the formation of a consonant sound; it is a narrowing of a degree that would cause audible friction. Because of this distinction, the sound represented by *ee* in the word *bee* is a vowel, while that represented by *s* in the word *see* is a consonant, although in both these cases there *is* a narrowing in the mouth.

2.23

The definition of 'vowels' and 'consonants' already given is in phonetic terms—i e in terms of the production of sounds. This definition is not dependent on any other criteria; nor is it related to any particular language. But if we want to define a sound as a vowel or a consonant in linguistic terms, then we must study the function of the sound in a given language, that is, in relation to the grammar of that language. This is explained in the following paragraph.

Take the initial sounds in the English words *yard* and *well*. In the production of these sounds, there is no obstruction or narrowing of such a degree in the mouth as would cause audible friction. The two sounds must therefore be regarded as vowels. And indeed, in strictly phonetic terms, they *are* vowels. Nevertheless, the English language regards them as consonants. This is so because the two sounds *function* in English grammar as consonants. For example, they take the article *a*, rather than *an*, in front of them (*a yard, a well*).

After the initial classification of all speech sounds into the broad categories of vowels and consonants, it is necessary to subclassify each category further. This we shall take up in Chapters 3 and 4.

2.3 Summary

A speech sound can be studied at three stages: the production stage, the transmission stage, and the reception stage. Correspondingly, a speech sound can be classified and described in articulatory terms, acoustic terms, and auditory terms. For the teaching of pronunciation, however, it suffices to describe certain sounds in articulatory terms and certain other sounds in auditory as well as articulatory terms.

Speech sounds are classified, first and foremost, into vowels and consonants. 'Vowels' are defined, in phonetic terms, as the speech sounds in the production of which there is, in the pharynx and the mouth, no obstruction or narrowing of a degree that would cause audible friction. All other sounds are regarded as 'consonants'. In terms of their function in a given language, however, some of the sounds determined in phonetic terms as vowels may be regarded as consonants. Such is the case with the initial sounds in the English words *yes* and *wet*, for example.

EXERCISES

I Say which of the following statements are incorrect, and then correct them:

1 Speech is always used for communication with other persons.

2 We can study how speech sounds are produced, how they travel from one speaker to another, and how a listener hears them.

3 A description of a sound is complete as soon as we have described how a speaker produces it.

4 In the production of vowels there should be no narrowing in the oral passage.

5 Vowels are best described in auditory as well as articulatory terms.

6 All consonants are produced with audible friction.

7 The sounds that are vowels in phonetic terms become consonants in linguistic terms.

8 How a sound functions in a language is, in linguistics, an important criterion for its classification.

II

1 Produce the sounds at the beginning of the following words:

tea	until	once
cat	unit	who
yet	one	fine
when	heir	bell

2 Say which of the sounds you produced in (1) are vowels in *strictly phonetic terms*.

3 Say which of these 'vowels' are regarded as 'consonants' in English.

III Say

1 three words in English, beginning and ending in a consonant;

2 five words in your mother tongue having one vowel followed by one consonant;

3 four words in English having, at their beginning, a consonant letter, but a vowel sound;

4 three words in English where the letter *y* occurs as a vowel in the middle of the word;

5 five words in English having two vowel letters, each standing for one vowel; and

6 three words in English in which one vowel (not just a vowel *letter*) is followed immediately by another vowel (not just a vowel *letter*).

3 The Description and Classification of Consonants

3.1 Introduction

Consonants are best described in terms of their articulation (see Section 2.1). For such description, however, we must answer the following questions:

(1) Is the airstream provided by the lungs or by some other organs?
(2) Is the air forced out or drawn inwards?
(3) Do the vocal cords vibrate or not?
(4) Is the soft palate raised or lowered?
(5) At what point does the articulation take place?
(6) What is the manner of articulation?

Ordinarily, all these questions are important to ask. In respect of many languages, however, questions (1) and (2) need not be asked every time because their answers are fixed for all the sounds of such languages: the airstream is provided by the lungs, and the air is forced *out*. That is, the airstream mechanism is *pulmonic egressive*. This is true of English and of all Indian languages, except Sindhi.

We now move to questions (3)–(6).

(3) If the vocal cords vibrate, the sound is voiced; if they do not, it is voiceless. And, by making the experiments given in section 1.33, we can ascertain whether the vocal cords vibrate or not.

(4) If the soft palate is raised, there is a velic closure, during which only oral sounds can be produced; if it is lowered, there is no such closure, and therefore either nasal or nasalized sounds can be produced (see section 1.47).

(5) The point (or place) of articulation is determined by the passive articulator. Thus, if the tip and blade of the tongue (active articulator) is raised to touch the teeth ridge (passive articulator), then the place of articulation is the teeth ridge.

(6) The manner of articulation specifies the kind of closure or narrowing involved in the production of a sound. To take an example, for the production of the **t**-sound as in the English word *tin*, there is, first, a complete closure in the mouth (at the teeth ridge), followed by a sudden release of it. As against this, for the production of the **s**-sound in the English word *sin*, there is no closure as such, but only a narrowing caused by the raising of the tip and blade of the tongue

towards the teeth ridge. Thus there is a difference between the two sounds with regard to their *manner of articulation*, although their place of articulation is obviously the same, i e the teeth ridge. Indeed, essentially it is this difference that makes **t** and **s** two different sounds.

Questions (5) and (6) call for some detailed discussion, which follows.

3.2 Place of Articulation

As discussed in Section 3.1, the place of articulation of a consonant is determined by the passive articulator involved in the production of it, and for this reason, the sound is also named after the passive articulator. Thus the **k**-sound in the English word *king* is called a *velar* sound because the passive articulator involved in its production is the velum, i e the soft palate. Similarly, the **s**-sound in the English word *sing* is called an *alveolar* sound because the passive articulator involved in this case is the alveolus, i e the teeth ridge.

The chief places of articulation of consonant sounds are the following:

(i) *Bilabial* The articulators are the two lips.

EXAMPLES The initial sounds in the English words *pen, bat, man, was*, and the Hindi words पल [pəl] 'moment', फल [phəl] 'fruit', भालु ['bha:lu] 'bear'. The Devanagari letters प [p], फ [ph], ब [b], भ [bh], म [m], all represent bilabial sounds.

(ii) *Labio-dental* The active articulator is the lower lip and the passive articulator the upper teeth.

EXAMPLES The initial sounds in the English words *fine* and *vine* and the Hindi word वही ['ʋəhi:] 'same'. (Indian learners may note that the English v-sound and the Hindi व [ʋ] sound are not the same, though they are similar in that both have the same *place* of articulation. They differ in the *manner* of articulation—see under *frictionless continuant* in Section 3.3.)

(iii) *Dental* The active articulator is the tip of the tongue and the passive articulator the upper teeth.

EXAMPLES The initial sounds in the English words *thin* and *that* and the Hindi words थकना ['t̪həkna:] 'to be tired' and दूर [d̪u:r] 'far'. The Devanagari series त, थ, द, ध, न represents dental sounds used in Hindi, Urdu, Marathi, and a number of other North Indian languages. (Indian learners should note that the initial sound in the English word *think* is not the same as the sound represented by the Devanagari letter थ [t̪h]; nor is the initial sound in the English word *that* the same as the sound represented by the Devanagari letter द [d̪]. The two English sounds spoken of here differ from the sounds represented by थ and द in respect of the manner of articulation.)

(iv) *Alveolar* The active articulator is the blade, or tip and blade, of the tongue, and the passive articulator the teeth ridge.

EXAMPLES The initial sounds in the English words, *tin, din, late, no, say, zoo*. In Hindi, while the स [s] sound as in सेब [se:b] 'apple' is alveolar, the ट, ठ, ड, ढ, ण [ʈ, ʈh, ɖ, ɖh, ɳ] sounds are retroflex (see below).

(v) *Post-alveolar* The active articulator is the tip of the tongue, and the passive articulator the rear part of the teeth ridge.

EXAMPLES The commonest variety of the **r**-sound in British English, as in the words *rail* and *tree*, and the र-sound in the Hindi word रात [ra:t̪] 'night'.

(vi) *Retroflex* The active articulator is the underside of the tip of the tongue, and the passive articulator the front of the hard palate. The tip of the tongue is curled back in such a way that only its underside articulates.

EXAMPLES The ट, ठ, ड, ढ, ण [ʈ, ʈh, ɖ, ɖh, ɳ] sounds in Hindi, Marathi, and a number of other Indian languages, and the **r**-sound found in the General American pronunciation of words such as *rain*, *rat*, and *right*.

(vii) *Palato-alveolar* Palato-alveolar sounds are produced by two simultaneous articulations: (i) the blade of the tongue as active articulator articulates against the teeth ridge as passive articulator, and (ii) the front of the tongue (active articulator) is raised towards the hard palate (passive articulator).

EXAMPLES The initial sounds in the English words *chair*, *jail*, and *share*, and the sound represented by *si* in the words *division*, *revision*. (For the Hindi च, ज [c, ɟ] sounds, see below.)

(viii) *Palatal* The active articulator is the front of the tongue, and the passive articulator the hard palate.

EXAMPLES The initial sound in the English word *yes*. The Devanagari series च, छ, ज, झ, ञ [c, ch, ɟ, ɟh, ɲ] represents palatal sounds found in Hindi, Urdu, Gujarati, and some other North Indian languages. (Of these, the च, ज [c, ɟ] sounds are often used by Indian speakers for the English sounds found initially in the words *chair* and *jail*.)

(ix) *Velar* The active articulator is the back of the tongue, and the passive articulator the soft palate.

EXAMPLES The final sounds in the English words *sock*, *sag*, and *sang*; the initial sounds in the Urdu words ख़त [xət̪] 'letter' and ग़म [ɣəm] 'sorrow'; the final sound in the Scottish word *loch* (which is the same as the initial sound in the Urdu word ख़त [xət̪] 'letter'). The Devanagari series क, ख, ग, घ, ङ represents velar sounds found in a number of North Indian languages.

(x) *Uvular* The active articulator is the back of the tongue, and the passive articulator the uvula. (Compare with the velar sounds for which too the active articulator is the back of the tongue.)

EXAMPLES The initial sounds in the Urdu words क़लम ['qələm] 'pen', क़रीब [qə'ri:b] 'near'. English has no uvular sounds; nor has Hindi.

(xi) *Glottal* The articulators for the glottal sounds are the two vocal cords. The sounds are produced by an obstruction, or a narrowing causing friction, but not by vibration, between the vocal cords.

EXAMPLES The sound of mild cough [ʔ], which some Englishmen use in place of the **p**, **t**, or **k** sounds at the end of words; the initial sound in the English word *hen* or the Hindi word हम [həm] 'we'.

This completes an account of the chief places of articulation of consonants. Before we proceed to discuss the manner of articulation, it may be pointed out that certain sounds require two simultaneous articulations—a primary articulation and a secondary articulation. A case in point is the initial sound in the English word *wood.* It is produced not only by bringing the lips together, but also by raising the back of the tongue towards the soft palate, the two articulations taking place simultaneously.

3.3 Manner of Articulation

As has been pointed out in question (6), Section 3.1, the *manner of articulation* specifies the kind of closure or narrowing involved in the production of a sound. In other words, it specifies the kind of *stricture* (or constriction) involved in the articulation of a sound. No consonant sound is fully identified, or described, without stating the *manner* of its articulation. Thus, a label such as 'voiceless alveolar consonant', which does not specify the manner of articulation, does not indicate whether we are referring to the **t**-sound or the **s**-sound, for both of them are voiceless, and both of them alveolar. To distinguish between them, we must also state *how* each of them is produced, that is, what kind of closure or narrowing is involved in their production. And this is what we shall discuss in this section.

Depending on the stricture involved, that is, on whether there is a complete closure, a partial closure, or only a narrowing that causes audible friction, consonants are classified into *plosive, affricate, nasal, roll, tap, flap, lateral,* and *fricative*. Then there are 'consonants' in the production of which there is no noise and no audible friction. These are called *frictionless continuants* and *semi-vowels*. All these classes are described below. It should be kept in mind that, except in the case of *nasals*, the nasal passage is shut off by raising the soft palate.

(i) *Plosive* It involves a *stricture of complete closure.* There is, first, a complete closure of the passage of air at some point in the vocal tract. As a result of it, air pressure is built up behind the closure. The closure is then suddenly removed, causing, in the process, a sudden release of the blocked air with some explosive noise.

> EXAMPLES The initial sounds in the English words *pit, bit, tell, deal, kit, gain.* Indian languages have a large number of plosives. This is reflected in the Devanagari script, which has twenty letters representing this class of consonants. These are:
> प [p], फ [ph], ब [b], भ [bh] (bilabial plosives);
> त [t̪], थ [t̪h], द [d̪], ध [d̪h] (dental plosives);
> ट [ʈ], ठ [ʈh], ड [ɖ], ढ [ɖh] (retroflex plosives);
> च [c], छ [ch], ज [ɟ], झ [ɟh] (palatal plosives); and
> क [k], ख [kh], ग [g], घ [gh] (velar plosives). Some examples of these are the initial sounds in the Hindi words पल [pəl] 'moment', फल [phəl] 'fruit', बल [bəl] 'force', भात [bha:t̪] 'cooked rice', ताल [t̪a:l] 'rhythm', थाल [t̪ha:l] 'plate', घर [ghər] 'home'.

(ii) *Affricate* It involves a *stricture of complete closure* followed by gradual release. As in the case of plosives, affricates too are produced in three stages, the first two of which are the same as for plosives—a complete closure of the air passage followed by the building up of pressure behind the closure. At the third stage, however, affricates are produced differently from plosives: the release of the blocked air is sudden for plosives; for affricates, it is slow. Because of a slow separation of the articulators, affricates are characterized by some audible friction, not by an explosive noise as heard in the case of plosives.

EXAMPLES The initial sounds in the English words *chair* and *jug*. The Hindi च, ज [c, ɟ], it may be noted, are plosives. Their substitution for the English affricates, as in *chair* and *jug*, it has already been pointed out, does not cause any problems of intelligibility.

(iii) *Nasal* It involves a *stricture of complete closure* of the oral passage only, the nasal passage remaining open. (Can you say what the state of the soft palate is, then?) The lung air can thus pass freely through the nose.

EXAMPLES The final sounds in the English words *ram*, *ran*, and *rang*; the final sounds in the Hindi words काम [ka:m] 'work', कान [ka:n] 'ear', गुण [guɳ] 'quality'.

(iv) *Roll* (or *Trill*) It involves a *stricture of intermittent closure*. As against the plosives, the affricates, and the nasals, the closure in this case is one of an interrupted kind. The tip of the tongue taps against the alveolar ridge (or just behind it), or the uvula against the back of the tongue, several times, so that the air can pass only intermittently between the articulators.

EXAMPLES The **r**-sound used by some English speakers in the word-initial position as in *rat*, *red*.

(v) *Tap* In the production of a tap, one articulator moves towards another, makes a momentary contact, and immediately withdraws to its position of rest.

EXAMPLES The [ɾ] sound often found in British English when the letter *r* occurs between vowels as in *very*. Also, the usual realization of the letters *t* and *d* between vowels in American English as in *letter, a lot of, ladder*. Thus in this variety of English, *matter* and *madder* are pronounced alike.

(vi) *Flap* As in the case of a tap, in the production of a flap too, one articulator starts out towards another and makes a momentary contact with it. But in this case, it does so only *in passing*, and then moves to another position.

EXAMPLE A typical example is the 'retroflex flap' [ɽ], a sound represented by the Devanagari letter ड़ [ɽ] as in Hindi word तोड़ना ['ʈoɽna:] 'to break'. The same sound is also used, though wrongly, by some Indian speakers in English words like *road, hard, board.*

(vii) *Lateral* It involves a *stricture of partial closure*. There is a partial closure at some point in the mouth, so that the airstream can escape on one or both sides of the contact. Since the air can pass continuously, the sound produced is a continuant, i.e. it can be continued, unlike the plosives and affricates, for example.

EXAMPLES The initial sound in the English word *let* or the Hindi word लेना ['le:na:] 'to take'.

In the production of the **l**-sound exemplified above, there is a contact between the tip of the tongue and the centre of the teeth ridge; but there is no such contact, at least on one side, between the rim of the tongue and the upper side teeth. And that is why the air can escape continuously through the mouth.

There is also a variety of the **l**-sound in the production of which there is a secondary articulation too: the back of the tongue is simultaneously raised towards the soft palate. Such a secondary articulation imparts a special 'colour' to the **l**-sound, which is then called 'dark' *l*, to distinguish it from the other **l**-sound, called 'clear' *l*.

EXAMPLES The last sound in the English word *tell* is a 'dark' *l*. In the word *little*, we have examples of both the varieties of the **l**-sound—the initial *l* being a 'clear' *l* and the final *l*, a 'dark' *l*.

(viii) *Fricative* It involves a *stricture of close approximation*: there is no closure anywhere; there is only a narrowing. The active articulator comes very close to the passive articulator, leaving only a narrow gap between the two. When the air passes through this narrow gap, it causes audible friction. Also, as the air can pass continuously, the sound produced in this manner can be continued. Thus fricatives are continuants, and they are accompanied by audible friction.

EXAMPLES The initial sounds in the English words *fail*, *very*, *think*, *that*, *see*, *zoo*, *shine*, and *hat*, and the Urdu words ख़राब [xə'raːb] 'bad' and ग़लत ['ɣələt] 'wrong'.

In respect of the manner of articulation, besides the classes of consonants described above, there are two more, which, in strictly phonetic terms, must be regarded as vowels, but since in many languages they function as consonants, they are grouped along with consonants (see section 2.23). These are now described.

(ix) *Frictionless continuant* In the oral passage of air, if there is a narrowing of such a degree that the sound produced is accompanied by audible friction, then the sound is called a fricative. If, on the other hand, the narrowing is of a lesser degree, i.e. the articulators do not come so close together, then no audible friction accompanies the sound produced. Such a sound is a *frictionless continuant*, now more often called an *approximant*. Like a fricative, it can be continued.

EXAMPLES The common variety of the **r**-sound in RP, the sound represented by the Devanagari letter व [ʋ] as in the Hindi word वीर [ʋiːr] 'brave'.

Notice that the English **v**-sound, as in the word *very*, is a fricative, whereas the Hindi व-sound is a frictionless continuant: audible friction accompanies the former, not the latter. And that indeed is the only difference between the two.

(x) *Semi-vowel* Semi-vowels are essentially very short approximants (see above). They are very rapid glides towards, or from, a vowel of greater steady duration. They differ from both approximants and vowels in that they are momentary in nature, and cannot be prolonged.

EXAMPLES The initial sounds in the English words *watch* and *yes*; the य [j] sound in the Hindi word यश [jəʃ] 'fame' (which is the same as the initial sound in the English word *yes*).

Notice, at this point, that the English v-sound is a fricative, the English w-sound a semi-vowel, and the Hindi व [ʋ] sound a frictionless continuant.

3.4 Description Illustrated

At the beginning of this chapter, we listed six points in the form of questions, the answers to which can provide a fairly exhaustive articulatory description of a consonant. Having furnished a possible classification under each of those six points, we are now in a position to attempt the description of some consonants.

I The sound represented by the letters *ch* in the English word *school*.

(1) The airstream is pulmonic.

(2) The air is forced out. Therefore, the airstream is *egressive*.

(3) The vocal cords do not vibrate. The sound is therefore *voiceless*.

(4) The soft palate is raised. The sound is therefore *oral*, not *nasal*.

(5) The articulation takes place at the soft palate. (The back of the tongue is the active articulator.) The sound is therefore *velar*.

(6) The sound is produced by (i) a complete closure in the mouth, (ii) the building up of air pressure behind the closure, followed by (iii) a sudden release of the blocked air with some explosive noise. The sound is thus a *plosive*.

II The sound represented by the letter *n* in the English word *lane*.

(1) The airstream is *pulmonic*.

(2) The airstream is *egressive*.

(3) The vocal cords vibrate. The sound is therefore *voiced*.

(4) The soft palate is lowered.

(5) The articulation takes place at the teeth ridge. (The blade, or tip and blade, of the tongue makes contact with the teeth ridge.) The sound is therefore *alveolar*.

(6) With the soft palate lowered and a complete closure in the mouth (see points (4) and (5) above), the air passes out through the nose *only*. The sound is therefore a *nasal*.

III The final sound in the Hindi word तोड़ [t̪oːɽ] 'break'.

(1) The airstream is *pulmonic*.

(2) The airstream is *egressive*.

(3) The vocal cords vibrate. The sound is therefore *voiced*.

(4) The soft palate is raised. The sound is therefore *oral*.

(5) The articulation takes place between the underside of the tip of the tongue (curled back) and the front of the hard palate. The sound is therefore *retroflex*.

(6) The underside of the tip of the tongue makes a single tap against the front of the hard palate. The sound is therefore a *flap*.

In the three descriptions given above, we have seen that the answers to questions (1) and (2) are the same—pulmonic, egressive. Indeed, as we pointed out in Section 3.1, this is the case with regard to all English sounds, all sounds of all Indian languages except Sindhi, and most of the sounds of most other languages of the world. Therefore, in the case of all those languages for which answers to questions (1) and (2) are *pulmonic* and *egressive*, we can take the two answers for granted. Further, except in the case of *nasal* or *nasalized* sounds, the answer to question (4) is that the soft palate is raised, thereby shutting off the nasal passage of air. In English, there is no special class of nasalized sounds. As for the identification of nasal sounds, it can be done in answer to question (6)—the manner of articulation. Thus, for classification and description of English consonants, questions (1), (2), and (4) need not be asked. Therefore, it becomes possible to assign just three-term labels to English consonants, for example,

(1) the consonant represented by the letters *ch* in the word *school* is *voiceless velar plosive*;

(2) the sound represented by the letter *n* in the word *lane* is voiced alveolar *nasal*; and

(3) the sound represented by the letters *ph* in the word *phone* is a *voiceless labio-dental fricative*.

3.5 Summary

Consonants are best described in terms of their articulation. For a good description in such terms, we must speak about the nature of the airstream, the state of the vocal cords (vibrating or not), the position of the soft palate (raised or lowered), the place of articulation, and the manner of articulation. If the vocal cords vibrate, the sound produced is *voiced*; if they do not, it is *voiceless*. If the soft palate is raised, the nasal passage gets shut off, and therefore the sound produced is *oral*; if, on the other hand, it is lowered, the nasal passage remains open, and therefore the sound produced is either *nasal* (when the oral passage is blocked) or *nasalized* (when the oral passage is also open).

Beyond this point, the classification of consonants depends on their place and manner of articulation. According to their place of articulation, consonants can be classified as *bilabial, labio-dental, dental, alveolar, post-alveolar, retroflex, palato-alveolar, palatal, velar, uvular*, and *glottal*. According to their manner of articulation, they can be classified as *plosives, affricates, nasals, rolls* (or *trills*), *taps, flaps, laterals, fricatives, frictionless continuants*, and *semi-vowels*.

For a brief description, or identification, of a consonant, especially in English, just three bits of information can suffice: (i) voice or voicelessness, (ii) place of articulation, and (iii) manner of articulation. Thus, *voiced bilabial plosive* is a good three-term label for the initial sound in the English word *bit*.

EXERCISES

I Say whether the following statements are true or false:

1 For the production of all English sounds, the airstream mechanism is pulmonic egressive.

2 No speech sound can be produced if the vocal cords do not vibrate.

3 Voiceless sounds cannot be heard.

4 If the soft palate is raised, no nasal sound can be produced.

5 To produce a nasal consonant, there must be an obstruction to the air passage at some point in the mouth.

6 In the production of a consonant sound, there must be a complete closure somewhere in the mouth.

7 It is the active articulator that determines the place of articulation.

8 In no variety of English are there any retroflex sounds.

9 The difference between a plosive and an affricate is that, for the latter, the closure in the mouth is not complete.

10 Semi-vowels are vowels that function as consonants.

II Give one example each of the following:

1 A nasalized sound.

2 A sound produced with the glottis open, i e with the vocal cords not vibrating.

3 A sound produced at the soft palate.

4 A sound in the production of which the active articulator is the underside of the tip of the tongue.

5 A palatal sound.

6 A voiceless fricative sound.

7 A vowel-like sound that functions as a consonant in English.

8 A glottal fricative.

9 A palatal semi-vowel.

10 A consonant sound produced at the same point as the initial sound of the English word *cat* is produced.

III Give three-term labels for the consonants represented by the italicized letters in the following English words:

a*p*t, *ch*at, *y*esterday, ma*ch*ine, runni*ng*, s*w*ing, a*ch*e, *s*ing, *ph*oto, *th*en

IV Look carefully at the figures given below, and choose the right answers from among those that follow them.

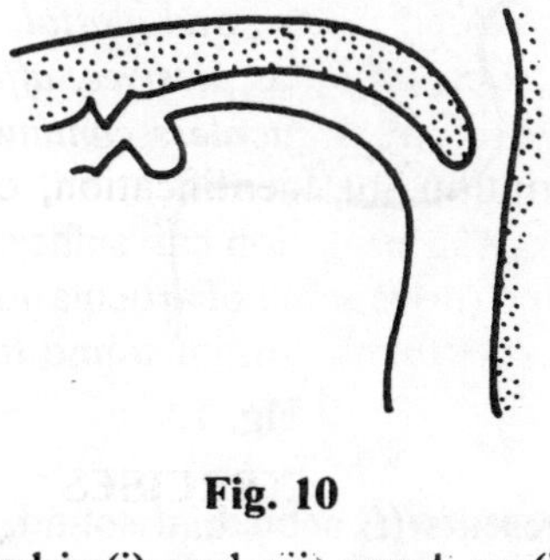

Fig. 10

1 The sound articulated is (i) oral, (ii) nasal, or (iii) nasalized.

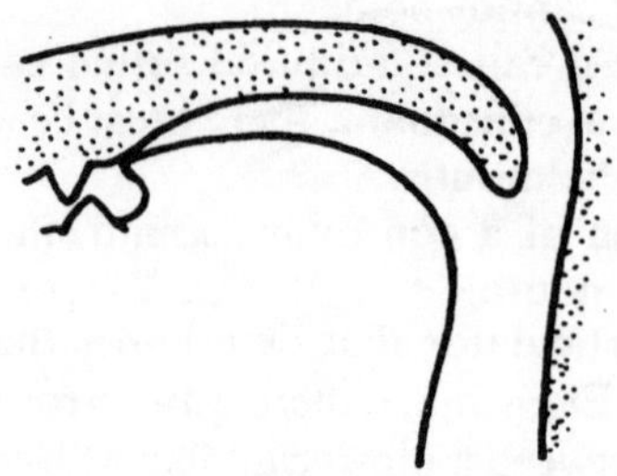

Fig. 11

2 The sound articulated is (i) velar, (ii) alveolar, or (iii) neither.

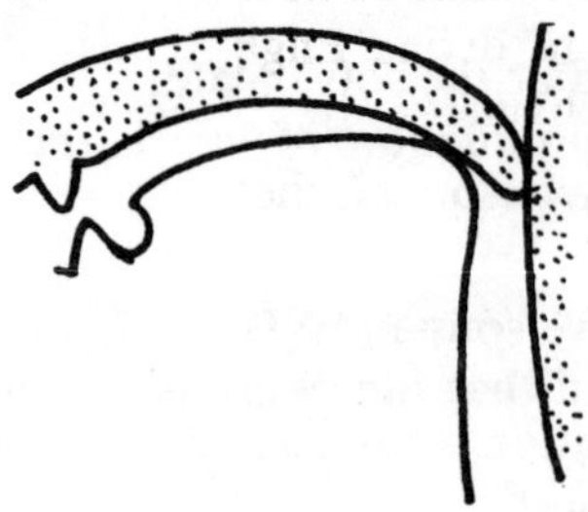

Fig. 12

3 The consonant represented can be (i) a velar plosive, (ii) a velar nasal, or (iii) either of these.

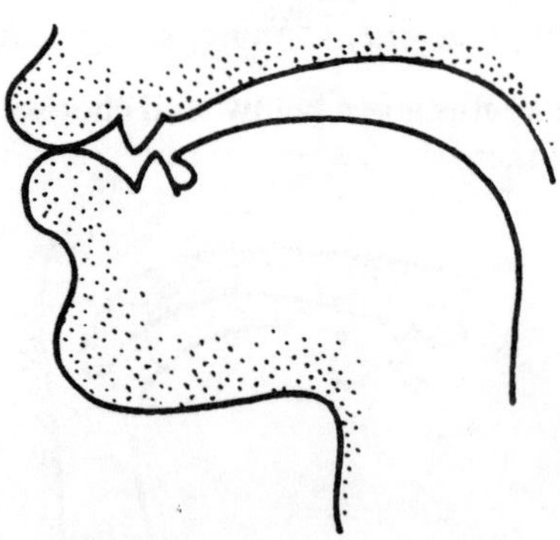

Fig. 13

4 The figure represents (i) a bilabial sound, (ii) an alveolar consonant, or (iii) a labio-dental consonant.

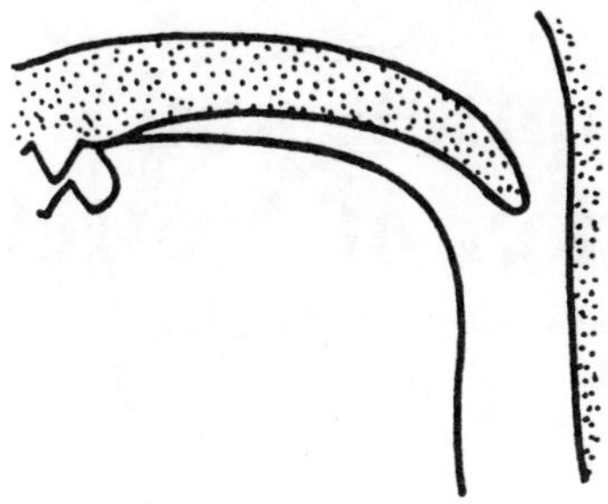

Fig. 14

5 The consonant articulated is (i) an alveolar plosive, (ii) a dental fricative, or (iii) an alveolar nasal.

V Answer the following questions in not more than 20 words each:

1 Why is it possible to define English consonants without stating the nature of the airstream mechanism?

2 To produce a nasal consonant, the soft palate must be lowered. Why is this so?

3 "The w-sound in the English word *wing* is a semi-vowel." What does this statement mean?

4 The place of articulation is named after the passive articulator. Why not after the active articulator?

5 In what way is the English sound at the beginning of the word *chance* different from the Hindi च [c] sound at the beginning of the word चांद [cã:d̪] 'moon'?

6 An English consonant, we have said, is identified by a three-term label. Why is this not possible for all languages?

7 Of all the manners of articulation described in this chapter, which would you regard as the least important for English? And why?

4 The Description and Classification of Vowels

4.1 Introduction

In Chapter 2, we saw how vowels, as a class, are distinguished from consonants. In particular, we noted that vowels are speech sounds in the production of which there is, in the pharynx and the mouth, no obstruction and no narrowing of a degree that would cause audible friction (see section 2.22). In this way, vowels are essentially a tone, or a 'hum', issuing from the glottis, with the vocal cords normally vibrating (since vowels are normally voiced).

Such a definition of vowels might be adequate—in most cases—in distinguishing vowels from consonants. But it does not help us in distinguishing vowels from vowels—in distinguishing, for example, between the vowels in the English words *beat* and *boot*, or between the vowels in the first syllables of the Hindi words पीटना ['piːt̪naː] 'to beat' and पिटना ['pit̪naː] 'to be beaten'. The answer to this question is that differences between vowels are broadly of two types: difference of quality, as illustrated by the pair *beat* and *boot*, and difference of quantity, as illustrated by the pair of the Hindi words cited above. To take the second one first, the difference of quantity is a difference in respect of the length of vowels. The other difference, viz the difference in respect of quality, is somewhat more complex, and it is this difference that will engage our attention through the rest of this chapter.

4.2 Vowel Description

In Section 4.1, we have seen that a vowel is essentially a tone or a 'hum'. Therefore, what distinguishes one vowel from another, in respect of quality, is the modification of the tone resulting from modification in the shapes and sizes of the resonating chambers through which the tone passes, viz the pharyngeal cavity, the nasal cavity, and the mouth. Mainly responsible for such modifications of the resonating chambers are the soft palate, the lips, and the tongue. For the identification and description of vowels, therefore, we must describe

(1) the position of the soft palate—whether it is raised to produce oral vowels, or lowered to produce nasalized vowels (see section 1.47);

(2) the shape assumed by the lips—spread, neutral, or rounded; and

(3) the shape assumed by the tongue—which part of it is raised and how high.

Of these, only the shape assumed by the lips can be clearly observed by the eye, and therefore described in articulatory terms. As against this, the position of the soft palate is judged only by auditory perception—the presence or absence of nasality in the vowel produced. As for the shapes assumed by the tongue, only certain extreme positions taken by it can be felt. For instance, in the production of the vowel in the English word *key*, it can be felt that the front of the tongue is being raised very high towards the hard palate. Such extreme positions apart, most other positions of the tongue may differ so minutely from one another that it may not be possible to notice the difference. Furthermore, since in the formation of vowels there is no contact of the tongue with the roof of the mouth, the sense of touch cannot help either. For these reasons, most of the positions of the tongue are judged by auditory perception only. Thus, all in all, vowels are best described in terms of both articulation and auditory impressions.

4.21

Of the three factors we have listed for the identification and description of vowels, the first—the position of the soft palate—does not need to be stated every time: by convention, it is understood that, unless otherwise stated, the soft palate is in its raised position so that the nasal cavity is shut off and therefore the vowel produced is oral, not nasalized.

4.22

Taking the second factor now, the lips can assume a number of positions: *spread*, as for the vowel in the English word *bead*; *neutral*, as for the vowel in *bird*; *open* for the vowel in *bard*; *open rounded* for the vowel in *hot*; and *close rounded* for that in *hoot*. It is common practice, however, to regard the *spread*, *neutral* and *open* positions as *unrounded*, and the other two positions as *rounded*.

4.23

We consider the third factor now: the shape assumed by the tongue. The tongue, being the most flexible organ of speech, can assume virtually a limitless number of shapes, every change in its shape resulting in a change in the quality of the sound produced. Thus, the differences in quality between the vowels in the English words *beat*, *bit*, *bet*, and *bat*, for example, are chiefly the differences caused by the assumption of different shapes by the tongue. Such shapes, in turn, are determined by two factors: which part of the tongue is raised and how high it is raised. These are now discussed.

4.231 The part of the tongue raised

The parts of the tongue which are responsible for the production of vowels are the front, the back, and that imaginary part where the front and the back are supposed to meet, viz the *centre*. The vowels produced when each of these parts is raised are, accordingly, called the *front vowels*, the *back vowels*, and the *central vowels*, respectively. Examples of the front vowels are the vowels in the English words *seat*, *sit*, *set*, and *sat*; those of the back vowels are the vowels in the words *cart*, *cot*, *caught*, and *cool*. Central vowels occur in the English words *curt*, *girl*, and in the second syllable in *actor*, for example.

4.232 The height of the tongue

Any part of the tongue can be raised, but only up to a certain point, in order to produce vowels; raising it beyond that point results in the production of audible friction, and hence of consonants. Similarly, any part of the tongue can be lowered, but only up to a certain point, in order to produce vowels. The vowels produced when any part of the tongue is raised to the highest point, or nearly so, are called *close vowels*, and those produced with any part of the tongue at or very near the lowest point are called *open vowels*. Thus the vowels in the English words *seat* and *suit* are close vowels because, in producing them, the tongue (the front in the case of *seat*, and the back in the case of *suit*) is near the highest point possible for the production of vowels. Again, the vowel in the English word *cart* is an open vowel because, in producing it, the back of the tongue is at the lowest point possible for the production of vowels.

Earlier, we cited the English words *seat*, *sit*, *set*, and *sat* as all containing front vowels, that is, the part of the tongue raised in their production is the front. The question that now arises is how to distinguish between these, which belong to the same class—in this case, the class of front vowels. Such distinction is possible mainly on the basis of the height of the tongue (apart also from the fact that the vowel in *seat* is longer than any other of this set). The vowel in *seat* is a close vowel and that in *sat* a fairly open vowel. The former is thus a *front close* vowel and the latter almost a *front open* vowel.

But, as we can see at once, even the close-open distinction does not enable us to distinguish between all of them. That is so because our scale with regard to the height of the tongue is not yet refined enough. To refine it, we mark two imaginary positions between *close* and *open*, and label them as *half-close* and *half-open*. This is done in such a way that the positions labelled as *close*, *half-close*, *half-open*, and *open* are equidistant. Now, we can distinguish between the vowels in the English words *seat* and *sit* by describing the former as a *front close* vowel and the latter a *front half-close* vowel. (Of course, they are distinguished in respect of length too.)

4.233 The vowel diagram

The discussion in sections 4.231 and 4.232 has brought us to a point where we can introduce a vowel scale, represented by a vowel diagram (Fig. 15). In this diagram, the horizontal lines AB, CD, EF, and GH represent four different positions vis-à-vis the height of the tongue, viz *close*, *half-close*, *half-open*, and *open*. Similarly, in relation to the part of the tongue raised, we show the divisions *front*, *central*, and *back*. (When the tongue is in its lowest position, the range of its horizontal movement is relatively small, and therefore, in that position, only two divisions—*front* and *back*—are generally recognized.) It should be remembered, with respect to Fig. 15, that the *close* and *open* positions represent, respectively, the highest and lowest positions of the tongue, the two outermost limits within which all vowel sounds are produced. The positions labelled as *half-close* and

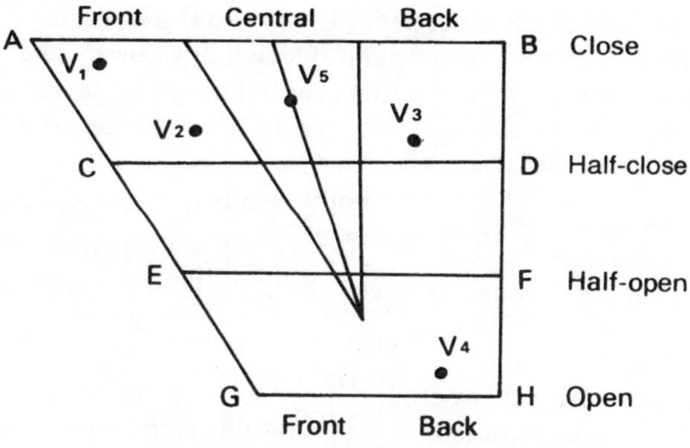

Fig. 15 The vowel diagram

half-open, on the other hand, are only imaginary positions, chosen in such a way that the points *A, C, E, G* (and similarly the points *B, D, F, H*) are equidistant. An important fact about these points is that they are equidistant not only spatially, but also auditorily. That is, a trained human ear perceives the vowels produced by raising the tongue to these points as equidistant in terms of vowel quality also. To illustrate this, if we call the vowels produced by raising the front of the tongue to the points *A, C, E, G* as Vowels A, C, E, G, respectively, then Vowel C is heard as equidistant, in quality, from Vowels A and E, and similarly Vowel E as equidistant, in quality, from Vowels C and G. The same is also true of the back vowels.

The vowel diagram (Fig. 15) given here (and in most books on this subject) is a highly conventionalized one, derived, by a process of simplification, from the total vowel area bounded by the extreme points *A* and *G*, beyond which the front of the tongue must not go, and the points *B* and *H*, beyond which the back of the tongue must not go, in order to produce vowels. The diagram was evolved by the English phonetician Daniel Jones, who also evolved the system of *Cardinal Vowels*. We do not intend to go into a description of that system in this book. It may, however, be mentioned in passing that the points *A, C, E, G, H, F, D, B* of our diagram are among the cardinal points of that system, and any vowels of any language can be identified, or described, with reference to such points.

4.234

Let us now describe a few vowels that may not necessarily belong to any particular language. For this, look at the five thick dots marked V_1, V_2, V_3, V_4, V_5, in Fig. 15.

V_1, a front vowel between close and half-close, but nearer close than half-close

V_2, a front (retracted) half-close vowel

V_3, a back (advanced) half-close vowel

V_4, a back open vowel, somewhat advanced

V_5, a central vowel between close and half-close

It will be noticed that all these descriptions are two-dimensional: they specify the part of the tongue raised and the height to which it is raised. The position of the lips is not represented on this two-dimensional diagram; it has therefore to be stated separately. When this is done, we arrive at three-term labels for the description of vowels such as

front close unrounded vowel : as in the word *beat*,
back open rounded vowel : as in the word *cot*,
back half-close rounded vowel: as in the Hindi word गोल [goːl] 'round',

and so on.

At this point, before we proceed, a word of caution may be in place. The conventional vowel diagram (Fig. 15) should not be mistaken as the shape the tongue assumes to produce vowels. It is only a visual, two-dimensional representation of the total vowel area, enclosing all the limitless points to which a given part of the tongue can be raised in order to produce vowels, and only vowels. Vowels of all languages must therefore, by definition, lie within this diagram; so too must any vowel sounds human beings can produce, whether or not they are used in any language.

4.24 Diphthongs

The description of vowels given so far assumes that the position of the tongue remains unchanged throughout the process of their production, and that therefore the quality of the vowel remains unchanged. This is by no means true of all vowels. To appreciate this point, let us say the vowels in the English words *be* and *by*. We notice that the quality of the vowel in the word *be* remains unchanged throughout the process of its production, whereas the quality of the vowel in the word *by* changes during the course of its production. We may also be able to feel that, for producing the vowel in the word *by*, the front of the tongue is, at first, raised to a point somewhere near the open position (point *A* in Fig. 16), and then it is gradually raised towards a point near the half-close position (point *B* in the same diagram). Further, the movement of the tongue from *A* to *B* (shown by an arrow in the diagram) is so smooth that it may be called a *glide*. The vowels produced as a result of such glides are called ***diphthongs***, and, to keep the distinction, other vowels are called ***monophthongs*** or ***pure vowels***. In the vowel diagram, the former are represented by arrows and the latter by thick dots. Some more examples of diphthongs are the vowels in the English words *town, tail, care, fear*; some more examples of monophthongs are the vowels in the English words *two, ten, can, feel*.

It should be noted here that a diphthong is not the same thing as a sequence of two monophthongs. In the English word *soil*, there is a diphthong, while in the word *sawing*, there is a sequence of two monophthongs—the monophthong that occurs in the word *saw* followed by the one that occurs in the suffix *-ing*. The diphthong we are speaking of is represented in the vowel diagram (Fig. 16) by the arrow CB, while the monophthongs in the word *sawing* by the point *D* and the point *B*. Another way of explaining this difference is to state that a diphthong

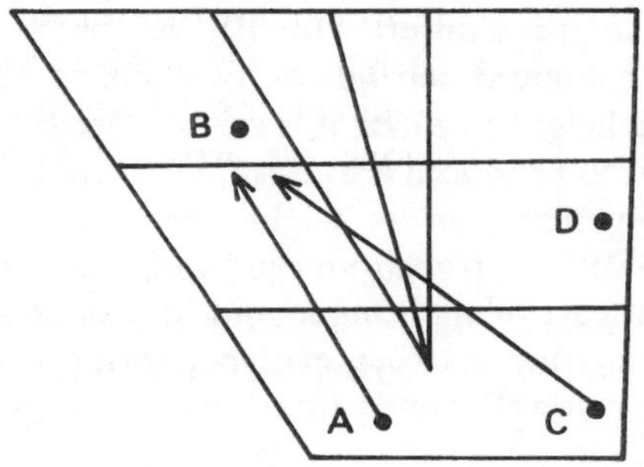

Fig. 16 Monophthongs and diphthongs

occupies one syllable, while a sequence of two monophthongs is spread over two syllables. This last point will become clearer after the concept of the syllable is explained (see Chapter 7).

Now, the manner in which a diphthong can be described is illustrated here with the help of the diphthongs AB and CB plotted in Fig. 16:

Diphthong AB: The tongue glide for this diphthong starts from a point in the front lying between half-open and open and moves towards half-close front (retracted).
Diphthong CB: Starting from a point in the back lying between half-open and open, the tongue glide moves towards half-close front (retracted).

Notice that, as in the case of monophthongs, the vowel diagram cannot show the lip positions for diphthongs, which have therefore to be stated separately. In certain diphthongs, the lip position does not change appreciably during their production; in other diphthongs, it may change. In the diphthong that occurs in the English word *tie*, for example, the lip position remains essentially the same throughout (unrounded); on the other hand, in the diphthong found in the English word *toy*, the lip position changes appreciably during the process of its production: the lips are rounded to start with, but they gradually become unrounded.

4.3 Summary

Vowels are essentially a tone or a 'hum', issuing from the glottis, with the vocal cords normally vibrating. They differ from one another in respect of quality, or quantity, or both. While the difference in quantity is merely a difference in respect of the comparative length of vowels, the difference in quality is more complex: it results from modification of the glottal tone brought about by modifications in the shapes and sizes of the resonating chambers—the pharyngeal cavity, the nasal cavity, and the mouth. Mainly responsible for such modifications of the resonating chambers are the soft palate, the lips, and the tongue. With the soft palate lowered, the vowels produced become nasalized; and with each different position assumed by the lips—spread, neutral, or rounded—

the vowels produced acquire a different quality. As for the role of the tongue, the quality of the vowel produced depends on two related factors: the part of the tongue raised and the height to which it is raised. Depending on the part of the tongue raised, the vowels produced are classified as front vowels, central vowels, and back vowels. Depending on its height, the vowels are classified as close vowels, half-close vowels, half-open vowels, and open vowels. Employing the two parameters—the part of the tongue and its height—a conventional two-dimensional vowel diagram has been evolved, within which the vowels of all languages, indeed any vowel sounds that human beings can produce, can be plotted.

If, during the process of production of a vowel, the tongue position remains unchanged, the vowel produced is a pure vowel, or a monophthong. If, on the other hand, the tongue position changes, through a smooth tongue glide, the vowel produced is a diphthong. A diphthong may, in some cases, involve a change in the lip position too. Further, a diphthong differs from a sequence of two monophthongs: the former occupies one syllable, and the latter two syllables.

EXERCISES

I Say which of the following statements are true:

1 In the production of vowels, no articulation of speech organs is involved.

2 Vowel quality changes with the change in the size and shape of the resonating chambers, i e the pharyngeal cavity, the nasal cavity, and the mouth.

3 When the soft palate is lowered, the air passes through the nose, and therefore no vowel sound is produced.

4 We can distinguish between one vowel and another by stating the height to which the tongue is raised in each case.

5 Auditory perception plays an important role in distinguishing one vowel from another.

6 All vowels are oral.

7 The conventional vowel diagram is a simplified diagram of the shape the tongue assumes at the time of producing vowels.

8 The line 'close' in the vowel diagram represents the highest point to which the tongue can be raised.

9 A half-close front vowel is as different in quality from a close front vowel as it is from a half-open front vowel.

10 Monophthongs can be fully identified by three-term labels.

11 Diphthongs consist of two monophthongs produced after one another.

II Complete the following statements, using one or more words in the blank spaces:

1 A vowel is a tone modified by __________.

2 Besides the position of the soft palate and the lips, the various __________ are also crucial in determining the quality of vowels.

3 Whether a vowel is nasalized or not is judged by ________.

4 English has no ________ vowels.

5 To produce vowels, rather than consonants, no part of the tongue should be raised above the ________ position.

6 The number of vowel sounds human beings can produce is ________.

7 The conventional vowel diagram can give ________ description of any vowel.

8 Vowel quality is determined by the position of the soft palate, ________, and ________.

9 A three-term label for a monophthong must state what part of the tongue has been raised, ________, and ________.

10 In the production of a diphthong, the position of the tongue ________.

III Assuming that, in a certain language, all front and central vowels are unrounded and all back vowels rounded, give a three-term description of the vowels of that language marked 1–9 in Fig. 17.

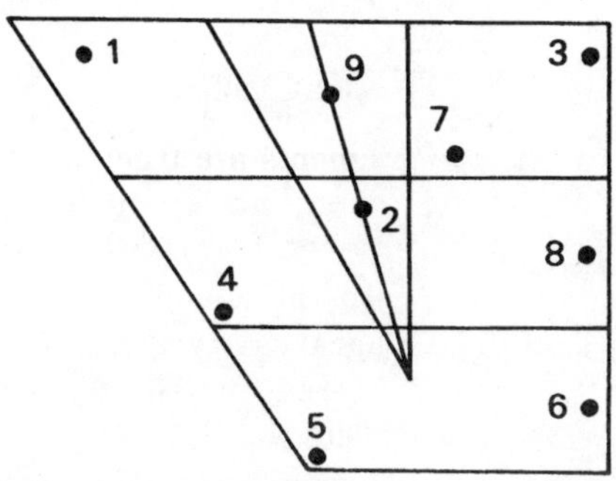

Fig. 17

IV Assuming that, in a certain language, the lips are unrounded for all diphthongs which occur completely in the front position, and rounded for all those which occur completely in the back position, describe, for that language, the diphthongs AB, CD, EF, and GH, as shown in Fig. 18.

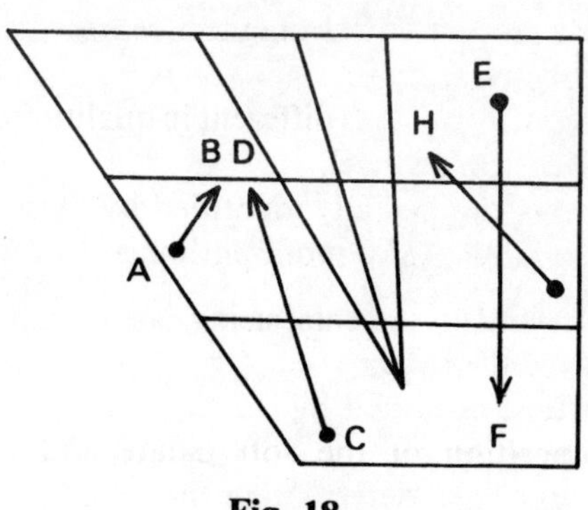

Fig. 18

V Now, with the same assumptions as in Exercise IV, attempt a description of the diphthongs PR, ST, and YZ in Fig. 19.

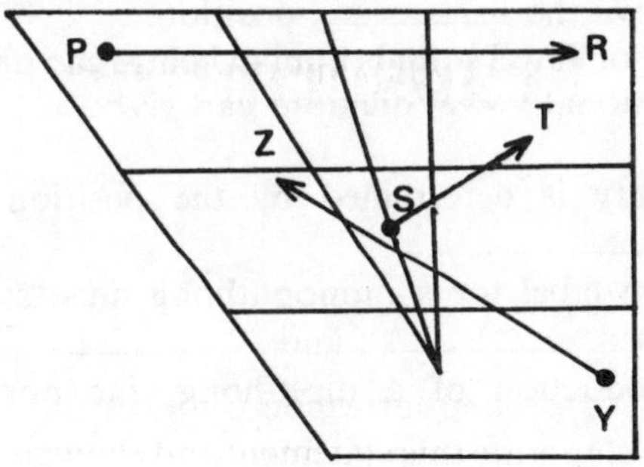

Fig. 19

5
Phonetic Transcription

5.1 Introduction

In English there is no one-to-one correspondence between spelling and sound. In this chapter, we shall elaborate this statement and show how the problem caused by such lack of correspondence can be overcome.

First, the problem. Barring a few languages such as Chinese and Japanese, the written form of a language is supposed to represent only the spoken form of its words, phrases, and sentences, and not directly the objects, actions, or concepts for which those words, phrases, and sentences stand. Thus, in English, the written form *cat* represents the spoken form of this word, viz the **k**-sound, the vowel sound that we find in words such as *sat*, *mat*, and *rat*, and the **t**-sound; it does not, by any means, represent directly the animal called 'cat'. Similarly, the written sentence 'the cat ran away' is a representation, in the written form, of the spoken sentence 'the cat ran away'; it is not a direct representation of the action denoted by the sentence. Now, since the written form is a representation of the spoken form, there ought to be, for perfect representation, a perfect correspondence between the sound and the symbol used to represent it in writing. Such correspondence, unfortunately, is not perfect for any language, and indeed in the case of languages like English and French, it is far from satisfactory. To illustrate this point from English, a letter of the alphabet may stand for different sounds, or combinations of sounds, in different words, and conversely, a given sound may be represented by different letters, or combinations of letters, in different words. An example of the first type is the letter *u* in the words *cut*, *put*, *rude*, *minute*, *bury*, and *university*. An example of the second type may be the **k**-sound represented differently in different words: by the letter *k* in *kit*, *ck* in *rock*, *c* in *cut*, *cc* in *acclaim*, *ch* in *chemistry*, and *qu* in *queen*.

Because of such a mismatch between spelling and sound, a learner of a language like English cannot be sure of how to pronounce a word that he encounters for the first time in the written form. Nor can he be sure of how a new word heard by him would be spelt. The latter is as much a problem of a child whose mother tongue is English as of another learner of English. In the case of a language like Hindi, the problem is not as acute as it is in English and French, for instance. But it exists nonetheless. In the word whose written form is करतब ['kərt̪əb], a person totally unfamiliar with the word may not know whether there is a vowel after each of the four consonant letters क, र, त, ब [k, r, t̪, b] or only after some; and in the latter case, after which. Again, since there are two letters श and ष to represent the only **sh**-sound in most accents of modern Hindi, there can be a spelling problem. Thus, even in a language like Hindi, where the sound-spelling relationship is far more systematic than in many other languages, the written form does not always represent the spoken form unambiguously. This, then, is the problem.

5.2 International Phonetic Alphabet

5.21

To overcome the problem discussed at length in Section 5.1, a need had been felt to evolve an alphabet in which words of any language could be written unambiguously. One such alphabet, which is used very extensively by phoneticians all over the world, is the *International Phonetic Alphabet* (or IPA), devised by the International Phonetic Association (see the chart in Section 5.3). It is claimed to have symbols to represent all the sounds that exist in the languages of the world; it can therefore be used to transcribe words of any language, i e to write them down more or less as one pronounces them. It is based primarily on the Roman alphabet; but since the 26 letters of the Roman alphabet are grossly inadequate to represent all the sounds that exist in all the languages of the world, some additional symbols have been devised by modification of the existing symbols of the alphabet, and some other symbols have been borrowed from the Greek alphabet. Examples of modification are the symbols ʌ and ə formed by modification of the letters *v* and *e* of the Roman alphabet. Examples of borrowing are the Greek letters *θ*, ð, Φ, *β*. Furthermore, in some cases, the small and capital letters of the Roman alphabet have been employed to stand for different sounds. Thus, the small *r* represents one sound, while the small capital ʀ represents another. Finally, there is also a set of *diacritics*, or modifiers, which are used to modify given sounds. Thus the diacritic ̪ put below the symbol of an alveolar plosive indicates that the plosive in question is dental, not alveolar: e g while t stands for the alveolar sound at the beginning of the English word *tea*, t̪ represents the first sound of the Hindi word तुम [t̪um] 'you'.

5.22

In this section, we shall describe and illustrate some of the symbols of the IPA.

p	voiceless bilabial plosive: s*p*in, प in Hindi पल [pəl] 'moment'
p^{h}	voiceless aspirated bilabial plosive: *p*in, फ in Hindi फल [p^{h}əl] 'fruit'
f	voiceless labio-dental fricative: *f*it, फ़ in Urdu फ़रेब [fə're:b] 'deceit'
t	voiceless alveolar plosive: s*t*ain, *t*oday
t̪	voiceless dental plosive: त in Hindi ताली ['t̪a:li:] 'clap'
ʈ	voiceless retroflex plosive: ट in Hindi टोकरी ['ʈokri:] 'basket'
g	voiced velar plosive: *g*et, ग in Hindi गोल [go:l] 'round'
ɣ	voiced velar fricative: ग़ in Urdu ग़रीब [ɣə'ri:b] 'poor'
c	voiceless palatal plosive: च in Hindi चल [cəl] 'go'
tʃ	voiceless palato-alveolar affricate: *ch*air
c^{h}	voiceless aspirated palatal plosive: छ in Hindi छल [c^{h}əl] 'deceit'

t̪ʰ voiceless aspirated dental plosive: थ in Hindi थाली ['t̪ʰaːliː] 'plate'

θ voiceless dental fricative: *th*in

ʈʰ voiceless aspirated retroflex plosive: ठ in Hindi ठोकर ['ʈʰoːkər] 'kick'

v voiced labio-dental fricative: *v*est

w voiced labio-velar semi-vowel: *w*est

ʋ voiced labio-dental frictionless continuant: व in Hindi विचार [ʋi'caːr] 'thought'

b voiced bilabial plosive: *b*it, ब in Hindi बीस [biːs] 'twenty'

i front close unrounded short vowel: इ in Hindi इस [is] 'this'

iː front close unrounded long vowel: *ea*t, ई in Hindi ईख [iːkʰ] 'sugarcane'

ə central unrounded short vowel: *a*go, अ in Hindi [əb] 'now'

əʴ central unrounded short *r*-coloured vowel: *ir* in American English pronunciation of g*ir*l, sh*ir*t

5.3 Phonetic Transcription

5.31

As already seen, the IPA can be used to represent in writing the sounds, words, phrases, and sentences of any language of the world. Such representation is called *phonetic transcription*. To illustrate how this is done, take the English words *cent* and *can't*, both beginning with the letter *c*. The first is transcribed as [sent] and the second as [kaːnt]. From the transcription it is clear that the letter *c* is pronounced differently in these two words. Now, take the word *access*, transcribed as ['ækses], from which it can be seen that the two *c*'s in this word are pronounced differently. On the other hand, if different spellings represent the same sound in different words, then, in their phonetic transcription, the sound in question will be represented by the same phonetic symbol. Thus, in the transcription of the words *kit*, *rock*, *cut*, *acclaim*, *chemistry* and *queen*, the **k**-sound will consistently be represented by the phonetic symbol [k], the different ways of writing this sound notwithstanding.

This particular characteristic of phonetic transcription, viz 'one sound one symbol', enables us to show the pronunciation of words unambiguously in writing, thereby making it possible to provide pronunciation in dictionaries. Any pronouncing dictionary of English (or any dictionary of English which gives pronunciation as well) will at once show that (i) the letter *g* in the word *target* is pronounced [g] (as in *get*), and not [dʒ] (as in *gem*); (ii) the letters *ee*, *e*, *ea*, *ie*, *ei*, *ey*, *i*, *ay*, *eo* are all pronounced [iː] in the words *tree*, *be*, *peace*, *piece*, *seize*, *key*, *machine*, *quay*, and *people*, respectively. Further, the dictionary can also show that the letters *b*, *l*, *p*, *c*, *n* are 'silent' in the words *lamb*, *talk*, *psychology*, *indict*, and *damn*, respectively. What is more, it can tell us that while *n* is silent in *damn*, it is not so in *damnable*. Examples can be multiplied.

To conclude, we may draw the reader's attention again to the fact that the IPA can be employed to write any language of the world. Indeed, so great is the

THE INTERNATIONAL

		Bilabial	*Labiodental*	*Dental, Alveolar, or Post-alveolar*	*Retroflex*
CONSONANTS (pulmonic air-stream mechanism)	*Nasal*	m	ɱ	n	ɳ
	Plosive	p b		t d	ʈ ɖ
	(Median) Fricative	ɸ β	f v	θ ð s z	ʂ ʐ
	(Median) Approximant		ʋ	ɹ	ɻ
	Lateral Fricative			ɬ ɮ	
	Lateral (Approximant)			l	ɭ
	Trill			r	
	Tap or Flap			ɾ	ɽ
(non-pulmonic air-stream)	*Ejective*	p'		t'	
	Implosive	ɓ		ɗ	
	(Median) Click	ʘ		ʇ ʗ	
	Lateral Click			ʖ	

DIACRITICS

̥ Voiceless n̥ d̥
̬ Voiced s̬ t̬
ʰ Aspirated tʰ
̤ Breathy-voiced b̤ a̤
̪ Dental t̪
̫ Labialized t̫
ʲ Palatalized tʲ
~ Velarized or Pharyngealized ɫ, ɫ
̩ Syllabic n̩ l̩
or ͜ Simultaneous sf (but see also under the heading Affricates)

˔ or ̝ Raised e˔, e̝, e̝ w̝
˕ or ̞ Lowered e˕, e̞, e̞ ʁ̞
̟ Advanced u+, u̟
- or ̠ Retracted i̠, i-, t̠
̈ Centralized ë
̃ Nasalized ɑ̃
˞, ˞, ʁ r-coloured ɑ˞
ː Long ɑː
ˑ Half-long ɑˑ
̆ Non-syllabic ŭ
˒ More rounded ɔ˒
˓ Less rounded y˓

OTHER SYMBOLS

ɕ, ʑ Alveolo-palatal fricatives
ʆ, ʓ Palatalized ʃ, ʒ
ɼ Alveolar fricative trill
ɺ Alveolar lateral flap
ɧ Simultaneous ʃ and x
ʃˢ Variety of ʃ resembling s, etc.
ɪ = ɩ
ʊ = ɷ
ɜ = Variety of ə
ɚ = r-coloured ə

PHONETIC ALPHABET (Revised to 1979)

Palato-alveolar	*Palatal*	*Velar*	*Uvular*	*Labial-Palatal*	*Labial-Velar*	*Pharyngeal*	*Glottal*
	ɲ	ŋ	ɴ				
	c ɟ	k ɡ	q ɢ		k͡p ɡ͡b		ʔ
ʃ ʒ	ç ʝ	x ɣ	χ ʁ		ʍ	ħ ʕ	h ɦ
	j	ɰ		ɥ	w		
	ʎ						
			ʀ ʀ				
		k' ɠ					

VOWELS

Front		*Back*	
i	ɨ	ɯ	*Close*
ɪ			
e		ɤ	*Half-close*
	ə		
ɛ		ʌ	*Half-open*
æ	ɐ		
a		ɑ	*Open*

Unrounded

Front		*Back*
y	ʉ	u
ʏ		ʊ
ø		o
	ɵ	
œ		ɔ
ɶ		ɒ

Rounded

STRESS, TONE (PITCH)

ˈ stress, placed at beginning of stressed syllable: ˌ secondary stress: ˉ high level pitch, high tone: ˍ low level: ˊ high rising: ˏ low rising: ˋ high falling: ˎ low falling: ˆ rise-fall: ˇ fall-rise.

AFFRICATES can be written as digraphs, as ligatures, or with slur marks; thus ts, tʃ, dʒ: ʦ ʧ ʤ: t͡s t͡ʃ d͡ʒ. c, ɟ may occasionally be used for tʃ, dʒ.

advantage of this alphabet that, in modern times, whenever a hitherto unwritten language is reduced to writing, the writing system given to it is very often kept as close to the IPA as possible.

5.32 *Types of Phonetic Transcription*

Our use of the term 'phonetic transcription' so far might give the impression that there is only one type of phonetic transcription. This is by no means true. Attempts have indeed been made from time to time to evolve scripts that might be easier than the IPA to teach and to use in writing, typing, and printing. Thus, for the vowel sounds in the English words *cat* and *cot*, some dictionaries and books on English pronunciation use the symbols **a** and **o** in place of æ and ɒ, respectively, which would represent the two sounds more accurately in terms of the IPA. This is one reason why more than one type of phonetic transcription may be available, even for the same variety of a language.

Another, and a crucial, reason for having more than one type of phonetic transcription is the following. Sometimes we wish to show in a phonetic transcription only the distinctive sounds of a language, called its *phonemes* (see Section 6.1), while at other times, our concern is to show even those sound features that are not distinctive within a given language. While a full appreciation of this point will have to wait till the concept of the *phoneme* is explained (in Chapter 6), an illustration from English might make this point clear. The **p**-sounds in the words *pin* and *spin* are not identical: the former is aspirated (i e it has a puff of breath following it); the latter is not. The former is more or less like the Hindi फ [p^h] sound as in फल [p^{h}əl] 'fruit', while the latter is like the Hindi प [p] sound as in पल [pəl] 'moment'. Such difference between the two **p**-sounds notwithstanding, they are regarded as essentially *one* sound so far as English is concerned. This is so because the use of one in place of the other might only 'sound odd' (to the native ears), but it does not effect any change of meaning in this language. So the two **p**-sounds, which we have represented as [p^h] and [p], are taken, in English, to constitute one phoneme, which is transcribed as /p/. When this is done, the two sounds, [p^h] and [p], are regarded as allophones of the English phoneme /p/. A transcription that disregards such distinctions, and represents only the phonemes of a language, is called ***phonemic transcription***, whereas the one that shows allophonic distinctions explicitly is called ***allophonic transcription***. The two English words exemplified above would be represented as /pɪn/ and /spɪn/ in their phonemic transcription, and as [p^{h}ɪn] and [spɪn] in their allophonic transcription. (Notice that we use the notation / / to enclose phonemic transcription, and [ ] for allophonic transcription. The latter notation is used in those cases too where the phonemic status of the sounds represented is of no concern to us, for example, in transcribing Hindi words in this book.

The reader should bear in mind that in some books on phonetics, the terms 'broad transcription' and 'narrow transcription' are also sometimes used to refer to phonemic and allophonic transcription, respectively. But we would not advise the reader to use these terms because their use can lead to some avoidable confusion.

5.4 Uses of Phonetic Transcription

One chief use of phonetic transcription might by now have become clear—to represent the pronunciation of a word, or a longer sequence, unambiguously. Such a use of phonetic transcription makes it possible for dictionaries to provide pronunciations of individual words and for language teachers to teach them. The use of phonetic transcription is particularly helpful in teaching a foreign or second language to adults, who cannot learn easily and economically entirely by imitation. Thus, such a learner might more readily get the right pronunciation of the English word *tortoise* by seeing it transcribed as /ˈtɔːtəs/ than by relying exclusively on imitation. Indeed, the transcription may at once tell him all that instructions like the following may do only slowly: (i) pronounce the first *o* as it is pronounced in *short*, (ii) make *r* silent (for a particular variety of British English), (iii) pronounce *oi* as the second vowel in *shaken*, (iv) pronounce *s* as in *see*, not as in *his*, and (v) make the final *e* silent.

What holds for the fresh teaching of pronunciation is also true of the remedial teaching of it. Indeed, in correcting a long-established instance of mispronunciation, resort to sheer imitation may be of no great help, for the learner may persistently hear the teacher's pronunciation as in no way different from his own.

Another use of phonetic transcription consists in comparing the sound systems of different languages. When we list the phonemic inventories of any two or more languages, we can at once see which sounds are common to them, and which are not. Thus the phonemic inventories of Urdu, Hindi, and English can at once reveal that (i) Urdu and Hindi have dental plosives (as word-initially in तुम [t̪um] 'you', दो [d̪oː] 'two'), whereas English has none; (ii) English and Urdu have **f** and **z** sounds, while Hindi has neither (except in the words borrowed from Urdu); and (iii) English has dental fricatives (as at the beginning of the words *thin* and *then*), while Hindi and Urdu have none; and so on.

Yet another use of phonetic transcription is found in comparing different varieties of the same language. Thus the English words *last*, *fast*, and *class* are transcribed /lɑːst/, /fɑːst/, and /klɑːs/ in their British pronunciation, and /læst/ /fæst/, and /klæs/, respectively, in their American pronunciation, thus explicitly bringing out the difference between the two varieties of English in respect of the vowel use in such words.

Finally, when a researcher in linguistics is for the first time writing down the text of a speech in a language unknown to him, he has to have recourse to phonetic transcription only. The script used by such a language, even if familiar to him, cannot go very far in informing him as to how the texts are actually pronounced. And indeed a researcher may sometimes have to deal with a language so far unwritten. In all such cases, phonetic transcription proves immensely useful.

5.5 Summary

The written forms of most languages of the world are a representation of their spoken forms. This fact notwithstanding, there exists no perfect correspondence between the spelling and the sound in any language. For some languages, however, the correspondence is fairly good (as in Hindi), while for some others it is far from satisfactory (as in English and French). Because of this mismatch between the spelling and the sound, a learner cannot know how to pronounce a new word encountered in his reading; nor can he decide how to spell a new word heard by him.

To overcome this problem, phoneticians have evolved an alphabet called the *International Phonetic Alphabet* (*IPA*). With the symbols and diacritics this alphabet provides, it is possible to transcribe words of any language of the world, that is, to write them as they are pronounced. Such a writing is called *phonetic transcription*. It makes speech visible, thereby making it possible to provide pronunciation of words in dictionaries. It helps language teachers to teach pronunciation, or to remedy it, especially when the learners are adults. With its help, it is possible to compare the sound systems of different languages or different varieties of the same language. Besides, researchers have recourse to phonetic transcription in investigating the sound systems of languages.

Phonetic transcription is of many types, of which the two most extensively employed are *phonemic transcription* and *allophonic transcription*. In phonemic transcription, only the distinctive sounds of a language, i e its phonemes, are represented; in allophonic transcription, on the other hand, even those features of sound are explicitly represented which are not linguistically significant in a given language, i e which do not bring about a change of meaning, e g in English, the aspiration of the **p**, **t**, and **k** sounds in certain positions.

EXERCISES

I Given here are the phonetic symbols for some of the vowels and consonants used in a particular variety of English. From the key-words given against the symbols, try to judge the sounds they stand for.

iː	as in *see* /siː/	p	as in *pack* /pæk/
e	as in *set* /set/	s	as in *sell* /sel/
æ	as in *sat* /sæt/	t	as in *tell* /tel/
ɒ	as in *pot* /pɒt/	θ	as in *thick* /θɪk/
		k	as in *kill* /kɪl/
		l	as in *leaf* /liːf/
		f	as in *feel* /fiːl/
		d	as in *deal* /diːl/
		r	as in *rat* /ræt/

Now attempt a phonemic transcription of the following English words:

cat	seat	thief	speak	peck	pat	deaf
top	read (past tense of *read*)			sack	tea	death

pea	pet	priest	drop	sad	soft	cease
dress	loss	steal	three	thread	quay	cock
ski	fleet	clot	slack	feast	trough	tread
wrap	wrest	spread	threat	lead (verb)		
lead (noun)		cough				

II For the variety of English mentioned above, a few more symbols are added in this exercise:

ɪ as in *sit* /sɪt/
ɑː as in *calm* /kɑːm/
ɔː as in *saw* /sɔː/
ʊ as in *put* /pʊt/
uː as in *two* /tuː/
ʌ as in *but* /bʌt/
ɜː as in *shirt* /ʃɜːt/
b as in *bed* /bed/
g as in *get* /get/
tʃ as in *check* /tʃek/
dʒ as in *jute* /dʒuːt/
v as in *vet* /vet/
ð as in *that* /ðæt/
z as in *zoo* /zuː/
ʃ as in *she* /ʃiː/
h as in *hen* /hen/
m as in *men* /men/
n as in *not* /nɒt/
ŋ as in *hang* /hæŋ/
j as in *yes* /jes/
w as in *wet* /wet/

With the help of the symbols you have learnt so far, look up the pronunciation of the following words in the *Oxford Advanced Learner's Dictionary of Current English* (Third edition, revised and updated), and then pronounce them:

knead	sieve	mete	says	hymn	mass	lamb
ring	gem	err	heard	tough	glove	hung
tooth	wool	truth	grew	threw	loose	juice
tomb	queue	nook	hall	bought	war	heart
dawn	shone	wasp	want	one	squat	clue
psalm	clerk	hearth	cruel	chord	alms	nerve
monk	song	wretch	thumb	wreath	wreathe	worse
path	tense	use(n)	paths	tens	fifth	rough
halve	thought	chew	chores	gin	won	suite
yacht	loss					

III We now give some English words in their phonemic transcription. Read them out.

iːtʃ	θriː	pɪŋk	bɔːl	dɜːt	djuːk
dɔːn	wɜːd	wɪdθ	bæk	gɜːl	kɒf
næk	kliːn	bɪlt	hɑːf	wɔːk	ʃʊd
nekst	niːl	dʒæk	sæŋ	rek	lɑːdʒ
lʌŋ	huː	θæŋks	ðæn	mɪθs	truːðz
skuːl	ʃʊə	breθ	briːð	θiːv	dʒem
wɪtʃ	wɒnt	wʌns	vɜːs	djuː	jɒt

Write each of these words in ordinary spelling.

IV Group the following words according to the vowels contained in them.

cheese	poor	rhythm	share	dead	ere	plait
how	monk	blood	know	curt	laugh	gone
dye	saw	great	would	err	chew	pure
pear	dear	found	toe	point	height	weigh
urge	lose	wolf	more	was	heart	son
mass	dead	said	sieve	key	eve	quay
Thames	done	tough	clerk	gone	cause	wool
fool	blue	food	foot	work	foe	

V Now look up the dictionary to check the grouping you have made.

6
The Phoneme

6.1 Introduction

The human speech mechanism is capable of producing an infinite number of speech sounds. From this vast human repertoire of speech sounds, every language makes its own selection. The selection that a particular language makes constitutes its sound system, which itself comprises a very large number of speech sounds. But not all of these sounds are significant. That is to say, not all of these sounds make any meaningful difference between words and help convey distinctions of meaning in communication between two individuals speaking that language. Let us study, for example, the English word *cake* [kʰeɪk˺]. Any native speaker of English will say that the first and last sounds in this word are the *same*. But the phonetician will make a distinction between them, though he knows that they are phonetically (i e in terms of both their place and manner of articulation, and the position of the vocal cords) *similar*. The first sound in this word is aspirated (i e pronounced with an accompanying puff of breath) and the last sound is unaspirated, and unexploded (i e pronounced without an audible release of the complete closure). In the English word *scale* [skeɪl], we have another **k**-sound, which is phonetically similar to, but not the same as, the above two sounds in the sense that it is neither aspirated nor unexploded. Now, these three sounds, which have been symbolized as [kʰ], [k˺], and [k] are not contrastive or *distinctive* in that the substitution of one for another in these words will not give a different word. Suppose a certain speaker of English (e g a non-native speaker) does not aspirate the initial [k] in *cake* and pronounces the word as [keɪk˺], it will not bring about any difference in the meaning, that is, the word *cake* will not change into another word. Again, if the word *scale* were pronounced as [skʰeɪl], it would remain the same word from the point of view of meaning. We can say, in other words, that though these three phonetically similar sounds, [kʰ], [k˺], and [k], are different in one way or other, the difference between them is not *functional* in English, i e it is not crucial for the purpose of communication. For communication, therefore, these sounds can be grouped together into one sound, say /k/, in English.

Let us now look at the English words *cake* [keɪk] and *bake* [beɪk]. The difference between them consists only in one sound in the initial position. But this difference is of a different order from that between [kʰ], [k˺], and [k]. The substitution of the sound [b] for the sound [k] in the same position gives us a different word; in other words, it brings about the difference of meaning between the words *cake* and *bake* (whereas, as we have seen, the substitution of [k] for [kʰ] in *cake* does *not* bring about any difference in the meaning of the word). The difference between [b] and [k] is thus taken to be *contrastive* in this position. It should also be noted that [b] and [k] are phonetically more *dissimilar* than [kʰ] and [k]. ([b] is bilabial and [k] is velar, apart from the first being voiced and the second voiceless.) Two phonetically dissimilar sounds like [b] and [k], which can occur in the same position (or 'environment') and are contrastive, are called *phonemes*. [Following the general practice of linguists, square brackets are being used, here and in the following chapters, to indicate allophones and oblique strokes to indicate phonemes (see Section 6.2).] If we now substitute some other sounds for /k/ in the word *cake* /keɪk/, we shall get *fake* /feɪk/, *lake* /leɪk/, *make* /meɪk/, *rake* /reɪk/, *sake* /seɪk/, *shake* /ʃeɪk/, *take* /teɪk/, and *wake* /weɪk/. The sounds /f/, /l/, /m/, /r/, /s/, /ʃ/, /t/, and /w/ are all phonemes because, according to the definition given above, they are phonetically dissimilar and contrast with /k/ in the same environment, i e in the initial position of the word *cake*. Similarly, by substituting sounds which contrast with /k/ in the final position of this word, we get the phonemes /dʒ/, /m/, /n/, /p/, /s/, /t/, and /v/ from the words *cage* /keɪdʒ/, *came* /keɪm/, *cane* /keɪn/, *cape* /keɪp/, *case* /keɪs/, *Kate* /keɪt/, and *cave* /keɪv/. And by substituting sounds which contrast with /eɪ/ in the medial position, we get the phonemes /ɪ/, /ɔː/, and /əʊ/ from the words *kick* /kɪk/, *cork* /kɔːk/, and *coke* /kəʊk/. By this process of *commutation*, we can establish all the phonemes of English and, for that matter, draw up an inventory of the phonemes of any language.

Every language makes use of a limited number of such contrastive sounds, or phonemes. English, for example, has 44 phonemes in its sound system, Hindi 46, Tamil 41, and Kannada 47. It must be borne in mind that, since phonemes are contrastive units of sound in the sound system of a given language, they have validity only in relation to that language. Sounds which are phonemes in respect of one language may be only positional variants, or allophones (see Sections 5.32 and 6.2), in relation to another. For instance, the sound [p] and [pʰ], which are allophones of the same phoneme /p/ in English, as in the words *spot* [spɒt] and *pot* [pʰɒt], are different phonemes in Hindi, as is clear from the words पल [pəl] 'moment' and फल [pʰəl] 'fruit'.

6.2 Allophones

Let us go back a little and look at the words *cake* [kʰeɪk˺] and *scale* [skeɪl] once again. We have already seen that [kʰ], [k˺] and [k] are phonetically *similar* sounds, and yet different from one another, and that the difference between them is not contrastive. It is also clear that the difference between them depends upon their position in the word. In English, [kʰ] can occur only in the initial position in an accented syllable, [k˺] only in the final position, and [k] only after [s]. None of them can be substituted for another. We can, therefore, say that these sounds occur in *predictable* and *mutually exclusive* positions, or environments, in English. In other words, they are in *complementary distribution* with one another. Such phonetically similar sounds in complementary distribution in relation to one another are called *positional variants*, or *allophones*, of the same phoneme. To give another example from English, we may take the case of the phoneme /l/. It has two positional variants, [l] and [ɫ], as in the words *loyal* [lɔɪɫ] and *field* [fi:ɫd]. [l] is articulated with the tip of the tongue making a complete closure with the teeth ridge; for [ɫ], in addition to this, the back of the tongue also goes up simultaneously to articulate with the soft palate. [l] occurs before vowels and /j/, and is called *clear* [l], and [ɫ] occurs before consonants (minus /j/) and word-finally, and is called *dark* [ɫ]. Thus the phoneme /l/ has two allophones—[l] and [ɫ]. As against this, the phoneme /r/, in English, has several, the chief ones being [ɹ], [ɹ̝], and [ɾ]. The first one, [ɹ], is a post-alveolar frictionless continuant, which occurs in the initial position in words as in *red* [ɹed]; [ɹ̝] is a post-alveolar fricative, occurring after /d/ as in *dress* [dɹ̝es]; and [ɾ] is an alveolar tap, which occurs between two vowels and after /θ/, as in the words *carry* ['kæɾɪ] and *throne* [θɾəʊn], respectively.

6.3 Summary

A phoneme is a contrastive unit of sound in the sound system of a particular language. It is realized differently, depending upon its position in words, or its environment. These positionally defined realizations, or variants, are its allophones. To put it differently, a phoneme is a group or family of positionally defined sounds. Every language has a limited number of phonemes in its sound system, though the selection it makes from the vast human repertoire of speech sounds is very large.

7
The Syllable

7.1 Introduction

In the earlier chapters, we studied speech sounds in general and discussed the 'minimal contrastive unit' of sound called the *phoneme*. Now, the phonemes of a language do not add up in a simple manner (i e in the sequence of a + b + c + ···) to form its utterances. They combine to form the next higher unit, which forms part of the next higher unit, and so on. The unit at the next higher level than the phoneme is called the *syllable*. The notion of the syllable as a unit, as distinct from the phoneme and the word, is very important since the syllable is a very significant unit in the production of speech, and, without taking it into account, we cannot analyse and describe speech.

Many attempts have been made in recent times to define the term 'syllable', but no agreed definition is yet available. Although it is very difficult to *define* the syllable, it is not so to *identify* syllables in a given word. And for our purpose here, we do not need to do more than be able to identify them and divide words into syllables.

7.2 Division of Words into Syllables

A word consists of one or more than one syllable. In the case of most words, it should be comparatively easy to point out how many syllables a given word has. For example, it is not difficult to identify the syllables in the English words *rat*, *redeem*, *humanist*, *degenerate*, *electricity*, and *characterization*, and say that they contain one, two, three, four, five and six syllables, respectively. The pronunciations of these words in phonemic transcription are: /ræt/, /rɪ-diːm/, /hjuː-mə-nɪst/, /dɪ-dʒe-nə-reɪt/, /ɪ-lek-trɪ-sɪ-tɪ/, /kæ-rɪk-tə-raɪ-zeɪ-ʃən/. It will be clear from these words (the syllable division is marked with a hyphen in each case) that the number of syllables in each corresponds to the number of vowel sounds (i e vowel phonemes) it contains. (It must be remembered here that the digraph—i e a sequence of two letters—e g eɪ in the words *degenerate* and *characterization*, represents a single vowel phoneme.) This rough and ready 'rule' of dividing words into syllables will apply to most words in English.

Another not-so-easy way of identifying syllables in a word could be to count the distinguishable postures (or movements) of a set of speech organs, assumed in the articulation of a given word. To each of these postures, in most cases, would correspond a syllable. If we listen to the pronunciations of the six words given above, or pronounce them ourselves, carefully and properly, we shall notice that the articulatory organs assume as many distinguishable postures as there are syllables in each of these words. Thus, either way, it is easy to determine the number of syllables in a word.

However, it may be sometimes difficult to decide where to draw the syllable boundary. The difficulty is generally of two kinds: The first is to do with the English spelling, and the second with the consonant clusters (see Section 7.5). In respect of spelling, there are many words in English having (i) double letters, and (ii) the letter **x**, in their spelling. In words containing double letters, if the syllable boundary is to be marked where the double letters occur, it is marked by putting a hyphen *between* the double letters:

ac-count, ag-grieve, com-mand
af-fect, al-lot, as-sume.

As, in each of these words, the two letters stand for a single sound, the hyphen *between* them obviously does not reflect the true division. The case with words having **x** in their spelling is however just the reverse in that the single letter **x** in such words stands for two sounds. For instance, in the words *exit*, *exempt*, and *luxury*, the letter **x** represents the sounds /ks/, /gz/, and /kʃ/, respectively. If we go by the spelling, it will not be possible to decide whether to divide these words as *ex-it*, *ex-empt*, and *lux-u-ry*, or as *e-xit*, *e-xempt*, and *lu-xu-ry*. Now, if we write down both these kinds of words (i e words having double letters and **x** in their spelling) in phonemic transcription, there will be no difficulty at all in dividing them into syllables. The phonemic transcription of these two sets of words with their syllable division marked will be:

(1) /ə-kaʊnt/, /ə-griːv/, /kə-mɑːnd/, /ə-fekt/, /ə-lɒt/, /ə-sjuːm/; and
(2) /ek-sɪt/, /ɪg-zempt/, /lʌk-ʃə-rɪ/.

It is clear from the transcription that the difficulty posed by these two kinds of words is more apparent than real. In their phonemic transcription, they easily lend themselves to syllable division. It would therefore be advisable to identify syllables in such words, and even in other words, after they have been reduced to their phonemic transcription.

The second difficulty in respect of syllable division is to do with words containing consonant clusters. Let us, in this connection, consider the English words *astray* /əstreɪ/, *estrange* /ɪstreɪndʒ/, *escape* /ɪskeɪp/, and *extra* /ekstrə/. The question arises whether to syllabify these words as /ə-streɪ/, /ɪ-streɪndʒ/, /ɪ-skeɪp/, and /ek-strə/, or as /əs-treɪ/, /ɪs-treindʒ/, /ɪs-keɪp/, and /eks-trə/. There is no fixed rule regarding this apart from the constraint that the division should not violate any rules of the phonology of the language. English admits of certain consonant clusters, and does not admit of certain others, in the beginning and the end of its syllables. Both the above divisions are possible because English allows of /sk-/, /str-/, and /tr-/ in the beginning of its syllables, and /-ks/ in the end. We may break up the word *astray* /əstreɪ/ even into /əst-reɪ/ because the cluster /-st/ can occur in the final position of an English word. For the same reason, the remaining three words, namely, *estrange*, *escape*, and *extra*, can be divided in more than two ways:

estrange	/ɪstreɪndʒ/:/ɪ-streɪndʒ/ or /ɪs-treɪndʒ/ or /ɪst-reɪndʒ/
escape	/ɪskeɪp/:/ɪ-skeɪp/ or /ɪs-keɪp/ or /ɪsk-eɪp/
extra	/ekstrə/:/ek-strə/ or /eks-trə/ or /ekst-rə/

Thus, while dividing English words containing consonant clusters into their constituent syllables, what we should bear in mind is that the rules of English phonology relating to the occurrence of these clusters are not violated.

7.3 The Structure of the Syllable

Being the next higher unit than the speech sound (i e the phoneme), the syllable is made up of one or more than one speech sound. Speech sounds are either vowels or consonants. The vowel element is essential to the structure of a syllable; that is, a syllable is not possible without the vowel element. Now, the vowel element being obligatory, if a syllable consists of only one sound, the sound will be a vowel. For example, the English syllables *oh* /əʊ/, *eh* /eɪ/, and *a* /eɪ/ consist of one vowel each. And if a syllable consists of more than one sound, one of them must be a vowel and the remaining one(s) consonant(s), as in the syllables *go* /gəʊ/, *on* /ɒn/, and *sit* /sɪt/. The vowel obviously is the obligatory element in a syllable and is called its *nucleus*. The consonant, on the other hand, occupies a marginal place and is optional, as is clear from the above examples. The consonant which begins a syllable is called the *releasing* consonant, and that which occurs at the end of a syllable is called the *arresting* consonant. In the syllable *bad* /bæd/, for instance, /b/ is the releasing consonant and /d/ the arresting consonant. Now, if we represent the vowel in this syllable by the symbol V and the consonant by the symbol C, the syllable *bad* /bæd/ will be represented by C V C, in which V is the nuclear element, and C's are the marginal elements.

7.31 Syllabic Consonants

In the foregoing account, we have seen that the vowel is the nucleus of a syllable, and the consonant occupies a marginal place in its structure. It might be argued that this is not always the case. There are syllables, of course, in which the nuclear place is occupied by certain consonants, but then, these consonants function like vowels. To give an example, let us look at the English words *button* /bʌtn/, *bottle* /bɒtl/, and *rhythm* /rɪðm/. It is generally agreed that each of these words has two syllables, and not one. Their syllable division is shown as /bʌ-tn/, /bɒ-tl/, and /rɪ-ðm/ in spite of the fact that the second syllable in each word has apparently no vowel. Here /-tn/, /-tl/, and /-ðm/ constitute independent syllables by themselves, without any intervening vowel. In such cases, the sounds /n/, /l/, and /m/ are said to form the nucleus, and are called *syllabic* consonants (i e they represent the V element in the syllable structure). The explanation generally given is that the nasal sounds [m] and [n] and the lateral sound [l] have the *inherent sonority* (i e their loudness relative to other consonant sounds) comparable to that of some vowels, and can therefore, like vowels, combine with consonants to form syllables. There are several other words of this kind in English in which /m/, /n/, and /l/ are syllabic. Some examples are:

prism	/prɪ-zm/
sudden	/sʌ-dn/
mutton	/mʌ-tn/
brittle	/brɪ-tl/
subtle	/sʌ-tl/

When /m/, /n/, and /l/ function as syllabic consonants, they are generally marked, in a slightly narrower transcription, with the diacritic [̩] as in [prɪzm̩], [sʌdn̩] and [brɪtl̩].

7.4 Types of the Syllable

With the help of the symbols V and C, representing the vowel and the consonant element, respectively, we can analyse the structure of different kinds of syllable. Analysed below are the types of syllable that we have in English.

Type 1	*Word*	*V* (Structure in terms of C and V)
	I	/aɪ/
	a	/ə/ or /eɪ/
	ah	/ɑː/
	heir	/eə/
Type 2	*Word*	*VC*
	an	/ən/ or /æn/
	ass	/æs/
	all	/ɔːl/
	ice	/aɪs/
Type 3	*Word*	*CV*
	no	/nəʊ/
	law	/lɔː/
	saw	/sɔː/
	sea	siː
Type 4	*Word*	*CVC*
	can	/kæn/
	boss	/bɒs/
	girl	/gɜːl/
	let	/let/
Type 5	*Word*	*CCV*
	play	/pleɪ/
	crow	/krəʊ/
	slay	/sleɪ/
	cry	/kraɪ/

Type 6	*Word*	*CCCV*
	straw	/strɔː/
	spray	/spreɪ/
	spree	/spriː/
	screw	/skruː/
Type 7	*Word*	*CCCVC*
	stream	/striːm/
	street	/striːt/
	spruce	/spruːs/
	sprawl	/sprɔːl/
Type 8	*Word*	*CCCVCC*
	strange	/streɪndʒ/
	strand	/strænd/
	sprained	/spreɪnd/
	screamed	/skriːmd/
Type 9	*Word*	*CCCVCCC*
	strands	/strændz/
	strengths	/streŋθs/
Type 10	*Word*	*VCCCC*
	pre-empts	/-empts/ (second syllable)
Type 11	*Word*	*CVCCCC*
	tempts	/tempts/
	texts	/teksts/
Type 12	*Word*	*CCVCCCC*
	twelfths	/twelfθs/
Type 13	*Word*	*CCVCCC*
	stunts	/stʌnts/
	brands	/brændz/
	trunks	/trʌŋks/
	stands	/stændz/
Type 14	*Word*	*CCVCC*
	brats	/bræts/
	crates	/kreɪts/
	spans	/spænz/
	snacks	/snæks/
Type 15	*Word*	*CVCC*
	tent	/tent/
	once	/wʌns/
	rains	/reɪnz/

Type 16	*Word*	*VCC*
	and	/ænd/
	ask	/ɑːsk/
	ilk	/ɪlk/
	earls	/ɜːlz/

A careful look at these sixteen types of English syllable will show that at the most three consonants can occur in the beginning of a syllable and four in the end. It will also be clear that the V element is obligatory and the C element optional. Using parentheses to indicate the optional elements, we can deduce (from the above types) the structure of a typical English syllable, which is of the kind (CCC) V (CCCC) or $C_{0-3}VC_{0-4}$. This means that in an English syllable there can be zero to three consonants in the beginning and zero to four in the end.

7.5 Consonant Clusters

We have seen that English permits up to three consonants to begin a syllable and up to four to end it. Such sequences of consonants at the beginning or the end of a syllable, occurring together, are called *consonant clusters*. For example, /-nd/ in the word *send* /send/ is a consonant cluster because it forms part of the same syllable, whereas /-mb-/ in the word *number* /nʌm-bə/ is not a cluster since /-m/ and /b-/ belong to two different syllables: /-m/ is the arresting consonant of the first syllable, and /b-/ the releasing consonant of the second. Now, consonants, like /m/ and /b/, which occur together in a word but form part of two different syllables, are called *abutting* consonants.

7.6 Summary

The unit of sound at the next higher level than the phoneme is called the *syllable*. Although it is difficult to define a syllable, it is certainly not so to identify syllables constituting a given word. The syllable is made up of one or more than one speech sound. The vowel forms its nucleus and is obligatory, whereas the consonant is optional. The structure of a typical English syllable is $C_{0-3}VC_{0-4}$, where C stands for the optional consonant element, and V for the obligatory vowel element.

EXERCISES

I Point out the number of syllables in the following words:

Bottom, following, phonemic, register, recede, succession, stupidity, terrific, trepidation, tweezers, twelfth, unprovided, unwieldy, universal, vitamin, vocabulary, vocational, wilderness, waive, wallet.

II Attempt a phonemic transcription of the following words and indicate their syllable division with a hyphen. Example: naughty: nɔː-tɪ

Attempt, collective, conspiracy, contrary, degrade, degree, dissertation, doxology, excite, exchange, exercise, foetus, gypsy, haughty, homonym, instance, misrepresent, organism, scuttle, chaos, appreciate, history, leopard, naive, shower.

III Transcribe the following words and show the structure of the syllables constituting them in terms of C V C. Example: about : ə-baʊt : V – C V C

Basked, blind, brevity, brushed, crumble, strict, strength, spring, spects, splashing, taunt, taxed, tearfully, twinkle, venue, wireless.

IV Write down 15 words to illustrate the use of /m/, /n/, and /l/ as syllabic consonants in English.

V Give five examples of abutting consonants in English.

VI Give five examples each of the following consonant clusters:

1 CC in the initial position
2 CCC in the initial position
3 CCC in the final position
4 CC in the final position
5 CCCC in the final position.

8 Various Accents of English

8.1 Introduction

When we refer to a language by labels, such as 'English', 'German', 'Arabic', or 'Hindi', we unwittingly suggest that it has only one speech form, which is uniform throughout. This, however, is far from the truth. In reality, most languages of the world have more than one clearly distinguishable form, or variety. Such varieties, when they differ from one another in respect of vocabulary, grammar, usage, and pronunciation, are called *dialects*. When, on the other hand, they differ in respect of pronunciation alone, they are called *accents*. Also, when only the pronunciation differences of different varieties of a language are being discussed, the varieties may be referred to as 'accents'. The word 'accent' is also used to speak about the relative prominence of a syllable in a word (see Chapter 12). In this chapter, however, 'accent' refers to a variety of a language in relation to pronunciation.

A language acquires a number of accents if it is spoken by large sections of people separated from one another geographically, socially, and/or educationally. This aptly applies to a language such as English, which is spoken so widely all over the world not only by those for whom it is the mother tongue, but also by many others, who use it for a variety of purposes (such as education, business, administration, and travel). It is meaningful, therefore, to distinguish between the native and non-native accents of English. Sections 8.2 and 8.3 will dwell upon this point.

8.2 Native Accents of English

As the mother tongue, English is spoken by the British, the Americans, the Canadians, the Australians, the New Zealanders, and the South Africans. All the various accents with which these people speak English are, by definition, native accents of English. There are, in some cases, wide variations within each of such regional accents. Thus there are very many accents of English within Britain, some of which are regional and others based on class or level of education. Generally, the accents of well-educated people are regarded as 'standard', and those of the uneducated as 'non-standard'. Non-standard native accents are also usually accompanied by non-standard grammar. Examples of such non-standard accents in Britain are the popular forms of pronunciation used in large cities such as London, Liverpool, and Birmingham, and certain regional accents such as the Yorkshire accent. Such non-standard accents are not formally taught at school; they are only imbibed from the older people in the family or community.

The accents of English generally recognized as the standard native accents are the following:

Educated South-eastern British
Educated Scottish
General American
Educated Canadian
Educated Australian
South African

The Educated Australian accent is supposed to subsume the Educated New Zealand accent as well.

These standard native accents enjoy, understandably, a much higher social status than non-native accents in their respective countries. But the degree of social status enjoyed by the Educated South-eastern British accent in England is far greater than that enjoyed by any other standard native accent in the country where it is spoken. It is the accent known variously as the King's (or Queen's) English, the BBC English, the Oxford English, or the Public School English. British phoneticians call it the 'Received Pronunciation' (RP) of England, and we shall refer to it as such in this book. We shall return to this accent in Section 8.4. At present, we shall state an important characteristic of all native English accents: They differ from one another chiefly (almost exclusively) in their vowel systems. Their consonant systems are the same (except for an additional consonant in Scottish English), although the distribution of such consonants may vary. (Witness, in General American, the use of [dʒ] in the final position in the English words *comouflage*, *sabotage*, *espionage* where RP uses [ʒ] instead.) What is of an even greater significance is the fact that all native accents of English evince almost complete identity in respect of word accentuation (see Chapter 12). This is one chief reason why there exists a fairly high degree of mutual intelligibility between speakers of various native accents of English, and also why any deviation from the standard accentual patterns causes greater problems of intelligibility than any other single factor.

8.3 Non-native Accents of English

Since English is used as an international language of trade, commerce, travel and tourism across many countries, and as a second language for administration, higher education, inter-state communication in a number of countries such as India and Pakistan, it has developed a large number of non-native accents as well. Thus in Germany, it is spoken with a distinct German accent, in India with clearly identifiable Indian accents, and in Ghana with a Ghanian accent. These non-native accents of English are marked by certain features of the mother tongues of the speakers. It is possible to discern in German speakers' English, for example, a good many phonological features of the German language. In India, an average Hindi speaker may pronounce the English word *school* as [isku:l], an average Punjabi speaker may pronounce it as [səku:l], and an average Tamil speaker may pronounce *egg* as [jeg], all these deviant pronunciations stemming mainly from the phonological characteristics of their respective mother tongues.

In India, for the last three decades or so, there have been attempts to establish, and institutionalize, an Indian accent of English, sometimes called General Indian English (GIE) or Standard Indian English. Such attempts began in the wake of the realization that, while there was a strong need for teaching better English pronunciation in India, there was no way of teaching every Indian learner a perfect native accent of English. We share the concern underlying such moves, but we do not believe that there exists a single accent that could be called General Indian English. The 'Englishes' that the Indians with different linguistic and regional backgrounds speak bear distinctive marks of their respective mother tongues. As a result, Assamese speakers' English and Malayalam speakers' English, for example, are no less different from each other than are any two native accents of English. Punjabi speakers' English and Tamil speakers' English differ vastly in many features, including the crucial feature of word accentuation, in respect of which the various native accents of English hardly differ. Indeed, some Indian accents are so different from one another that they are "sometimes not even mutually intelligible".* And this should not surprise anyone, for the various mother tongues of which these varieties of English bear distinct marks are themselves quite different. (Indeed, some even belong to different language families!) In such a situation, the existence of one common accent of English in India cannot even be expected.

8.4 The Choice of a Model

The question to ask now is: which accent of English should we choose as a model? We have already stated that there is no pan-Indian model, and to choose a regional Indian accent would just not do. We learn English for communication not so much with the people of our own state or region (with whom we can, anyway, communicate in our mother tongue or a regional language), but with people from other regions and other countries. The obvious choice therefore would be a native accent—a widely understood native accent—rather than any non-native accent or any particular accent employed in any particular state or region of India.

There is yet another reason why we should choose a native accent for teaching English pronunciation in India: Those recognized as 'good' speakers of English in India, namely, those who are easily understood nationally and internationally (for example, AIR and Doordarshan newsreaders) are recognized as such only by virtue of their attempt to use a native accent of English, i e RP. Most native speakers of English hear their pronunciation as a kind of approximation to RP—that is, an attempt in the direction of RP—rather than as good examples of 'Indian' English.

* R.K. Bansal and J.B. Harrison, *Spoken English for India* (Madras: Orient Longman, 1983), p. 3.

We take the stand, therefore, that for the teaching of English pronunciation in India, we must choose a native accent as a model. This does not mean, though, that we expect to turn all Indian speakers of English into native speakers of the language. There is no such expectation, and there is no such need either. Individual learners will no doubt remain at varying distances from the model presented to them, but ambitious learners will at least know in which direction to keep relentlessly moving for continuous improvement of their pronunciation and international intelligibility.

The question that now naturally follows from the foregoing discussion is: which accent of native English should we choose as a model for the teaching of English in India? Our answer to this is the RP of England, and before we explain why, we must say something about this accent.

Received Pronunciation (RP), initially no more than an educated South-eastern British English accent, is today more of a social than regional accent, the word 'Received' in its label implying social acceptance. It acquired such acceptance largely because the public schools in England adopted it in the nineteenth century, and the products of such schools held positions of authority. Moreover, its dissemination as a class pronunciation throughout England led to its recognition as a marker of high social status, rather than just another regional accent. It is, therefore, used all over England by educated upper classes, and its prestige in England is such that people seeking social advancement (or sometimes even career advancement) learn it through conscious effort and training. The flower-girl in Shaw's *Pygmalion* is a case in point. The BBC uses it in its announcements and newscasts, and its attempts to use announcers who have even a mild regional accent have provoked protests even from the regions whose accent was used.

This situation is constantly changing, though. Today, many Englishmen with high education, but without public school background, not only retain their regional accents, but also claim a place for them. In a democratic set-up, therefore, RP speakers, who constitute a minority, cannot openly assert their superiority any more. Nonetheless, RP still retains a position, which it may no longer afford to openly display.

It is, however, not for this reason that we choose RP as a model for teaching English pronunciation in India (and many other countries similarly placed). Our choice of this model is for practical reasons. As English came to India from Britain, rather than the USA, Australia, or any other English-speaking country, we understand British English, and in particular RP, more easily than we do any other accent of native English, the influence of American movies notwithstanding. Indeed, we understand RP more readily than even an Indian accent of English from a distant region of the country. And, most curiously, in some cases, the people of a particular region in India are found to comprehend RP better than their own regional accent of English. (This may, however, be due to the fact that RP maintains more distinctions in its vowel and consonant inventories than do most Indian accents of English.)

Another good reason for choosing RP as a teaching model is that the best speakers of English in India (some newsreaders, for example) model their speech on RP. And since many of such speakers come from good social and educational background, their accent enjoys a certain degree of prestige in India, which other native accents do not. Furthermore, in all known teacher-training programmes in English language teaching in India, the accent described, and given practice in, is RP. This is understandably so, because most of the teacher-trainers themselves have been trained in this, rather than in any other, accent. Another reason for the choice of this accent in teacher-training programmes is the ready availability of descriptions of RP, practice books and recordings in RP, and dictionaries giving RP pronunciations. Even the authors of books on English pronunciation published in India are themselves trained in RP. Finally, the greatest advantage of learning RP is that it is readily understood in most parts of the English-speaking world, including the USA.

At this point, a distinction must be made between what is being recommended here as a model for description and teaching and what we expect most learners to attain. What we expect teacher-trainers to impart to teachers of English is a description of the essentials of RP and a good amount of practice in listening and speaking. We expect them to draw up their own lists of priorities, which may differ from region to region, and to spend more time on the items they regard as relatively more important for their respective regions. For instance, while teacher-trainers in all regions of India should spend a good deal of time on word-accentuation, those in Kashmir and Punjab should also profitably spend some time on teaching consonant clusters, about which teacher-trainers in South India need not bother. Similarly, teacher-trainers in Assam and some other north-eastern states would do well to spend an appreciable amount of time on teaching the distinction between **s**, **sh**, and **ch** sounds.

As against this, what we expect teachers under training to attain may remain far short of RP for a variety of reasons: inadequate exposure, an unsatisfactory model, insufficient practice and use, and so on. Naturally, therefore, what the ultimate learners receive from such teachers in schools and colleges will be quite short of RP. But—and this is our main contention—what they will learn will be, in varying degrees, an approximation to RP, and their further attempts at improvements with the help of dictionaries, practice books, and recordings will bring them still nearer to RP. Perfect RP may still never be attained; but that is neither necessary, nor, in some cases, even desirable for foreign learners of English. A good approximation will do. And that can be achieved only by setting up RP itself, rather than any other accent, as our aim.

Considering all the factors discussed above, and taking into account the question of practicability, we have decided to choose RP as a model for teaching. This course, therefore, describes and attempts to teach RP.

8.5 Summary

Different varieties of a language are called *accents* when they differ in pronunciation only, or when their pronunciation differences alone are being referred to. Since English is spoken very widely, it has acquired a large number of accents. And since it is spoken both as the mother tongue and as another tongue, it has acquired both native accents and non-native accents. The standard ones among the native accents are the Educated South-eastern British (called RP), Educated Scottish, General American, Educated Canadian, Educated Australian, and South African. The non-native accents are very many, such as the German accent, the Ghanian accent, the Punjabi accent, the Tamilian accent, and so on. The different native accents of English differ, chiefly, in their vowel systems, whereas the different non-native accents may differ in a number of phonological and distributional features. The different Indian accents of English may differ vastly from one another. We do not, therefore, believe that there exists a pan-Indian accent of English.

Of the native accents of English, RP is the most widely understood one. In England it enjoys considerable prestige, too.

For teaching English pronunciation in India, RP can be recommended as a model. It is better understood in this country than even various Indian accents of English are; it has a fair amount of prestige; the best Indian speakers of English attempt to approximate to it; a number of teacher-training programmes choose it as a model for description and practice; and books, recordings, and practice materials on it are readily available.

EXERCISES

I Say whether the following statements are true or false:

1 Different accents of a language differ from one another in vocabulary and pronunciation.

2 Different native accents of English differ from one another largely in their vowel systems.

3 The patterns of word accentuation in Australian English are very different from those of RP.

4 The standard native accents of English are those which the people in large cities in England and elsewhere use.

5 The most prestigious accent of English in the world is RP.

6 In England many people who want to advance socially try to acquire RP.

7 In India many speakers' pronunciation of English is marked by some features of their mother tongue.

8 The English spoken in one part of India is not understood by people in another part.

9 By choosing RP as a model for teaching English pronunciation in India, we do not expect to turn out perfect RP speakers, but such speakers as would attempt to constantly improve their pronunciation in that direction.

II Complete the following statements:

1 In different parts of the world, English is spoken ———— which are called ————.

2 The chief difference between different native accents of English ————.

3 Native speakers of English find it difficult to understand a foreign accent of English in which word accentuation is different from theirs because ————.

4 Of all the standard native accents of English, RP is ————.

5 It is no use teaching a regional accent of English in India because ————.

6 As a model for India, RP has many advantages over any other model. They are ————.

III Argue the following cases:

1 We should learn to speak with an internationally acceptable accent of English.

2 It is not possible to teach General American English in India.

3 It is not realistic to expect every learner of English as a second language in India to acquire perfect RP.

4 A good approximation to RP is what we should aim at.

9
The Sounds of English–Vowels

9.1 Introduction

In this chapter and in Chapter 10, we shall be dealing with the sounds of English (RP). This chapter is devoted to the vowels of RP and Chapter 10 to the consonants of RP. In describing the vowels and consonants of RP, we shall follow the classificatory systems explained in Chapters 4 and 3, respectively. Accordingly, the vowels of RP will be described in terms of the vowel diagram introduced and explained in section 4.233. The description of RP monophthongs will therefore be in terms of (i) the part of the tongue raised, (ii) the height of that part of the tongue, and (iii) the position of the lips. Such a description will lead on to a three-term label for each RP monophthong as illustrated in section 4.234. In the case of diphthongs, the description will indicate the starting point of the glide, the direction of its movement, and the position of the lips, which may in some cases undergo a change during the process of production of the diphthongs (see section 4.24).

9.2 Vowels of RP

In RP there are twenty vowels (or vowel phonemes, to be precise). These are listed below, along with examples that illustrate their occurrence in the initial, medial, and final positions. A blank space in the table indicates the non-occurrence of a vowel in that position. The phonetic symbols used for the vowels are those of the *Oxford Advanced Learner's Dictionary of Current English*, third edition (revised and updated).

Vowel	*Initial*	*Medial*	*Final*
Monophthongs			
iː	east	seen	key
ɪ	it	hit	duty
e	end	lend	
æ	and	land	
ɑː	arm	harm	car
ɒ	on	cot	
ɔː	all	caught	saw
ʊ		put	
uː	ooze	choose	shoe
ʌ	up	cup	

ɜː	earn	turn	sir
ə	*ago*	p*o*lice	tail*or*
Diphthongs			
eɪ	eight	straight	stray
əʊ	oak	joke	slow
aɪ	ice	mice	my
aʊ	out	shout	how
ɔɪ	oil	boil	boy
ɪə	ear	beard	clear
eə	air	shared	care
ʊə		cured	poor

Of the 12 monophthongs, 7 are short: /ɪ, e, æ, ɒ, ʊ, ʌ, ə/ and 5 long: /iː, ɑː, ɔː, uː, ɜː/.

Diphthongs are all long vowels.

It must be stated here that 'long' vowels are only comparatively longer than the 'short' vowels: they are always longer than the 'short' vowels in identical phonetic environments. Thus /iː/ in a word like *beat* /biːt/ is always longer than /ɪ/ in a word like *bit* /bɪt/. Apart from this, each vowel has different degrees of length, depending upon the phonetic environment in which it occurs. Generally speaking, a vowel is longer when it is followed by a voiced consonant or when it occurs finally in a word than when followed by a voiceless consonant. Thus the /uː/ in *sued* and *sue* is longer than the /uː/ in *suit*; the /eɪ/ in *made* and *may* is longer than the /eɪ/ in *make*; and the /ɪ/ in *bid* and *be* (unstressed) is longer than in *bit*. Further, a still finer distinction in the relative length of a vowel can be made. A vowel is slightly longer when it occurs finally in a word than when it is followed by even a voiced consonant. Thus in the above examples, the vowel /uː/ in *sue* is longer than the same vowel in *sued*; /eɪ/ in *may* is longer than it is in *made*; and so on. Length is therefore one dimension along which the variants of a vowel may occur.

Another dimension along which a vowel may vary is the relative height of the tongue. A vowel is usually lower (or opener) when it occurs finally in a word than otherwise. Thus the word-final vowel /ə/ in *data* /'deɪtə/ is opener than the /ə/ in *datum* /'deɪtəm/ (see Fig. 20).

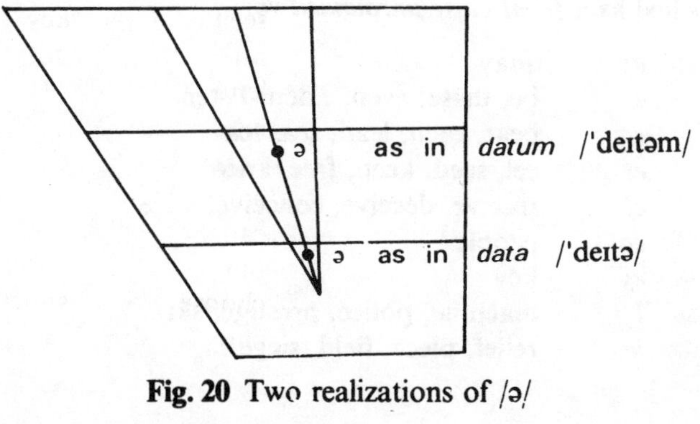

Fig. 20 Two realizations of /ə/

The variants of a vowel along the dimensions of length and the height of the tongue are its positional variants in that they are determined by the position of that vowel in a given word. They are thus phonologically-conditioned variants, or *allophones*, of the vowel.

All vowels are voiced, and in English there is no nasalized vowel. Therefore in the description of the production of English vowels, the vocal cords are assumed to be vibrating and the soft palate is taken to be raised.

9.3 Detailed Description of the Vowels of RP

9.31 Monophthongs

Of the 12 monophthongs, (i) four are front vowels: /iː, ɪ, e, æ/, (ii) five back vowels: /ɑː, ɒ, ɔː, ʊ, uː/, and (iii) three central vowels: /ʌ, ɜː, ə/. These are now discussed.

9.311 Front vowels: /iː, ɪ, e, æ/

/iː/ as in *seat*

/ɪ/ as in *sit*

/e/ as in *set*

/æ/ as in *sat*

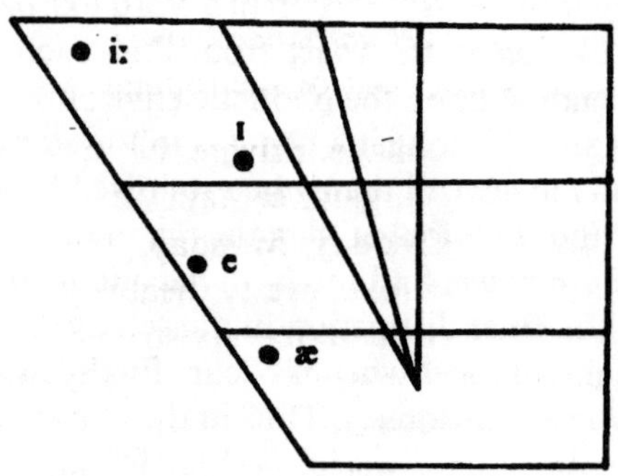

Fig. 21 Front vowels

/iː/

DESCRIPTION The front of the tongue is raised to a height just below the close position (Fig. 21); the lips are spread; and the tongue is tense. It is a long vowel. It can be labelled as a *front close unrounded vowel.*

SPELLING		
	ay	quay
	e	be, these, even, Eden, Peter
	ea	beat, each, lead, sea, tea
	ee	eel, seed, keep, free, knee
	ei	receive, deceive, conceive, seize
	eo	people
	ey	key
	i	machine, police, prestige, ski
	ie	relief, piece, field, siege

OCCURRENCE The vowel occurs more frequently in accented than in unaccented positions:

Accented	*Unaccented*
'even	*e*'conomist
com'plete	*se*'crete
re'ceive	
emplo'yee	

The occurrence of /iː/ in unaccented positions is, however, decreasing. More RP speakers now use the vowel /ɪ/, instead, in all such positions.

/iː/ occurs initially (e g *eat*, *east*, *eve*, *eel*), medially (e g *sheet*, *please*, *thief*, *relief*), and finally (e g *sea*, *tree*, *payee*, *bee*). But it does not occur before the consonant /ŋ/.

/ɪ/

DESCRIPTION To produce the RP vowel /ɪ/, the rear part of the front of the tongue is raised just above the half-close position (Fig. 21); the lips are loosely spread, and, unlike in the production of /iː/, the tongue is lax. It can be called a *centralized front half-close unrounded vowel*, the phrase *centralized front* referring to the rear part of the front of the tongue. It is a short vowel.

SPELLING		
	a	village, private, bagg*a*ge, surface
	ai	bargain, captain, mountain
	ay	Sunday, Monday, Tuesday
	e	*e*voke, pretty, heat*e*d, ticket, system, harmless, horses, *e*xtempor*e*, apostroph*e*
	ee	coffee
	ei	foreign
	ey	monkey, money, honey
	i	it, hill, fifth, lift
	ia	carriage, marriage
	ie	cities, dailies, ladies, lobbies
	o	women
	u	busy, minute (n)
	ui	build, guilt
	y	rhythm, symbol, city, hilly, easy

OCCURRENCE /ɪ/ occurs in accented as well as unaccented positions:

Accented	*Unaccented*
o'mit	'need*e*d
com'mit	'troll*ie*s
'bigger	*re*'fer
'Indian	*ex*'haust
'simple	*ex*'clude

The vowel occurs initially, medially, and finally:

Initial	*Medial*	*Final*
it	fit	volley

ill	fill	holy
if	stiff	lady
enjoy	engine	simile
except	prefix	Sunday, coolie

The distinction between /iː/ and /ɪ/ must be clearly maintained by differentiation of length and quality. Otherwise, distinction between many pairs of words, such as the following, can be lost:

/iː/	/ɪ/	/iː/	/ɪ/
beat	bit	heel	hill
feel	fill	seat	sit
leave	live	feet	fit
sleep	slip	field	filled

/e/

DESCRIPTION In the production of the RP vowel /e/, the front of the tongue is raised to a point about half-way between the half-open and half-close positions (Fig. 21); the lips are loosely spread and a little wider apart than for /ɪ/; the tongue is not as lax as for /ɪ/. The vowel can be described as a *front unrounded vowel between half-close and half-open*. Like /ɪ/, it is a short vowel.

SPELLING		
	a	any, many, Thames, ate (/et/ or /eɪt/)
	ai	said, again (/ə'gen/ or /ə'geɪn/)
	ay	says
	e	end, send, let, get
	ea	dead, spread, health, leant, jealous
	ei	leisure, Leicester
	eo	leopard, Leonard, Geoffrey
	ie	friend
	u	bury
	ue	guess, guest

OCCURRENCE Essentially, /e/ occurs in syllables carrying the primary accent. Sometimes, however, it may occur in syllables having the secondary accent, e g *recollect* (to remember) /ˌrekə'lekt/ (first syllable). It may also occur in an unaccented syllable, but in such cases an alternative pronunciation with the weak vowel /ə/, instead of /e/, may also be available. Examples:

	with unaccented /e/	*with* /ə/
lieutenant (first syllable)	/lef'tenənt/	/ləf'tenənt/
tempestuous (first syllable)	/tem'pestʃʊəs/ or /tem'pestjʊəs/	/təm'pestʃʊəs/ or /təm'pestjʊəs/

In the case of the word *tempestuous*, it is easy to see that the retention of /e/ in the first syllable, which is unaccented, is a vestige of the /e/ that occurs in the accented first syllable of the stem *tempest*. Such examples are many: *sensation*, *sententious*, *tendentious*, *temptation* (first syllables).

The vowel occurs initially and medially only:

Initial	*Medial*
end	lend, send, friend
any	many
egg	leg
else	sense

/æ/

DESCRIPTION The vowel is produced by raising the front of the tongue to a little below the half-open position (Fig. 21). The lips are in the neutral position and the mouth is more open than for /e/. The vowel can be called a *front unrounded vowel just below the half-open position.* It is a short vowel, but in front of voiced consonants it becomes as long as the 'long' vowels in similar environments. Thus, while in *bat* /bæt/ it is much shorter than the /iː/ in *beat*, in *bad* /bæd/ it is almost as long as the /iː/ in *bead.*

SPELLING		
	a	ass, sat, hand, match
	ai	plaid, plait

OCCURRENCE It occurs in both accented and unaccented syllables:

Accented	*Unaccented*
'accent (n)	*ac*'cent (v)
con'tact (v)	'cont*a*ct (n)
'absent (adj)	*a*b'normal
'damage	*ca*n'teen
'marriage	m*a*s'seur

Like /e/, the vowel /æ/ also occurs only initially and medially:

Initial	*Medial*	*Initial*	*Medial*
add	sad	axe	lax
and	sand	apt	rapt
ass	lass	ant	sat

The distinction between /e/ and /æ/ must be clearly maintained by making /æ/ sufficiently opener than /e/, and by making it sufficiently long in front of voiced consonants. If such distinction is not maintained, the distinction between a good many pairs of words, such as the following, can be lost:

/e/	/æ/	/e/	/æ/
hem	ham	head	had
said	sad	bend	band
men	man	mess	mass
bet	bat	beg	bag
bed	bad	gem	jam
set	sat	lend	land
pen	pan	merry	marry
met	mat	r*e*bel (n)	r*a*bble
guest	gassed	k*e*ttle	c*a*ttle

9.312 Back vowels: /ɑː, ɒ, ɔː, ʊ, uː/

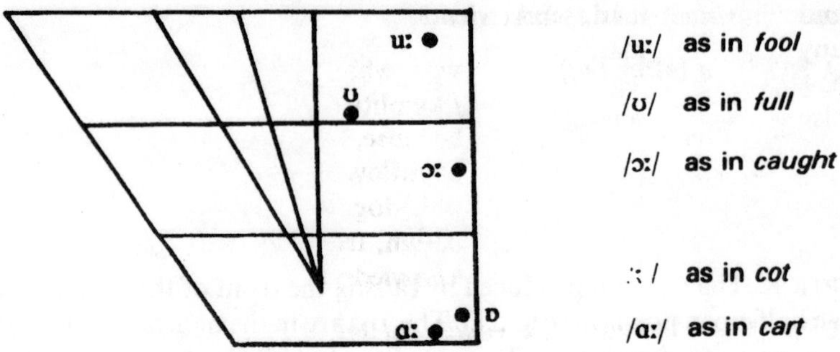

Fig. 22 Back vowels

/ɑː/

DESCRIPTION To produce this vowel, the jaws are kept considerably separated; the lips are neutrally open; and a part of the tongue between the centre and the back is in the fully open position (Fig. 22). It is a long vowel, and can be called a *back open unrounded vowel.*

SPELLING		
	a	ask, dance, bath, after, mam*a*
	ah	ah
	al	balm. calm, palm, psalm, half
	ar	park, part, march, car
	au	aunt, laugh
	ear	heart, hearth
	er	clerk, Derby, sergeant, Berkeley

OCCURRENCE /ɑː/ occurs mostly in accented syllables. Its occurrence in unaccented syllables is restricted generally to English words of foreign origin, e g 'camoufl*a*ge, 'espion*a*ge, 'gar*a*ge, 'mass*a*ge, 'rhub*a*rb, 'sabot*a*ge.

The vowel occurs in all the three positions—initial, medial, and final:

Initial	*Medial*	*Final*
arms	charm	car
art	starve	star
arch	heart	papa
arc	laughter	mama
ask	martyr	far
army	disaster	debar
artificial	ex*a*sperate	aha
articulate	aghast	
arson		

/ɒ/

DESCRIPTION During the articulation of this vowel, the back of the tongue is raised slightly above the open position (Fig. 22); the jaws are widely open and the lips are slightly rounded. The vowel is therefore a *back rounded vowel just above the open position*. It is a short vowel.

SPELLING	*a* (after /w/)	was, what, want, watch, wash, quality /ˈkwɒlɪtɪ/
	au	because, sausage, Austria, Australia, cauliflower
	o	pot, dog, lorry, gone
	ou	cough, trough, Gloucester
	ow	knowledge

OCCURRENCE Like /ɑː/, the vowel /ɒ/ tends to occur in accented syllables. Indeed, the tendency is so strong that where it occurs in unaccented syllables, it may often be replaced by /ə/.

EXAMPLES *despot* /ˈdespɒt/ or /ˈdespət/, and *occult* /ɒˈkʌlt/ or /əˈkʌlt/. (Also possible: /ˈɒkʌlt/.)

The vowel /ɒ/ occurs in the initial and medial positions only:

Initial	*Medial*
on	gone
odd	rod
ox	fox
often	s*o*ften
opt	dropped
off	scoff
object (n)	trough
obverse	w*a*nder
obstacle	squ*a*nder
obstinate	qu*a*lity
obsolete	c*o*nstant
occupy	pr*o*mise
office	pr*o*verb
olive	conc*o*ct
October	comm*o*dity
obvious	pr*o*bable

/ɔː/

DESCRIPTION The vowel /ɔː/ is articulated with the back of the tongue raised between the half-open and half-close positions (Fig. 22); the lips are considerably more rounded than for /ɒ/. It can thus be described as a *back rounded vowel between half-open and half-close*. It is a long vowel.

SPELLING	*a*	all, tall, wall, talk, chalk, salt, water
	ar	warm, towards, quarter, war
	au	cause, daughter, fault, slaughter, caught, caution
	aw	awkward, law, raw, saw, straw, flaw, yawn, lawn
	oa	broad

oar	oar, board
oor	door, floor
or	or, nor, cord, sword, born, morning
ore	more, store, before
ou	ought, bought, fought, thought, nought
our	four, court, pour

OCCURRENCE The vowel occurs more often in accented than in unaccented positions. Some examples of its occurrence in unaccented positions are: *au*'thority, *au*'tocracy, *au*'tonomy, *or*'ganic.

The vowel occurs in all the three positions—initial, medial, and final:

Initial	*Medial*	*Final*
all	stall	law
aught	brought	jaw
ought	bored	store
aweful	sword	tore
ordinary	w*a*rrior	floor
author	dawn	roar
organ	story	lore

The distinction between /ɑː/, /ɒ/, and /ɔː/ must be maintained to prevent certain pairs and triplets of words from getting confused. Practising the pronunciation of the following words in pairs and triplets can help in learning the distinction:

/ɑː/	/ɒ/	/ɔː/
dark	dock	
last	lost	
guards	gods	
heart	hot	
sharp	shop	
mark	mock	
large	lodge	
lark	lock	
caste	cost	
	cock	cork
	fox	forks
	not	naught
	knotty	naughty
	odd	awed
	shot	short
art		ought
hard		hoard
barn		born
lard		lord
hearty		haughty
m*a*rtyr		m*o*rtar
card	cod	cord
cart	cot	caught

darn	don	dawn
part	pot	port
hark	hock	hawk
tart	tot	taught

/ʊ/

DESCRIPTION The vowel /ʊ/ is articulated by raising a part of the tongue nearer to centre than to back just above the half-close position (Fig. 22); the lips are closely but loosely rounded, and the tongue is lax. The vowel can be described as a *centralized back rounded vowel just above half-close*. It is a short vowel.

SPELLING		
	o	wolf, woman, b*o*som
	oo	foot, good, book, look, wood, wool
	ou	could, should, would, courier
	u	put, bull, sugar, push, butcher

Also note /ʊ/ in *worsted* (a kind of cloth) /'wʊstɪd/.

OCCURRENCE The vowel occurs in both accented and unaccented syllables. All the words listed under "Spelling" are instances of the occurrence of /ʊ/ in accented syllables. Examples of its occurrence in unaccented syllables are: 'manh*oo*d, 'imp*u*dent, f*u*l'fil, 'conc*u*bine, 'bedr*oo*m /'bedrʊm/ (also pronounced /'bedru:m/).

/ʊ/ occurs in the word-medial position only (except in the case of the 'weak forms' of *to* and *you*, where it can occur word-finally). It does not occur before final /ŋ/.

/u:/

DESCRIPTION To produce this vowel, the back of the tongue is raised to very near the close position (Fig. 22); the lips are closely rounded and the tongue is tense. It is thus a *back close rounded* vowel. It is a long vowel.

SPELLING		
	eau (pronounced /ju:/)	beauty, beautiful
	eu (pronounced /ju:/)	eulogy, eunuch, euphony
	ew	crew, blew, chew, grew
	o	do, to (strong form), who, tomb, womb, prove
	oe	shoe, canoe
	oo	moon, room, food, soon, brood, troop
	ou	group, through, route, you
	u	flute, rude, June
	ue	blue, true
	ui	juice, fruit
	wo	two

Note: In words spelt with *u*, *ue*, *ui*, and *ew*, representing the vowel /uː/, the semivowel /j/ (see Chapter 10) is sometimes inserted before /uː/ (as in *unit*, *few*), and sometimes not (as in *grew* and *juice*). The rules for this are as follows:

(1) /j/ is not inserted after /tʃ, dʒ, r, l/; examples: *chew*, *June*, *rule*, *blue*. (*Lute* and *absolute* are now more often pronounced without /j/ than with /j/.)

(2) /j/ is regularly inserted after /p, b, t, d, k, g, m, n, f, v, h/; examples: *pure*, *beauty* (*eau* representing /juː/), *tutor*, *duty*, *curious*, *argue*, *mute*, *new*, *few*, *view*, *hue*.

(3) Usage varies after /s, z, θ/. Thus, *suit*, *presume*, *enthuse* are pronounced with /j/ by some, and without /j/ by others.

OCCURRENCE The vowel occurs in both accented and unaccented syllables. All the words listed under 'Spelling' are instances of its occurrence in accented syllables. Examples of its occurrence in unaccented syllables are: 'absol*u*te, 'resol*u*te, 'arg*ue*, m*u*'sician, t*u*'torial.

/uː/ occurs in the initial, medial, and final positions, but not before /ŋ/:

Initial	*Medial*	*Final*
oof	bluebird	sue
ooze	student	stew
	shrewd	flew
	routine	drew
	truth	through
		threw
		true

The distinction between /ʊ/ and /uː/ must be clearly maintained; otherwise, the distinction between the following pairs of words can be lost:

/ʊ/	/uː/	/ʊ/	/uː/
pull	pool	soot	suit
full	fool	wood	wooed
could	cooed	should	shoed

Further, the distinction between several other pairs of words such as the following can get blurred if the two vowels are not properly distinguished:

/ʊ/	/uː/	/ʊ/	/uː/
foot	food	shook	shoot
stood	stool	book	boot
look	loop	brook	brood

9.313 Central vowels: /ʌ, ɜː, ə/

/ʌ/

DESCRIPTION The vowel /ʌ/ is articulated with the centre of the tongue raised to a point nearly half-way between open and half-open positions (Fig. 23), with the lips neutrally open and with a considerable separation of the jaws. The vowel can thus be described as a *central unrounded vowel between open and half-open*. It is a short vowel.

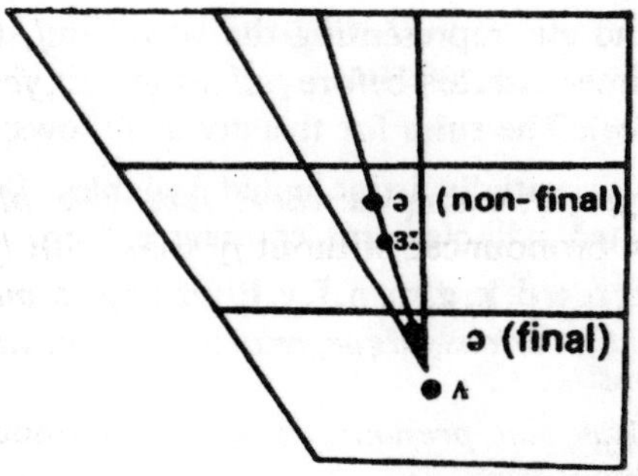

/ə/ (non-final) as in *ago*
/3ː/ as in *shirt*
/ə/ (final) as in *china*
/ʌ/ as in *bus*

Fig. 23 Central vowels

SPELLING	*o*	ton, son, one, monkey, c*o*lour, *o*nion, oven, tongue, won, th*o*rough
	oe	does
	oo	blood, flood
	ou	trouble, double, southern, enough, young
	u	sun, cut, shut, but

OCCURRENCE The vowel /ʌ/ occurs essentially in accented syllables. Some examples of its occurrence in unaccented syllables are: 'catap*u*lt, 'hicc*u*p (or: 'hicc*ou*gh), 'cuc*u*mber.

It does not occur before /ŋ/.

It occurs in the initial and medial positions only:

Initial	*Medial*	*Initial*	*Medial*
up	cup	udder	s*u*dden
us	bus	uncle	plunder
umber	slumber	ugly	c*u*pboard
upper	supper		c*o*mpass
utter	mutter		c*o*vet
oven	g*o*vern		wonder
			front

/3ː/

DESCRIPTION To produce the vowel /3ː/, the centre of the tongue is raised between half-close and half-open (Fig. 23); the lips are in the neutral position. The vowel can therefore be called a *central unrounded vowel between half-close and half-open*. It is a long vowel.

SPELLING	*ear*	early, earth, learn, heard
	er	serve, term, perfect, concern
	err	err
	ir	bird, firm, first, girl, shirt
	or (when preceded by *w*)	word, world, work, worship
	our	journey, adjourn
	ur	burn, turn, hurt, murder, surface

urr	purr, currish
yr	myrtle

Note: /ɜː/ in *colonel* /'kɜːnl/.

OCCURRENCE The vowel /ɜː/ occurs essentially in accented syllables. Some examples of its occurrence in unaccented syllables are: 'comm*e*rce, 'forew*o*rd, 'pennyw*o*rth.

It does not occur before /ŋ/.

/ɜː/ occurs in all the three positions:

Initial	*Medial*	*Final*
earth	mirth	fir
erred	first	stir
early	curly	spur
earl	curl	prefer
earn	stern	refer
irk	shirk	occur
urn	burn	blur
earnest	f*u*rnace	whir

/ə/

DESCRIPTION The vowel /ə/ has at least two positions—the non-final and the final. The non-final /ə/ is articulated exactly the same way and at more or less the same place as the vowel /ɜː/. In that position, it differs from /ɜː/ mainly in respect of length, /ə/ being a short vowel. The final /ə/, however, is produced with the centre of the tongue raised just below the half-open position (Fig. 23). In both cases, the lips are in the neutral position. /ə/ can therefore be described as a *central unrounded short vowel.*

SPELLING		
	a	*a*gain, allow, woman, anim*a*l, dram*a*, China
	ar	p*ar*ticul*ar*, beggar, dollar
	e	governm*e*nt, gentlem*e*n, problem, refer*e*nce
	er	bothersome, otherwise, better, mother, singer
	i	possible, terrible
	ia	musician, magician, partial
	o	consume, obtain, pr*o*long
	or	comfort, effort, actor, doctor, governor
	ou	jealous, frivolous, famous
	ough	thorough
	our	labour, neighbour, colour
	re	metre, centre
	u	succeed, s*u*ccumb, suspect (v)
	ur	surprise, surmise (v), surpass
	ure	treasure, measure, feature

OCCURRENCE The vowel occurs in unaccented syllables only. It occurs in all the three positions:

Initial	*Medial*	*Final*
alert	am*o*r*ou*s	bitter
alarm	t*o*wards	rector
alas	treach*er**ou*s	valour
among	backw*a*rd	odour
allow	c*o*mpare	mixture
about	c*o*rrect	saga
away	p*e*rhaps	pressure
arrest	p*o*tato	collar
alive	t*o*mato	theatre
ago	p*o*lite	data
around	c*o*nductor	sofa

Care must be taken to keep the three central vowels, /ʌ/, /ɜː/, and /ə/, distinct. The first two have a strong tendency to occur in accented syllables, while the last one occurs in unaccented syllables only. If the first two are not kept distinct, pairs of words such as the following cannot be distinguished:

/ʌ/	/ɜː/	/ʌ/	/ɜː/
bud	bird	cud	curd
gull	girl	hut	hurt
shut	shirt	ton	turn
luck	lurk	fussed	first
such	search	bust	burst
study	sturdy		

Words containing /ə/ do not form such pairs with any of the words containing /ʌ/ or /ɜː/ (or, for that matter, any vowel). The vowel /ə/ must, nonetheless, be kept distinct from both—from /ʌ/ by maintaining the quality distinction, and from /ɜː/ by maintaining, mainly, the length distinction.

9.32 Diphthongs

Of the eight diphthongs, (i) three glide towards [ɪ]: /eɪ, aɪ, ɔɪ/; (ii) two towards [ʊ]: /aʊ, əʊ/; and (iii) three towards [ə]: /ɪə, eə, ʊə/. In the diphthongs grouped under (i) and (ii), the movement of the glide is towards closer positions, and in those under (iii), it is towards the centre of the vowel diagram. Accordingly, the diphthongs grouped under (i) and (ii) are called the *closing diphthongs*, and those under (iii) the *centring diphthongs.* There are two other terms, which must not be confused with *closing* and *centring* diphthongs. These are *falling* and *rising* diphthongs. These latter terms apply to two diphthongs only — /ɪə/ and /ʊə/— and are explained under the description of [ɪə] in section 9.323.

(Remember that in the diagrams for diphthongs, the dot represents the starting point and the arrow the direction in which the glide moves.)

9.321 Closing diphthongs gliding to [ɪ]: /eɪ, aɪ, ɔɪ/

/eɪ/

DESCRIPTION The glide starts from a point just below the half-close front position and moves in the direction of RP /ɪ/ (Fig. 24). The movement of the

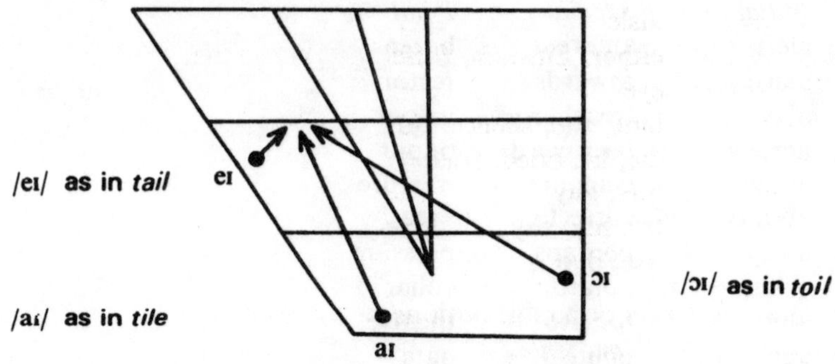

Fig. 24 Closing diphthongs gliding to [ɪ]

tongue is accompanied by a slight closing movement of the lower jaw. The lips are spread.

SPELLING		
	a	ace, race, take, bass (in music)
	ai	aim, brain, slain, straight
	ay	day, may, pray, say, stay
	ea	break, great
	ei	veil, eight, weigh, neighbour
	ey	they, grey

OCCURRENCE The vowel occurs in both accented and unaccented syllables:

Accented	*Unaccented*
'favour	'earthqu*a*ke
a'fraid	'consul*a*te
ar'range	'popul*a*te
a'vailable	de'liber*a*te
re'lation	

Also, it occurs in all the three positions:

Initial	*Medial*	*Final*
age	sage	stay
ache	take	pray
ale	bale	tray
aid	raid	neigh
eight	fate	defray
acre	taker	convey

/aɪ/

DESCRIPTION The glide for /aɪ/ begins at a point slightly behind the front open position and moves in the direction of RP /ɪ/ (Fig. 24). The movement of the tongue is accompanied by an appreciable closing movement of the lower jaw. The lips have a neutral position at the beginning, but they gradually change to a loosely spread position.

SPELLING	*ai*	aisle
	ei	either, *Ei*nst*ei*n, Eiffel, height, neither
	eye	eye
	i	lime, site, silence, tidy, nice, fight, might
	ie	die, lie, cried, tried
	uy	buy, guy
	y	try, my, shy, fry, type
	ye	bye, dye

OCCURRENCE The vowel occurs in both accented and unaccented syllables:

Accented	*Unaccented*
'idle	*i*'dea
'island	'advert*i*se
'icicle	'valent*i*ne
de'cline	'fructif*y*
des'pite	'marit*i*me

Also, it occurs in all the three positions:

Initial	*Medial*	*Final*
ice	rice	rye
ivory	syphon	dry
item	siren	deny
eyes	rhyme	awry
identity	knight	hi
isolate	sleight	belie

/ɔɪ/

DESCRIPTION Beginning at a point between the back half-open and open positions, the glide for this vowel moves in the direction of RP /ɪ/ (Fig. 24). The jaw movement is not as considerable as for the diphthong /aɪ/. The lips are open rounded at the beginning, changing to neutral towards the end.

SPELLING	*oi*	oil, boil, toil, voice, noise, join
	oy	toy, boy, annoy, employ

Also notice /ɔɪ/ in *buoy* pronounced like *boy* /bɔɪ/.

OCCURRENCE Generally, the vowel occurs in accented syllables. Very few examples can be found of its occurrence in unaccented syllables: 'expl*oi*t (n), empl*oy*'ee.

The vowel occurs in all the three positions:

Initial	*Medial*	*Final*
oil	boil	coy
ointment	appointment	enjoy
oyster	loiter	deploy
	rejoice	cloy
	poison	employ

If /aɪ/ and /ɔɪ/ are not properly distinguished, confusion can arise between pairs of words such as the following:

/aɪ/	/ɔɪ/	/aɪ/	/ɔɪ/
tile	toil	isle	oil
file	foil	kine	coin
by	boy	lines	loins
tie	toy	bile	boil
vice	voice	imply	employ

9.322 Closing diphthongs gliding to [ʊ]:/aʊ, əʊ/

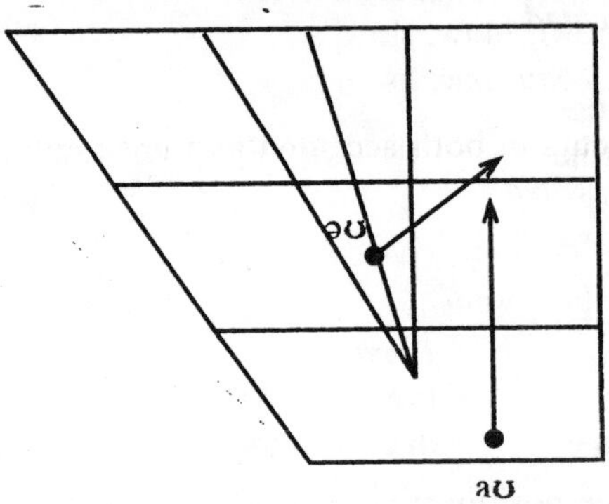

Fig. 25 Closing diphthongs gliding to [ʊ]

/aʊ/

DESCRIPTION The glide for /aʊ/ begins at a point between the back and front open positions and moves towards RP /ʊ/. The starting point may be almost half-way between the back and the front, often nearer the back than the front, as shown in Fig. 25. The jaw movement is as extensive as for the diphthong /aɪ/, with which this vowel has a symmetrical relationship. Lips are neutral at the beginning of the glide, but become rounded towards the end.

SPELLING *ou* out, round, doubt, sound, mouth
ow how, cow, town, allow, now

OCCURRENCE The vowel occurs mostly in accented syllables. Examples of its occurrence in unaccented syllables are, for the most part, confined to compounds formed by the affixation of *out-* and *-how*, where the affixes are unaccented (e g when *out-* is prefixed to verbs and adjectives): out'do, out'live, out'dated, out'moded, 'somehow, 'anyhow. (Also notice: 'eyebr*ow*.)

The vowel occurs initially, medially, and finally:

Initial	*Medial*	*Final*
owl	bounce	plough
oust	mountain	endow
ounce	scoundrel	bow (incline the body)
out	thousand	row (quarrel)
	allowed	

/əʊ/

DESCRIPTION The glide for /əʊ/ begins at a central position almost midway between half-close and half-open, and moves in the direction of RP /ʊ/ (Fig. 25). The jaw movement is very slight; the lips, which are neutral at the beginning of the glide, become rounded towards the end.

SPELLING		
	o	old, open, bold, home, go, no, don't, won't
	oa	oak, oaf, boat, road, goal, boast
	oe	toe, doe, foe, hoe
	ou	though, mould, soul, smoulder
	ow	own, bowl, blow, slow

Also note /əʊ/ in *mauve, beau, sew, brooch.*

OCCURRENCE The vowel occurs in both accented and unaccented syllables:

Accented	*Unaccented*
'open	'sorr*ow*
'owner	to'mat*o*
'photograph	N*o*'vember
im'pose	'fell*ow*
de'note	'sparr*ow*
be'low	'bill*ow*

/əʊ/ occurs in all the three positions:

Initial	*Medial*	*Final*
oats	boats	borrow
ownership	shoulder	potato
owed	ghost	go
over	fold	dough
overt	supp*o*se	though
ovum	coat	know
ovation	mould	so
oval	c*o*count	lo
ogre	comb	sow

To distinguish between /aʊ/ and /əʊ/, the following words should be practised in pairs:

/aʊ/	/əʊ/
bow[1]	bow[2]
noun	known
loud	load
bouts	boats
found	phoned
row[3]	row[4]

[1] Bending the head
[2] Piece of wood for shooting arrows
[3] Quarrel
[4] Persons or things in a line

9.323 Centring diphthongs gliding to [ə]: /ɪə, eə, ʊə/

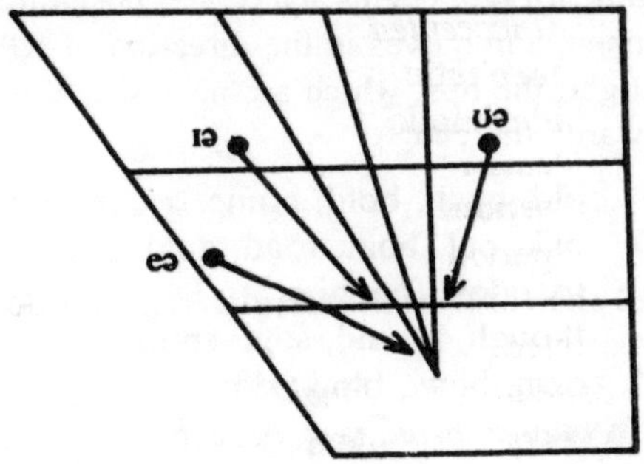

Fig. 26 Centring diphthongs in the word-final position

/ɪə/

DESCRIPTION The glide for /ɪə/ begins at approximately the half-close centralized front RP vowel /ɪ/ and moves in the direction of the opener variety of RP /ə/, when /ɪə/ is final in the word (as in *fear*, *clear*), and towards the less open variety of /ə/, when it is not final in the word (as in *feared*, *clears*). The lips are neutral throughout.

In this vowel the first element [ɪ] is more prominent than the second element [ə] when the vowel occurs in an accented syllable as in *theory* /'θɪərɪ/ and *idea* /aɪ'dɪə/. In such cases, the diphthong is called a *falling diphthong*. The opposite is the case when the diphthong occurs in an unaccented position: here the second element [ə] is more prominent than the first element [ɪ] as in *idiom* /'ɪdɪəm/ and *theoretical* /θɪə'retɪkl/. The diphthong, in such cases, is called a *rising diphthong*. In words like *period* /'pɪərɪəd/ and *serious* /'sɪərɪəs/, where the diphthong occurs in both the accented and unaccented syllables, the first is a falling diphthong and the second a rising diphthong.

The rising diphthong can generally be replaced by [jə], but not when preceded by /r/ (as in *period* and *serious*), for the cluster /rj/ does not occur in English.

SPELLING		
	e	zero, serious, period
	ea	idea, theatre, real
	ear	dear, clear, fear
	eer	deer, cheer, beer, sheer
	eir	weird
	ere	here, mere, severe
	eo	theory, theorem, theological
	eu	museum
	ia	Ian, India
	ier	fierce, bier, tastier
	io	period
	iou	serious, impious

OCCURRENCE As is clear from the description given above, /ɪə/ occurs in both accented and unaccented syllables:

Accented	*Unaccented*
'theory	th*eo*'retic
'clearly	id*eo*'matic
'cheerful	'easier
's*e*rious	'ser*iou*s
'p*e*riod	'per*io*d

/ɪə/ occurs in all the three positions, although its occurrence in the initial position is highly restricted.

Initial	*Medial*	*Final*
era	dreary	dear
eerie	impious	clear
ears	s*e*ries	interfere
	f*ear*less	appear
	beard	bier

/eə/

DESCRIPTION The glide for RP /eə/ begins in the front, above the half-open position, and moves in the direction of RP /ə/. As in the case of /ɪə/, the glide is in the direction of the opener variety of /ə/ if /eə/ occurs word-finally (*care*, *stare*), and in the direction of the less open variety of /ə/ if it occurs non-finally in a word (*airy*, *compared*). The lips are neutrally open throughout.

SPELLING		
	a	various, hilarious, aqu*a*rium, Mary
	air	air, chair, fair, despair
	ar	scarce
	are	care, share, stare, beware
	ear	bear, pear, wear, tear (v)
	eir	their, heir
	ere	there, where, ere, compere

OCCURRENCE /eə/ occurs in both accented and unaccented syllables, with a strong tendency to occur in accented syllables:

Accented	*Unaccented*
'airy	'hardware
'airport	'compere
im'pair	'bugbear
question'naire	'ploughshare

The diphthong occurs in all the three positions:

Initial	*Medial*	*Final*
airy	careless	compare
aeroplane	shared	flair
aerodrome	scarecrow	pear
heirs	impaired	prayer (supplication)
		pair

/ɪə/ and /eə/ can often get confused. To learn to avoid such confusion, the following words should be practised in pairs:

/ɪə/	/eə/	/ɪə/	/eə/
hear	hair	ear	air
beer	bear	fear	fair
piers	pears	tear (n)	tear (v)
cheer	chair	steer	stair
weary	wary	spear	spare
dear	dare	mere	mare
sheer	share	beard	bared
really	rarely		

/ʊə/

DESCRIPTION The glide for RP /ʊə/ starts from the tongue position for RP /ʊ/ and moves in the direction of RP /ə/. As in the case of /ɪə/ and /eə/, the glide is towards the opener variety of /ə/ if the diphthong occurs word-finally (*poor*, *sure*); otherwise, it is towards the less open variety of /ə/ (*dual*, *steward*). The lips are loosely rounded at the beginning of the glide and neutral at the end.

As in the case of the diphthong /ɪə/, /ʊə/ is a falling diphthong when it occurs in an accented syllable, as in *fluency* /'flʊənsɪ/ and *injurious* /ɪn'dʒʊərɪəs/, where the first element [ʊ] is more prominent than the second, [ə]. The diphthong is a rising one, on the other hand, when it occurs in an unaccented syllable, as in *influence* /'ɪnflʊəns/, *individual* /ɪndɪ'vɪdʒʊəl/. The rising diphthong can often be replaced by [wə].

SPELLING

oor	poor, moor
our	tour, gourd, gourmet
u	jury, rural, mural, lux*u*rious
ua	manual, truant, casual
ue	fluent, influence, fuel
uou	tortuous
ure	sure, pure, cure

OCCURRENCE /ʊə/ occurs in both accented and unaccented syllables:

Accented	*Unaccented*
'curious	'manual
ma'nure	'casual
mer'curial	re'sidual
obs'cure	indi'vidual
en'durance	'virtuous

/ʊə/ occurs in the medial and final positions only:

Medial	*Final*
mural	poor
jury	allure
tort*uou*s	endure
st*ew*ard	sure
fluent	cure

9.33 Diphthongs + /ə/

All the five closing diphthongs, /eɪ, aɪ, ɔɪ, aʊ, əʊ/, may be followed by /ə/ within a word, either as an inseparable part of the word, as in *tyre, hire, our, shower* /'taɪə, 'haɪə, 'aʊə, 'ʃaʊə/, or as a suffix, as in *player, higher, employer, rower* ('a boat rower') /'pleɪə, 'haɪə, ɪm'plɔɪə, 'rəʊə/.

In some descriptions, the sequence diphthong + /ə/ is treated as one vowel phoneme—a *triphthong*; in others it is taken as a sequence of two phonemes—the diphthong and the vowel /ə/. We follow the latter kind of treatment. In this treatment, the sequence diphthong + /ə/ constitutes two syllables (not one). Accordingly, the words *tyre, hire, our, shower, player, higher, rower*, all consist of two syllables each, their first syllable containing the diphthong and the second, the monophthong /ə/.

In rapid speech, the sequence diphthong + /ə/ may generally get reduced. What happens in such a case is that the second element of the diphthong is omitted, and the first element is lengthened, thus reducing the sequences /eɪə, aɪə, ɔɪə, aʊə, əʊə/ to [eːə, aːə, ɔːə, aːə, əːə]. The words *player, higher, employer, shower, mower* are then pronounced as ['pleːə, 'haːə, ɪm'plɔːə, 'ʃaːə, 'məːə]. As a result of such reduction, some word-distinctions that are otherwise available are lost, e g *tire* and *tower* are then both pronounced ['taːə].

9.4 Summary

In RP, there are twenty vowels, all of them oral, each represented in the writing system by different letters and their combinations. Of them, twelve are monophthongs, or pure vowels, and the remaining eight, diphthongs. All the diphthongs and five monophthongs are long; the remaining seven monophthongs are short (see below). It is, however, only in identical phonetic environments that the 'long' vowels are always longer than the 'short' vowels. Apart from this, each vowel is longer when it occurs finally in a word or is followed by a voiced consonant than when followed by a voiceless consonant.

The monophthongs can be divided into *front* /iː, ɪ, e, æ/, *back* /ɑː, ɒ, ɔː, ʊ, uː/, and central /ʌ, ɜː, ə/. Of these, /iː, ɑː, ɔː, uː, ɜː/ are long, and the rest short. Only four back vowels, /ɒ, ɔː, ʊ, uː/, are rounded; all the other monophthongs are unrounded. In the case of the rounded vowels, the degree of lip-rounding increases as the height of the tongue increases. As for distribution, /ʊ/ occurs only medially; /e, æ, ɒ, ʌ/ initially and medially; and the rest in all the three positions. Furthermore, while /ə/ occurs in unaccented syllables only, /iː, e, ɑː, ɒ, ɔː, ʌ, ɜː/ have a strong tendency to occur in accented syllables generally. Besides, /ə/ is much opener when final in a word than otherwise.

Of the eight diphthongs, three glide towards [ɪ]: /eɪ, aɪ, ɔɪ/, two towards [ʊ]: /aʊ, əʊ/, and the remaining three towards [ə]: /ɪə, eə, ʊə/. The first two categories are called *closing diphthongs* (the glide being in the direction of the closer vowels [ɪ] and [ʊ]), while the third category is called *centring diphthongs* (the glide being towards the central vowel [ə]). In the case of the centring diphthongs, the glide is towards the opener variety of the RP /ə/ when the diphthongs occur word-finally. Furthermore, two of them, /ɪə, ʊə/, have still other variants: if they occur in accented syllables, their first element, [ɪ] or [ʊ], is more prominent than the second, [ə]; otherwise, the reverse is the case. The former are called *falling diphthongs*, and the latter *rising diphthongs*. (The rising diphthongs /ɪə, ʊə/ can generally be replaced by the sequences [jə] and [wə] respectively.) In the case of /ɔɪ, aʊ, eə/, the occurrence in unaccented syllables is rather restricted. All diphthongs except /ʊə/ occur in all the three positions—initial, medial, and final; /ʊə/ occurs medially and finally only.

The closing diphthongs (/eɪ, aɪ, ɔɪ, aʊ, əʊ/) may sometimes be followed by /ə/ in the same word, forming the sequences [eɪə, aɪə, ɔɪə, aʊə, əʊə]. We treat such sequences as consisting of two syllables each, the first syllable containing the diphthong and the second the monophthong /ə/. The middle element of such sequences, [ɪ] or [ʊ], generally gets deleted in rapid speech.

EXERCISES

I In each of the subdivisions (1), (2), and (3), group the words according to the vowel contained in them. On the top of each group, write the vowel symbol.

(1) Clean, head, caught, breath, learn, heart, eve, said, breathe, third, thought, wall, clerk, key, wealth, friend, worse, chalk, saw.

(2) Tall, lunch, brook, blood, cough, threw, bought, should, gone, want, loose, wool, touch, move, June, watch, boot, good, through.

(3) Like, lake, look, poor, dear, plait, quay, jew, sew, joy, say, care, sky, plough, own, town, crowd, weight, tie, toy, fair, pair, pear, clear, tour, sieve, thief, heal, sow, brow, brew, fuel, signed, bye.

II The teacher will read the following words. Write only the symbol of the vowel contained in each.

1 dawn	6 dough	11 spur	16 blood
2 isle	7 sue	12 we're	17 bland
3 heart	8 sleight	13 all	18 dead
4 ought	9 scarce	14 tomb	19 says
5 vice	10 ere	15 knew	20 bee

III For each of the vowels given below, cite three examples of your own of words containing them:

/e, æ, ʊ, eɪ, eə, aɪ, ɔɪ, ɒ, ɔː/

IV On the pattern of the two examples given below, provide a three-term label for each of the vowels contained in the following words:

True, sad, fraud, hearth, spot, breed, head, hill, pull, but.

Examples:

(1) Word: seen
Vowel: /iː/
Label: front close unrounded vowel

(2) Word: ball
Vowel: /ɔː/
Label: back rounded vowel between half-open and half-close

V Cite two words as examples for each of the following:

1 /iː/ spelt *ie*
2 /ɒ/ at the beginning of words
3 /e/ spelt *ea*
4 /ɔː/ spelt *aw*
5 /ɜː/ spelt *ir*
6 /ɔː/ in an unaccented position
7 /uː/ spelt *o*
8 the back open unrounded vowel
9 /ɒ/ spelt *a*
10 /ɪə/ in the word-final position
11 /ʊə/ in unaccented position
12 /eɪ/ spelt *ei*
13 The letter *e* representing the front unrounded vowel between half-close and half-open
14 /ʊə/ spelt *oo*
15 /aʊ/ in the word-initial position
16 /aɪ/ spelt *y* in the middle of words
17 /iː/ at the end of words
18 The sequence /aɪ/ + /ə/
19 The sequence /aʊ/ + /ə/ in the word-final position
20 The sequence /iː/ + /eɪ/ in the middle of words

VI Give three pairs of words to distinguish between each of the following pairs of vowels:

1 /e/, /æ/
2 /ɑː/, /ʌ/
3 /ɒ/, /əʊ/
4 /aɪ/, /ɔɪ/
5 /ɑː/, /ɒ/
6 /ɪə/, /eə/
7 /ʌ/, /ɜː/
8 /əʊ/, /ɔː/
9 /e/, /eɪ/
10 /ɑː/, /ɔː/

VII The teacher will dictate the words contained in the following sets, choosing one set at a time. First, the serial number will be announced and, then, each word will be said twice. Write down the serial number and the word. (Some words may occur more than once in the same set.)

(a)

1 wheel	6 field	11 filled	16 grin
2 filled	7 green	12 will	17 tick
3 sleep	8 risen	13 slip	18 risen
4 chick	9 teak	14 hill	19 heel
5 reason	10 heel	15 cheek	20 wheel

(b)

1 fed	6 kettle	11 gem	16 cattle
2 jam	7 mat	12 beg	17 met
3 bag	8 bag	13 men	18 rabble
4 fed	9 merry	14 marry	19 merry
5 man	10 fad	15 jam	20 guessed

(c)

1 cot	6 caught	11 shut	16 tall
2 short	7 wonder	12 folks	17 tart
3 cut	8 taught	13 wander	18 shot
4 fox	9 lodge	14 shirt	19 tot
5 shot	10 cart	15 large	20 toll

(d)

1 buy	6 tie	11 boy	16 file
2 lines	7 foil	12 loins	17 employ
3 toy	8 imply	13 vice	18 bile
4 toil	9 lines	14 tile	19 lions
5 isle	10 boil	15 oil	20 voice

VIII First look up the following words in an English pronouncing dictionary to ascertain what vowels they contain, and then pronounce them correctly. (Some words contain more than one vowel, and so, more than one syllable. In such cases, be sure to put the accent on the right syllable as shown in the dictionary.)

> Axe, earth, among, truer, none, measure, church, judge, Eden, police, loiter, pretty, rout, health, dough, ravage, rebel (noun), review, colonel, indict, furnace, towel, refer, pious, impious, theatre, preserve, ago, square, treacherous, player, Mary, enough, freight, monk, wonder, wander, bier, pier, pyre, oven, weird, onion, front, sponge, feud, suit, soot, sergeant, olive, shone, martyr, mortar.

IX Transcribe the following words without looking up the dictionary. (You can, however, look up the "Key to phonetic symbols" in the dictionary.)

> Cruel, sky, cook, ache, guest, guard, thread, meant, tough, dumb, tomb, heart, light, crowd, choice, sew, comb, plough, though, sought, laugh, tear (eye-water), tear (v), turn, death, knead, breath, breathe, health, healthy, lamb, threw, woollen, squash, cough, sphere, ghost, thumb, sure, first, share, hear, hair, here, wrong, bury.

Now look up the dictionary for each word, and make corrections in your transcription. Looking at the corrected transcription, say each word three times with the correct pronunciation.

10 The Sounds of English– Consonants

10.1 Introduction

As already stated in Chapter 9, in the description of the consonants of English (RP), we shall follow the classificatory system explained in Chapter 3. Accordingly, the consonants of English will be described in terms of (i) voice or voicelessness, (ii) the place of articulation, and (iii) the manner of articulation (see Section 3.5). Such a description will lead on to a three-term label for each consonant of English, for example, the label *voiceless bilabial plosive* for the initial consonant in the English word *pit*.

10.2 Consonants of RP

In RP there are 24 consonants (or consonant phonemes, to be precise). These are listed below along with examples that illustrate their occurrence in the initial, medial, and final positions. A blank space in the table indicates the non-occurrence of a consonant in that position. The phonetic symbols used for the consonants are the same as those used in dictionaries such as the *Oxford Advanced Learner's Dictionary of Current English* (Revised and updated) by A S Hornby, *Longman Dictionary of Contemporary English*, and *English Pronouncing Dictionary* (14th ed.) by Daniel Jones.

Consonant	*Initial*	*Medial*	*Final*
p	pin	spin	ship
b	bit	clubs	hub
t	take	stone	lit
d	day	heads	lid
k	key	sky	talk
g	go	eggs	bag
tʃ	chain	fetched	teach
dʒ	jail	barged	large
m	main	small	sum
n	nail	snake	shine
ŋ		thi*ngs*	si*ng*
l	late	slate	tell
f	fan	sphere	half

Consonant	*Initial*	*Medial*	*Final*
v	view	thieves	live
θ	thin	months	bath
ð	then	bathes	clothe
s	sit	taste	loss
z	zoo	buzzed	lose
ʃ	ship	wished	fresh
ʒ		divi*s*ion	rou*g*e
h	hat	behave	
r	run	shrewd	
w	win	swim	
j	yes	tune	

When classified according to the manner of articulation, the English consonants fall into the following groups:

Plosives (6)	/p, b, t, d, k, g/
Affricates (2)	/tʃ, dʒ/
Nasals (3)	/m, n, ŋ/
Lateral (1)	/l/
Fricatives (9)	/f, v, θ, ð, s, z, ʃ, ʒ, h/
Frictionless continuant (1)	/r/
Semi-vowels (2)	/w, j/

On the other hand, when classified according to the place of articulation, they fall into the following groups:

Bilabial (4)	/p, b, m, w/
Labio-dental (2)	/f, v/
Dental (2)	/θ, ð/
Alveolar (6)	/t, d, n, l, s, z/
Post-alveolar (1)	/r/
Palato-alveolar (4)	/tʃ, dʒ, ʃ, ʒ/
Palatal (1)	/j/
Velar (3)	/k, g, ŋ/
Glottal (1)	/h/

Nine consonants are voiceless: /p, t, k, tʃ, f, θ, s, ʃ, h/, and the remaining 15 voiced: /b, d, g, dʒ, m, n, ŋ, l, v, ð, z, ʒ, r, w, j/.

All the classificatory information given above is summarized in Table 1.

The consonant /w/ is shown under *Velar* as well as under *Bilabial*. This is done in order to indicate that this consonant has a second articulation at the soft palate. This point is explained in the detailed discussion of /w/.

As already stated in Chapter 3, the airstream mechanism for all English sounds is *pulmonic* and *egressive*. Besides, except in the case of the nasal consonants, the soft palate is raised, thus shutting off the nasal passage. Therefore, in the detailed description of English consonants that follows, we shall not state the above facts.

Table 1 Classification of English Consonants

Place	Bilabial	Labio-dental	Dental	Alveolar	Post-alveolar	Palato-alveolar	Palatal	Velar	Glottal
Manner	vl vd	vl vd	vl vd	vl vd	vl vd	vl vd	vl vd	vl vd	vl vd
Plosive	p b			t d				k g	
Affricate						tʃ dʒ			
Nasal	m			n				ŋ	
Lateral				l					
Fricative		f v	θ ð	s z		ʃ ʒ			h
Frictionless continuant					r				
Semi-vowel	w						j	(w)	

10.3 Detailed Description of the Consonants of RP

In the description of the consonants of RP, we shall follow the order determined by the manner of articulation—plosive, affricate, nasal, lateral, fricative, frictionless continuant, and semi-vowel.

10.31 Plosives

The production of a plosive is completed in three stages:

(1) The *closing* stage, during which the articulatory organs come together and make a firm contact with each other.

(2) The *hold* or *compression* stage, during which, as a result of lung action, the air behind the closure is compressed.

(3) The *release* or *explosive* stage, during which the articulatory organs part rapidly, resulting in the escape of the compressed air with explosion.

RP has three pairs of plosives:

bilabial /p, b/
alveolar /t, d/
velar /k, g/

/p, t, k/ are voiceless, and /b, d, g/ voiced.

Other notable features of the RP plosives are discussed under (i) voicing, (ii) aspiration, (iii) lip position, and (iv) release stage in the following paragraphs.

Voicing

The voiced plosives /b, d, g/ may be fully voiced only when they occur between voiced sounds, e g in *about, ado, sugar, rub in, read out, fag-end, to buy, I do, you go*. In initial and (especially) in final positions, they may be only partially voiced or completely voiceless. When they occur initially, as in *bell, do, go*, the vocal cord vibration begins only towards the last part of the second stage (the compression stage). When, on the other hand, they occur finally, as in *cub, read, egg*, the vocal cord vibration ceases before the release stage. (Note: Here, 'initially' means 'following silence'; 'finally' means 'preceding silence'.)

Aspiration

The voiceless plosives /p, t, k/, when they occur at the beginning of accented syllables, are *aspirated*, that is, a puff of breath follows the release of the plosive. Thus, *pen, ten*, and *cool* are pronounced as [pʰen, tʰen, kʰuːl], the symbol [ʰ] standing for *aspiration*. When these plosives are followed by other consonants, the aspiration is manifested in the devoicing of those consonants, i e in the loss of voice during the earlier part of their articulation. Thus the consonants [l, r, w, j] are devoiced in words such as *plate, pray, tray, twice, tune, clean, cry, quite*, and *cue*. When, however, /s/ precedes the plosives, there is no aspiration. Compare, for example, *pin* [pʰɪn] with *spin* [spɪn], *till* [tʰɪl] with *still* [stɪl], and *cool* [kʰuːl] with *school* [skuːl]. Also, there is no aspiration if /p, t, k/ occur in unaccented syllables as in *police* [pə'liːs], *tomorrow* [tə'mɒrəʊ], *concern* [kən'sɜːn]. (Cf [kʰ] in *conduct* (n) ['kʰɒndəkt] and the initial [k] in *conduct* (v) [kən'dʌkt].)

Lip position

During the articulation of a plosive, the lips may be spread or rounded, depending upon the nature of the vowel that immediately follows it. If the vowel that follows immediately is unrounded, then there is no rounding in the articulation of the plosive either. If, on the other hand, the vowel that follows immediately is rounded, then there is an anticipatory lip-rounding in the articulation of the plosive too. Some examples follow:

	Spread-lip variety of the plosive	*Rounded-lip variety of the plosive*
/p/	peak	pork
/b/	beast	boost
/t/	tea	two
/d/	dean	dawn
/k/	can	corn
/g/	get	got

The release stage

In certain cases, at the release stage of the plosives in English, there may not be a sudden escape of air. Instead, the release may be accomplished in one of the following ways:

(i) *Inaudible release in final positions* In the final position, as in *ship, mob, meet, need, sack, sag*, the release of the plosive may be achieved by a gentle, and therefore relatively inaudible, opening of the oral closure. Although careful speakers usually tend to release such plosives audibly in formal situations, in ordinary conversational style, they too may often use the inaudible unexploded variety.

(ii) *No audible release in stop clusters* If two stops (plosives, or plosive plus affricate) occur in a cluster, either within a word or at word boundaries, then the first plosive has no audible release, e g in *act* /ækt/, *clubbed* /klʌbd/, *good boy* /'gʊd 'bɔɪ/, *subject* (n) /'sʌbdʒɪkt/, *black jacket* /'blæk 'dʒækɪt/. In such cases the closure for the second stop (plosive or affricate) is made before the release of the first is achieved inaudibly. The release of the first plosive is also delayed in cases of *gemination*, that is, when the same plosive occurs twice in a sequence, e g in *book case* /'bʊk 'keɪs/, *hot toast* /'hɒt 'təʊst/, *big girl* /'bɪg 'gɜːl/.

(iii) *Nasal release* When a plosive is followed by a homorganic nasal consonant, that is, a nasal consonant articulated at the same place, the oral closure, made initially for the plosive, is retained and the compressed air is released through the nose by lowering the soft palate, e g in *topmost* /'tɒpməʊst/, *sudden* /'sʌdn/.

(iv) *Lateral release* When the alveolar plosive /t/ or /d/ is followed by /l/ (which is also alveolar), the plosive is released laterally, that is, by lowering one or both sides of the tongue, while retaining the contact of the tip of the tongue with the teeth ridge, e g in *kettle* /'ketl/, *bottle* /'bɒtl/, *at last* /ət 'lɑːst/, *headless* /'hedlɪs/, *bad light* /'bæd 'laɪt/.

10.311 Bilabial plosives /p, b/

/p/

DESCRIPTION In the articulation of /p/, the soft palate is raised to shut off the nasal cavity, the obstacle to the passage of the lung air being provided by the closure of the lips. The lung air is compressed behind this closure, during which stage the vocal cords are kept wide apart. When the lip closure is released, the compressed air escapes with force. Thus /p/ is a *voiceless bilabial plosive*.

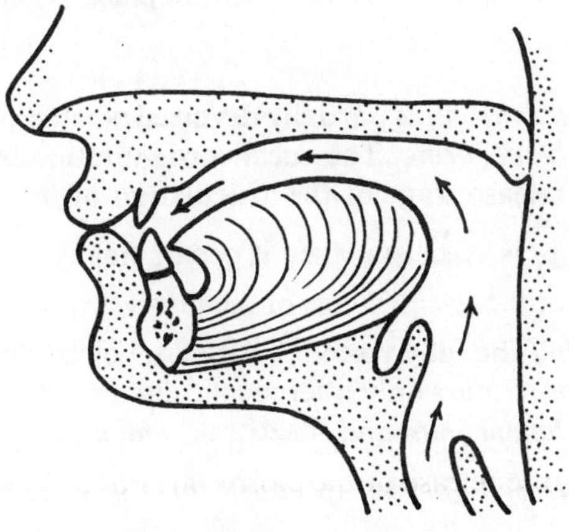

Fig. 27 /p, b/

SPELLING The consonant /p/ is always spelt with the letter *p*, the only exception being the word *shepherd* /ˈʃepəd/, in which it is spelt with *ph*.

The letter *p* is, however, silent in *cupboard, pneumonia, psalm, receipt*, and so on.

Allophones of /p/

(i) *Aspirated /p/* /p/ is aspirated when it occurs initially in an accented syllable as in *pot, pull, aˈpart, apˈply* /əˈplaɪ/, *play, prove, pure*. In all such cases, the consonant that immediately follows /p/ becomes devoiced.

(ii) *Unaspirated /p/* /p/ is unaspirated when
   (1) it occurs in unaccented syllables as in *preˈvent, ˈleper, ˈtaper*;
   (2) it is preceded by /s/ as in *spot, spool, spy, sporadic*; and
   (3) it occurs medially in a syllable as in *apt, lapse, helped.*

(iii) *Inaudibly released (or unexploded) /p/* /p/ is released without an explosion when
   (1) it occurs finally, i e before silence, as in *cup, sleep, type*; and
   (2) it occurs before another plosive or affricate as in *wept, captain, stop cheating.*

(iv) *Nasally released /p/* /p/ is released through the nose when it is followed by /m/ or /n/ as in *happen, help me, cheap meal.*

OCCURRENCE /p/ occurs in all the three positions in a word.

/b/

DESCRIPTION The articulation of /b/ differs from that of /p/ only in respect of voicing: while for /p/ the vocal cords do not vibrate, for /b/ they do. Thus /b/ is a *voiced bilabial plosive.*

SPELLING /b/ is regularly spelt with the letter *b*. The letter *b* is, however, silent when preceded by *m* or followed by *t* in the word-final position as in *climb, comb, thumb, tomb, bomb; debt, doubt*. It is also silent in *plumber, bomber*, and *subtle.*

Allophones of /b/

(i) *Partially devoiced /b/* /b/ is partially devoiced when it occurs initially in a word as in *boy, boat, blade, bring*. The vocal cord vibration in such words may start only during the release stage of the articulation of /b/.

(ii) *Voiceless /b/* /b/ is voiceless when it occurs finally in a word as in *club, mob, robe.*

(iii) *Fully voiced /b/* The fully voiced /b/, that is, voiced through all the three stages of its articulation, occurs only intervocalically, or between voiced sounds, as in *about, rebound, labour, husband* /hʌzbənd/, *ambush.*

(iv) *Inaudibly released (or unexploded) /b/* /b/ is released without an explosion when

(1) it occurs finally, i e before silence as in *rob, tub*; and

(2) it is followed by another plosive or affricate as in *rubbed, subcontinent, subject, object*.

(v) *Nasally released /b/* /b/ is released through the nose when it is followed by /m/ or /n/ in *sub-marine, submit, ribbon*.

OCCURRENCE Like /p/, /b/ occurs in all the three positions in a word.

Distinction between /p/ and /b/

As the description of the two sounds suggests, they are distinguished by the absence of voicing in /p/ and its presence in /b/. Such distinction is very difficult when /p/ and /b/ occur word-finally, where both are voiceless; it is only the context that can tell the difference between *mop* and *mob*, *rope* and *robe*, *tap* and *tab*, for example. In the initial position, too, on account of the partial devoicing of /b/, the distinction can be rather difficult. But in this position, the distinction is restored, if /p/ occurs in an accented syllable, by aspirating it. Thus the following pairs of words, among others, are distinguished, in RP and other native accents of English, chiefly by the aspiration of /p/:

pin	bin	pig	big
pit	bit	pad	bad
pill	bill	pack	back
pat	bat	pull	bull
peach	beach	played	blade

10.312 Alveolar plosives /t, d/

/t/

DESCRIPTION For the articulation of /t/, the soft palate is raised to shut off the nasal passage of air, and the primary obstacle to the airstream is formed by a closure made between (i) the tip of the tongue and the teeth ridge, and (ii) the rims of the tongue and the side teeth. The lung air is compressed behind the closure, during which stage the vocal cords are wide apart. When the closure is released, the compressed air escapes with force. /t/ is thus a *voiceless alveolar plosive*.

SPELLING The consonant /t/ is regularly spelt with *t* and *tt* as in *tank, actor, prompt*, and *butter, cattle, nett* (also spelt *net*). It is sometimes spelt with *th* as in *Thomas, Thames*. Also, the past and past participle marker *-ed*, when suffixed to verbs ending in voiceless consonants other than /t/, is pronounced as /t/, e g *heaped* /hiːpt/, *booked* /bʊkt/, *passed* /pɑːst/, *hatched* /hætʃt/.

The letter *t* is, however, silent in *castle, Christmas, hustle, bustle*, etc.

Allophones of /t/

(i) *Aspirated /t/*. Like /p/, /t/ is aspirated when it occurs initially in an accented syllable as in *tin, tear, ob'tain, attire* /əˈtaɪə/; *try, twice, tune*. In all such cases, the vowel or consonant that immediately follows /t/ becomes devoiced.

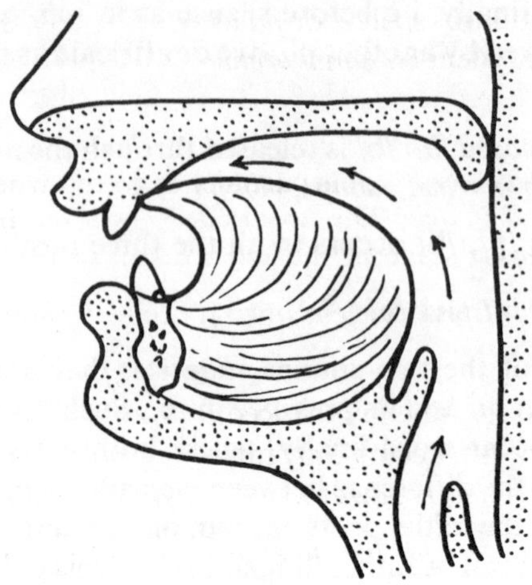

Fig. 28 /t, d/

(ii) *Unaspirated /t/* Again, like /p/, /t/ is unaspirated when

(1) it occurs in unaccented syllables as in *to'day*, *'filter*, *'later*;
(2) it is preceded by /s/ as in *stain*, *stray*, *stupendous*; and
(3) it occurs medially in a syllable as in *hats*, *bits*.

(iii) *Inaudibly released (or unexploded) /t/* /t/ is released inaudibly, that is, without an explosion, when

(1) it occurs finally, i e before silence as in *hot*, *wet*, *late*; and
(2) it is followed by another plosive or affricate as in *hotbed*, *white dog*, *fat child*, *that jug*.

(iv) *Nasally released /t/* /t/ is released through the nose if it is followed by /n/ as in *button*, *mutton*, *cotton*.

(v) *Laterally released /t/* /t/ is released laterally when it is followed by /l/ as in *settle*, *metal*, *cattle*.

(vi) *Dental /t/* /t/ becomes a dental plosive (like the Hindi त [t̪] as in तुम [t̪um] 'you') if it is followed by the dental fricatives /θ, ð/ as in *eighth*, *sit there*.

(vii) *Post-alveolar /t/* /t/ is realized as a post-alveolar plosive if it is followed by /r/ as in *trick*, *true*, *betray*.

OCCURRENCE /t/ occurs in all the three positions in a word.

/d/

DESCRIPTION /d/ is articulated in the same way as /t/, except for voicing: while the vocal cords do not vibrate for /t/, they do for /d/, which is therefore a *voiced alveolar plosive*.

SPELLING /d/ is regularly spelt *d* or *dd* as in *door*, *ado*, *sad*; *sudden*, *hidden*. The letter *d* is, however, silent in *handkerchief*, *handsome*.

Allophones of /d/

(i) *Partially devoiced /d/* /d/ is partially devoiced when it occurs initially in a word as in *dig*, *do*, *dry*, *dew*. The vocal cord vibration in such words may start only during the release stage of the articulation of /d/.

(ii) *Voiceless /d/* /d/ is voiceless when it occurs finally in a word as in *bid*, *said*, *shoved*, *roused*.

(iii) *Fully voiced /d/* The fully voiced /d/, that is, voiced through all the three stages of its articulation, occurs only intervocalically, or between voiced sounds, as in *ado*, *render*, *model*, *roadways*.

(iv) *Inaudibly released (or unexploded) /d/* /d/ is released without an explosion when

(1) it occurs finally, i e before silence as in *head*, *road*, *pleased*; and

(2) it is followed by another plosive or affricate as in *headgear*, *bad times*, *good day*, *good judge*.

(v) *Nasally released /d/* /d/ is released through the nose when it is followed by /n/ as in *sadden*, *bad name*, *good night*.

(vi) *Laterally released /d/* /d/ is released laterally when it is followed by /l/ as in *saddle*, *middle*, *bad light*.

(vii) *Dental /d/* /d/ becomes a dental plosive (like the Hindi द [d̪] as in दान [d̪a:n] 'donation') when it is followed by the dental fricatives /θ, ð/ as in *sad thought*, *add this*.

(viii) *Post-alveolar /d/* /d/ is realized as a post-alveolar plosive if it is followed by /r/ as in *dry*, *drain*, *adrift*.

OCCURRENCE /d/ occurs in all the three positions in a word.

Distinction between /t/ and /d/

As in the case of /p/ and /b/, the distinction between /t/ and /d/ can also get lost in all those positions in which /d/ is partially or fully devoiced (see above). However, in the initial position in accented syllables, such distinction can be maintained, nevertheless, by aspirating /t/. It is chiefly by the aspiration of /t/, therefore, that the following pairs of words, among others, are distinguished:

tin	din	tale	dale
tip	dip	try	dry
ten	den	tune	dune
tell	dell	tie	die

Pronunciation of the past tense marker *-d* or *-ed*

The past tense marker *-d* or *-ed* is pronounced in three different ways:

(1) It is pronounced /t/ after voiceless consonants other than /t/.

EXAMPLES:

heaped	/hi:pt/	*passed*	/pɑ:st/
looked	/lʊkt/	*rushed*	/rʌʃt/
laughed	/lɑ:ft/	*reached*	/ri:tʃt/

(2) It is pronounced /d/ after voiced sounds other than /d/. (Voiced sounds mean all vowels and voiced consonants.)

EXAMPLES:

clubbed	/klʌbd/	*hinged*	/hindʒd/
tagged	/tægd/	*prayed*	/preɪd/
lived	/lɪvd/	*tried*	/traɪd/
praised	/preɪzd/	*sued*	/su:d/
		bowed	/baʊd/

(3) It is pronounced /ɪd/ after /t, d/.

EXAMPLES:

hated	/'heɪtɪd/	*headed*	/'hedɪd/
batted	/'bætɪd/	*raided*	/'reɪdɪd/

10.313 Velar plosives /k, g/

/k/

DESCRIPTION For the articulation of /k/, the main obstacle to the airstream is formed by a firm contact of the back of the tongue against the soft palate, which itself is raised in order to shut off the nasal passage. The lung air is compressed behind the closure, during which stage the vocal cords are wide apart. When the closure is released, the compressed air escapes with force. /k/ is thus a *voiceless velar plosive*.

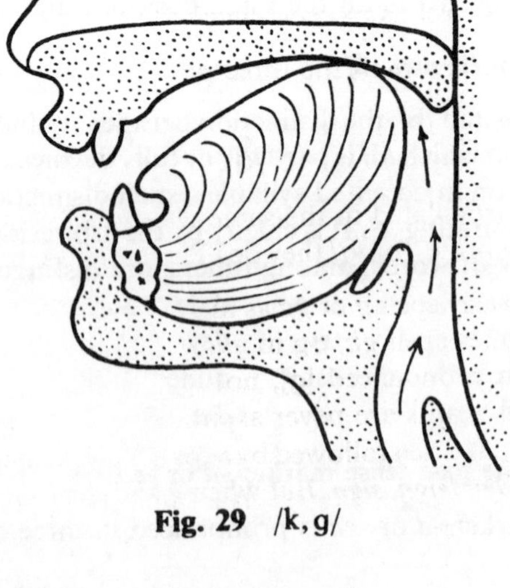

Fig. 29 /k, g/

SPELLING /k/ is spelt in a number of ways:

k	keen, speaker, peak
c	cut, act, metric
cc	when followed by *a*, *o*, or *u*: *occasion*, according, occur
ck	pack, sick, luck
ch	chemist, alchemy, stomach
qu	(pronounced /kw/) quarter, queen, quiet

The letter *k* is silent in *know*, *knee*, *knit*, and so on. The letter *c* is silent in *muscle*.

Allophones of /k/

(i) *Aspirated /k/* Like /p/ and /t/, /k/ is aspirated when it occurs initially in an accented syllable as in *king*, *cat*, *account* /ə'kaʊnt/; *clay*, *cry*, *queue*, *quit*. In all such cases, the consonant that immediately follows /k/ becomes devoiced

(ii) *Unaspirated /k/* Again, like /p/ and /t/, /k/ is unaspirated when

(1) it occurs in unaccented syllables as in *con'tain*, *'basking*, *'bouquet*, *'marker*;

(2) it is preceded by /s/ as in *sky*, *school*, *square*; and

(3) it occurs medially in a syllable as in *act*, *checked*, *packs*.

(iii) *Inaudibly released (or unexploded) /k/* /k/ is released inaudibly, that is, without an explosion, when

(1) it occurs finally, i e before silence as in *lack*, *cheque*, *take*; and

(2) it is followed by another plosive or affricate as in *backed*, *back door*, *blackboard*, *deckchairs*.

(iv) *Advanced variety of /k/* /k/ is articulated nearer the palate if it is followed by a front vowel as in *keen*, *kit*, *cat*.

(v) *Retracted variety of /k/* /k/ is articulated further back in the mouth if it is followed by a back vowel as in *cool*, *caught*, *cart*.

OCCURRENCE /k/ occurs in all the three positions in a word.

/g/

DESCRIPTION /g/ is articulated in the same way as /k/, but, whereas for /k/ the vocal cords do not vibrate, for /g/ they do. Therefore, /g/ is a *voiced velar plosive*.

SPELLING /g/ is regularly spelt *g* or *gg* as in *gate*, *get*, *give*, *go*, *again*, *bag*; *juggle*, *begged*. It is sometimes spelt *gh*, e g in *ghost*, *aghast*. (Students must note that *gh* in such words is pronounced [g], not [gh], that is, it is not aspirated. In English, voiced consonants are never aspirated.)

The letter *g* is silent when followed by *m* or *n* in the same syllable as in *phlegm*, *diaphragm*, *gnat*, *gnaw*, *feign*, *sign*. But when *g* and the following *m* or *n* occur in two different syllables, *g* is not silent, e g *phlegmatic*, *signature*, *ignore*, *ignite*.

Allophones of /g/

Like /b/ and /d/ discussed earlier, /g/ is also partially devoiced, voiceless, or fully voiced, depending on its position in a word or phrase. These three varieties (allophones) are now discussed.

(i) *Partially devoiced* /g/ /g/ is partially devoiced when it occurs initially in a word as in *girl, gate, good.* In such words, the vocal cord vibration may start only during the release stage of the articulation of /g/.

(ii) *Voiceless* /g/ /g/ is voiceless when it occurs finally in a word as in *bag, smog, tug.*

(iii) *Fully voiced* /g/ The fully voiced /g/, that is, voiced through all the three stages of its articulation, occurs only intervocalically, or only between voiced sounds, as in *ago*, *against*, *begin*, *tiger*.

(iv) *Inaudibly released (or unexploded)* /g/ /g/ is released without explosion when

(1) it occurs finally, i e before silence, as in *tag*, *drug*, *fog*; and

(2) it is followed by another plosive or affricate as in *bagpipe*, *eggcup*, *big chin*, *big jacket*.

(v) *Advanced variety of* /g/ /g/ is articulated nearer the palate when it is followed by a front vowel as in *get*, *geese*, *gander*.

(vi) *Retracted variety of* /g/ /g/ is articulated further back in the mouth when it is followed by a back vowel as in *goose*, *good*, *gone*.

OCCURRENCE /g/ occurs in all the three positions in a word.

Distinction between /k/ and /g/

As in the case of the pairs /p/, /b/, and /t/, /d/, the distinction between /k/ and /g/ becomes very difficult when these two sounds occur finally in words, for, in that position, both are voiceless. It is only the context, therefore, that brings out the distinction between *back* and *bag*, *lock* and *log*, and *smock* and *smog*, for example. In the initial position, too, on account of the partial devoicing of /g/, the distinction between /k/ and /g/ can sometimes be lost. But in this position, the distinction is restored in those cases where /k/ is aspirated, i e when /k/ occurs initially in an accented syllable. Thus the following pairs of words, for example, are distinguished, in all native varieties of English, chiefly by the aspiration of /k/:

cane	gain	cot	got
class	glass	cable	gable
crew	grew	curl	girl
cold	gold	come	gum
card	guard	call	gall

10.32 Affricates

The production of an affricate is similar to that of a plosive: there is a closing stage, a compression stage, and a release stage. But, whereas in the case of a plosive the release is sudden, for an affricate it is gradual. Because of a gradual separation of articulators (at the release stage), an affricate is accompanied by friction at the same point where the complete closure is made. For this reason, the closure part of the affricate is represented in the phonetic alphabet by the symbol of the appropriate plosive, and the release part, by that of the fricative produced at the same point. Thus an affricate is symbolized by what is called a digraph (i e a sequence of two letters used in a phonetic transcription to represent a single phoneme), e g the symbol /tʃ/ to represent the consonant at the beginning of words such as *chess*, *chain*, and *choose*.

In English there are two affricates, and these are palato-alveolar: /tʃ/ and /dʒ/.

10.321 Palato-alveolar affricates /tʃ, dʒ/

/tʃ/

DESCRIPTION With the soft palate raised to shut off the nasal passage, the obstacle to the airstream is formed by a closure made between the tip and blade of the tongue and the alveolar ridge, the rims of the tongue making a contact with the upper side teeth. At the same time, the front of the tongue is also raised in the direction of the hard palate (see Fig. 30). The closure is released slowly, with the blocked air escaping with friction, which takes place between the blade-to-front section of the tongue and the alveolar ridge-to-hard palate section of the roof of the mouth. The vocal cords are wide apart. Thus /tʃ/is a *voiceless palato-alveolar affricate*.

During the articulation of the affricate, there is a certain amount of protrusion and rounding of lips irrespective of the nature of the following vowel.

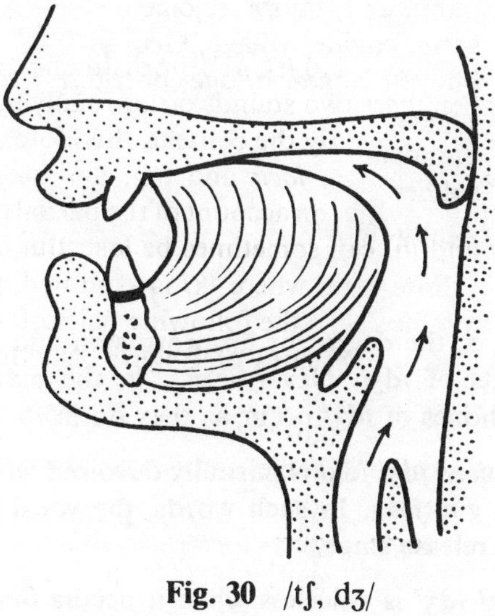

Fig. 30 /tʃ, dʒ/

However, the protrusion is greater if the following vowel is a rounded one as in *choose*. (Contrast with *cheese*.)

SPELLING	*ch*	chair, achieve, orchard, march, church
	tch	butcher, watch, catch
	t + *eous* (pronounced /tʃəs/)	righteous
	t + *ion* (pronounced /tʃən/) when *t* is preceded by *s*	question, suggestion
	t + *ure* (pronounced /tʃə/)	picture, nature, culture, furniture (But *mature* is pronounced without /tʃ/: /mə'tjʊə/.)

Allophones of /tʃ/

No important variants of /tʃ/ occur, except in the matter of the degree of lip-protrusion and rounding. As already stated, such lip-protrusion and rounding is greater when /tʃ/ is followed by a rounded vowel than when it is followed by an unrounded vowel.

OCCURRENCE /tʃ/ occurs in all the three positions in a word.

/dʒ/

DESCRIPTION /dʒ/ is articulated in the same way as /tʃ/, except for the state of the vocal cords: whereas for /tʃ/ the vocal cords are wide apart, for /dʒ/ they vibrate. /dʒ/ is therefore, a *voiced palato-alveolar affricate*.

As in the case of /tʃ/, there is a certain amount of protrusion and rounding of lips in the articulation of /dʒ/. Also, as in the case of /tʃ/, such protrusion and rounding is greater when the consonant is followed by a rounded vowel than otherwise. Thus it is greater in *jaws* than in *jazz*.

SPELLING	*j*	jump, ajar, injure, rejoice
	g	germ, engine, village, George
	dg	budget, ledger, bridge, porridge
	gg	suggest
	de	grandeur
	di	soldier
	dj	adjoin, adjacent

Allophones of /dʒ/

Except in the matter of the degree of lip-protrusion and rounding, there are no important variants of /dʒ/. Nevertheless, in the matter of voicing, the following three allophones of /dʒ/ occur as they do in /b, d, g/:

(i) *Partially devoiced* /dʒ/ /dʒ/ is partially devoiced when it occurs initially in a word as in *jam, gin, joke*. In such words, the vocal cord vibration may start only during the release stage.

(ii) *Voiceless* /dʒ/ /dʒ/ is voiceless when it occurs finally in a word as in *large, age, huge*.

(iii) *Fully voiced* /dʒ/ The fully voiced /dʒ/, that is, voiced through all the stages of its articulation, occurs only intervocalically, or only between voiced sounds, as in *adjust*, *margin*, *major*.

OCCURRENCE /dʒ/ occurs in all the three positions in a word.

10.33 Nasals

Nasals are like plosives in that a complete closure is made in the mouth for their articulation; they are at the same time different from plosives in that the soft palate is in its lowered position, allowing the air to escape freely through the nose. Since the air can escape freely through the nose, nasals can be continued, whereas plosives cannot. In this respect, therefore, they are like fricatives (see section 10.35), except that they are not accompanied by any audible friction, which is characteristic of fricatives. Further, since they can be continued, and have no audible friction, they are somewhat like vowels.

English has three nasals, which, in respect of the place of articulation, correspond to the three pairs of plosives: the bilabial nasal /m/ corresponds to the plosives /p, b/; the alveolar nasal /n/ to /t, d/; and the velar nasal /ŋ/ to /k, g/. They are all voiced.

As nasals are in some respect like vowels, they can perform the syllabic function of vowels. This is particularly true of the English nasal /n/. Thus the words *button*, *cotton*, and *mutton*, for example, which have two syllables each, are pronounced without any vowel in the second syllable: /ˈbʌtn, ˈkɒtn, ˈmʌtn/. In such cases, /n/ performs the function of a vowel.

10.331 Bilabial nasal

/m/

DESCRIPTION For the articulation of /m/, a closure is formed at the lips (as for /p, b/); the soft palate is lowered to allow a free passage of air through the nose. The vocal cords vibrate. /m/ is thus a *voiced bilabial nasal*.

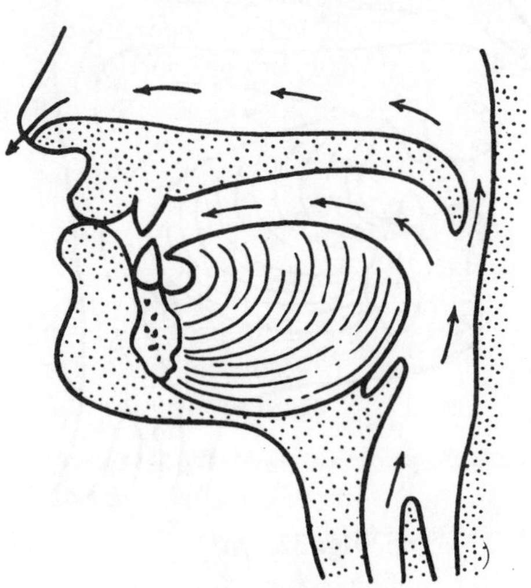

Fig. 31 /m/

SPELLING /m/ is regularly spelt *m* and *mm* as in *mad, amid, sum*; *summer, dimmer*. Other spellings for it are the following:

mb climb, plumber /'plʌmə/
comb /kəʊm/, tomb /tu:m/

mn autumn, damn

(Note that when the juxtaposing *m* and *n* are assigned to two different syllables, neither of them is silent, e g *autumnal* is pronounced as /ɔ:'tʌmnəl/ and *damnable* as /'dæmnəbl/.)

Allophones of /m/

(i) *Labio-dental /m̪/* /m/ is realized as a labio-dental nasal when it is immediately followed by the labio-dental /f, v/ as in *comfort, nymph, come first, same vest, circumvent*.

(ii) *Partially devoiced /m̥/* /m/ is partially devoiced when /s/ precedes it as in *small, smooth, science master*.

(iii) *Syllabic /m̩/* /m/ becomes syllabic in words such as *prism* and *rhythm* if the vowel /ə/ ordinarily occurring in their second syllables is dropped.

OCCURRENCE /m/ occurs in all the three positions in a word.

10.332 Alveolar nasal

/n/

DESCRIPTION For the articulation of /n/, a closure is formed in the mouth between (i) the tip of the tongue and the teeth ridge, and (ii) the rims of the tongue and the upper side teeth, exactly as for /t, d/; the soft palate is lowered to allow a free passage of air through the nose. The lip position will depend on the adjacent vowel: e g spread lips when preceded or followed by /i:/, as in *seen, niece*; neutral lips when preceded or followed by /ʌ/, as in *shunt, nut*; and somewhat rounded

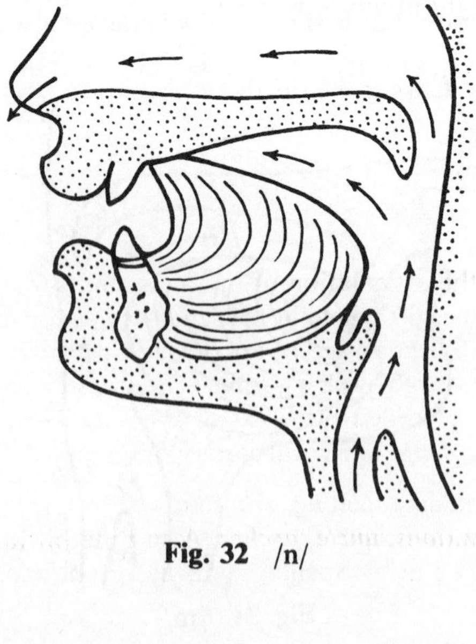

Fig. 32 /n/

lips when preceded or followed by /uː/, as in *soon*, *nude*. The vocal cords vibrate. /n/ is thus a *voiced alveolar nasal*.

SPELLING /n/ is regularly spelt with *n* and *nn* as in *not*, *ant*, *run*; *running*, *funny*. Other spellings for /n/ are the following:

gn	gnat, sign
kn	know, knit, knife
pn	pneumonia, pneumatic

Note that when the juxtaposing *g* and *n* or *k* and *n* belong to two different syllables, *g* and *k* are not silent. Contrast (i) *signature* /'sɪgnɪtʃə/ and *signal* /'sɪgnəl/ with *sign* /saɪn/, and (ii) *acknowledge* /ək'nɒlɪdʒ/ with *knowledge* /'nɒlɪdʒ/.

Allophones of /n/

The articulation of /n/ is particularly affected by the following consonant, resulting in the following allophones:

(i) *Labio-dental /n/* /n/ is realized as a labio-dental nasal when it is immediately followed by /f, v/ as in *infant*, *inform*, *in view*, *invite*. Such a labio-dental realization is the same as the labio-dental realization of /m/.

(ii) *Dental /n/* When followed by /θ, ð/, /n/ is realized as a dental nasal as in *month*, *tenth*, *on them*.

(iii) *Post-alveolar /n/* When followed by /r/, /n/ is realized as a post-alveolar nasal as in *sunrise*, *unrest*, *enrol*.

In addition to these, /n/ has the following allophones:

(iv) *Partially devoiced /n/* /n/ is partially devoiced when it is preceded by /s/ or /t/ as in *snack*, *snow*, *cotton*, *button*, *mutton*.

(v) *Syllabic /n/* /n/ becomes syllabic in words such as *button*, *sudden*, *often*, *listen*, *dozen*, *vision*.

OCCURRENCE /n/ occurs in all the three positions in a word.

10.333 Velar nasal

/ŋ/

DESCRIPTION For the articulation of /ŋ/, a closure is formed between the back of the tongue and the soft palate in the same way as for /k, g/; the soft palate is lowered to allow a free passage of air through the nose. The lip position will depend on the preceding vowel: e g somewhat spread when preceded by /ɪ/ as in *sing*; neutral when preceded by /ʌ/ as in *sung*; and somewhat rounded when preceded by /ɒ/ as in *song*. The vocal cords vibrate. /ŋ/ is thus a *voiced velar nasal*.

SPELLING /ŋ/ is regularly spelt *ng*, or *n* followed by a letter representing /k/, e g *sing*, *rung*; *brink*; *anxious*, *uncle*, *anchor*. Also note /ŋ/ in *anxiety* /æŋ'zaɪətɪ/.

The word-final *ng* in the spelling is always pronounced /ŋ/, never /ŋg/, e g

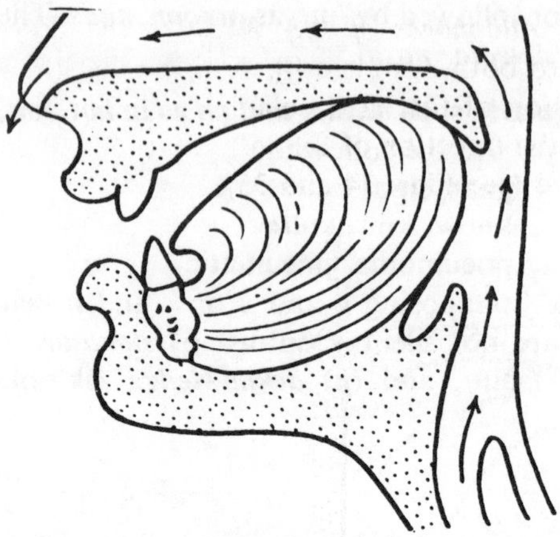

Fig. 33 /ŋ/

running /'rʌnɪŋ/, *sing* /siŋ/. The medial *ng*, however, is pronounced

(1) /ŋ/ in derivatives of verbs ending in /ŋ/, e g *singer* /'sɪŋə/, *ringing* /'rɪŋɪŋ/, *hanger* /'hæŋə/; and

(2) /ŋg/ in other words, e g *finger* /'fɪŋgə/, *anger* /'æŋgə/, *hunger* /'hʌŋgə/.

(Note: *longer* /'lɒŋə/: one who longs for something, but *longer* /'lɒŋgə/: comparative degree of the adjective *long*.)

Allophones of /ŋ/

Ordinarily, there are no allophonic variants of /ŋ /. However, occasionally, a syllabic /ŋ / may occur in the final position where /ən/ is generally expected in words such as *bacon, thicken, organ*.

OCCURRENCE /ŋ/ does not occur in the word-initial position. Besides, it occurs only after the short vowels /ɪ, æ, ɒ, ʌ/, e g *sing* /sɪŋ/, *sang* /sæŋ/, *song* /sɒŋ/, *sung* /sʌŋ/.

10.34 Lateral

A lateral consonant is produced when there is a closure, essentially, in the centre of the oral passage, so that the air can escape on one or both sides of such a closure.

English has only one lateral, the alveolar lateral /l/.

10.341 Alveolar lateral

/l/

DESCRIPTION In the articulation of /l/, the tip of the tongue is in contact with the teeth ridge, with one or both sides of the tongue remaining low so that the lung air can escape freely without friction through the side(s). The soft palate is in its raised position, shutting off the nasal passage, and the vocal cords vibrate. /l/ is thus a *voiced alveolar lateral*.

RP has two distinct varieties of /l/: a clear [l] and a dark [ɫ]. (See their distribution under *Allophones of /l/*.) Whereas the description in the above paragraph applies to both, for clear [l], additionally, the front of the tongue is raised in the direction of the hard palate, while, for dark [ɫ], the back of the tongue is raised in the direction of the soft palate, the front of the tongue being somewhat depressed (see Figs. 34 and 35).

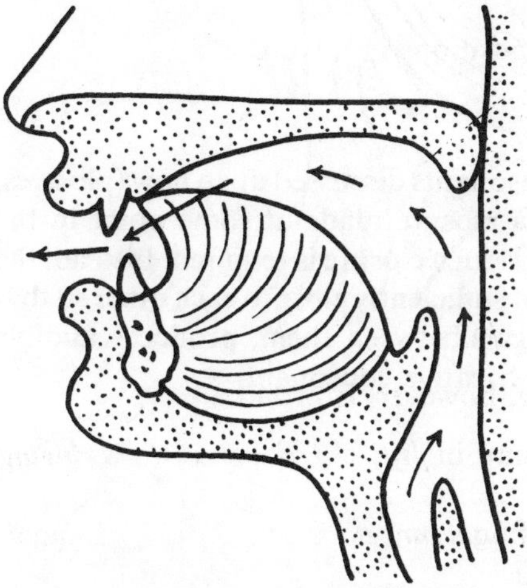

Fig. 34 Clear [l]

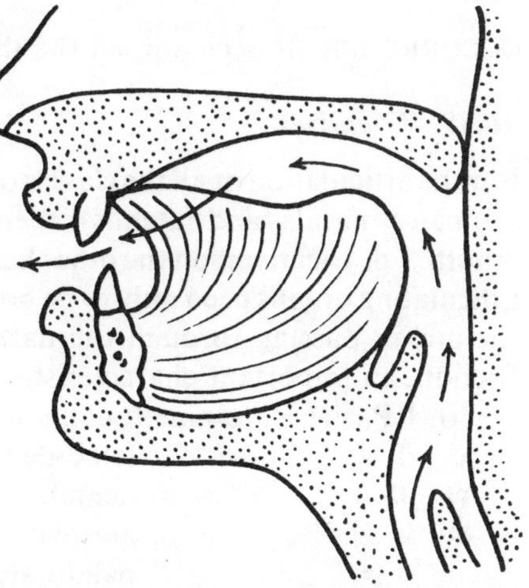

Fig. 35 Dark [ɫ]

The lip position, during the articulation of /l/, is determined by the nature of the adjacent vowel, e g *lease, feel* are said with spread lips, but *loose, fool* with somewhat rounded lips.

SPELLING /l/ is regularly spelt *l* or *ll*, e g *let, halt, seal; killed, hill*. The letter *l* is, however, frequently silent in front of certain other consonants, as in *chalk, would, half, balm, salmon, folk*.

Allophones of /l/

As already stated, the two chief allophones of /l/ are the clear [l] and the dark [ɫ]. The other allophones of /l/ (to be discussed now) must also, at the same time, be either clear or dark /l/, depending on the rules given now under Clear [l] and Dark [ɫ].

(i) *Clear* [*l*] Clear [l] is used only when the lateral is followed by a vowel or the semi-vowel /j/ as in *lean, let, lose, flute, ply; billion, lure*.

(ii) *Dark* [ɫ] Dark [ɫ] is used whenever the lateral is not followed by a vowel, e g word-finally as in *heal, hell, call*, and before consonants other than /j/ as in *health, helm, milk, called*.

(iii) *Dental* [l̪] /l/ is realized as a dental lateral when it is followed by the dental fricative /θ/ as in *health, wealthy, stealth*

(iv) *Voiceless* /*l*/ /l/ is rendered voiceless when it is preceded by aspirated /p, k/, e g in *play, apply, climb, decline*. (Note that /t/ cannot occur before /l/ in a syllable-initial or word-initial position.)

(v) *Partially devoiced /l/* /l/ becomes partially devoiced when it is preceded by an unaspirated /p, k/ or by /s, f, ʃ, θ/, as in *pla'centa, plan'tation, 'droplet, clan'destine, cli'matic, uncle; slate, flee, flushless, ruthless.*

(vi) Syllabic /l/ /l/ becomes syllabic in words such as *bottle, kettle, settle, shackle.* Syllabic /l/ is always a dark [ɫ].

OCCURRENCE /l/ occurs in all the three positions in a word.

10.35 Fricatives

For the articulation of all the classes of consonants discussed up to now (plosives, affricates, nasals, and laterals), there is a closure made at some point in the mouth. For fricatives, on the other hand, no such closure is required. Instead, the articulating organs need only to be brought sufficiently close to each other so that the air, in passing through the narrow gap between them, produces audible friction, an important characteristic of a fricative consonant.

In RP, there are nine fricatives:

/f, v/	labio-dental
/θ, ð/	dental
/s, z/	alveolar
/ʃ, ʒ/	palato-alveolar
/h/	glottal

of these, /f, θ, s, ʃ, h/ are voiceless and /v, ð, z, ʒ/ voiced. The 'voiced' fricatives, however, are fully voiced only when they occur between voiced sounds as in *govern, rather, razor, vision, in vain, all this, a zebra, a genre* [ə 'ʒɑ̃:rɹ]. In other positions, they may be only partially voiced or completely voiceless, e g initially (i e following silence as in *vet, that, zoo*), only the latter part of the fricative may be voiced, and finally (i e before silence as in *love, bathe, whose, beige*), the fricative is generally voiceless. The 'voiceless' fricatives, on the other hand, with the only exception of /h/, are voiceless in all positions. Generally, /h/ has some voicing when it occurs between voiced sounds as in *behave, enhance, a hat, the headmaster*.

As for the position of the lips, some RP speakers use slight lip-rounding for /ʃ, ʒ/ in all positions; for other speakers the lip position is determined by the nature of the adjacent vowel, as it is, for all speakers, in the case of the other fricatives, /f, v, θ, ð, s, z, h/. In the articulation of these fricatives, the lips are spread if the adjacent vowel is produced with spread lips; otherwise they will be rounded. Examples of the above fricatives with spread lips are *feed, leaf; veal, leave; think, sheath; this, with; see, hiss; zebra, fees; heat*; examples with rounded lips are *food, roof; voice, move; thought, broth; smooth; sue, loose; zoo, ooze; who.*

10.351 Labio-dental fricatives /f, v/

/f/

DESCRIPTION During the articulation of /f/, the soft palate is raised, shutting off the nasal passage of air. The inner surface of the lower lip makes a light contact with the front upper teeth, leaving a narrow gap through which the lung air escapes, producing audible friction. The vocal cords are wide apart. /f/ is thus a *voiceless labio-dental fricative*.

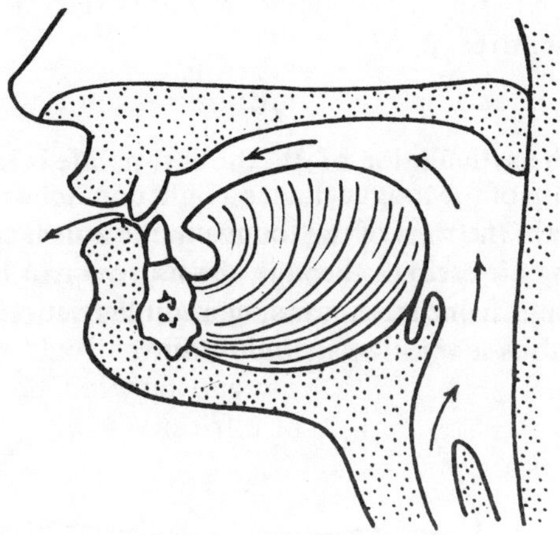

Fig. 36 /f, v/

SPELLING	*f*	fit, after, leaf, fly, cleft, soften
	ff	offer, affair, gruff, stiff
	gh	laughter, enough, trough
	ph	photo, trophy, graph

Allophones of /f/

No important allophonic variants of /f/ occur except in respect of the position of the lips, which, as stated earlier (see section 10.35), depends on the lip position required by an adjacent vowel.

OCCURRENCE /f/ occurs in all the three positions in a word.

/v/

DESCRIPTION /v/ is articulated in the same way as /f/, except that in the articulation of /v/ the vocal cords vibrate. /v/ is thus a *voiced labio-dental fricative*.

SPELLING /v/ is regularly spelt *v* as in *vain*, *invite*, *love*, the only exceptions being the preposition *of* and *nephew*, where the letters *f* and *ph*, respectively, are pronounced /v/.

Allophones of /v/

(i) *Partially voiced /v/* /v/ is only partially voiced when it occurs initially (i e after silence) as in *vain, vine, verse*.

(ii) *Devoiced /v/* /v/ may be completely devoiced when it occurs finally (i e before silence) as in *leave, prove, calve*.

Further, as in the case of /f/, the lip position for /v/ will depend upon the adjacent vowel (see section 10.35), e g spread lips for /v/ in *veal*, *vain*, and somewhat rounded in *move, prove*.

OCCURRENCE /v/ occurs in all the three positions in a word.

10.352 Dental fricatives /θ, ð/

/θ/

DESCRIPTION In the articulation of /θ/, the soft palate is raised, shutting off the nasal passage; the tip of the tongue makes a light contact with the inner surface of the upper front teeth; the rims of the tongue make a firm contact with the upper side teeth. The lung air escapes through the narrow gap between the tip of the tongue and the upper front teeth, causing audible friction. The vocal cords are wide apart. /θ/ is thus a *voiceless dental fricative*.

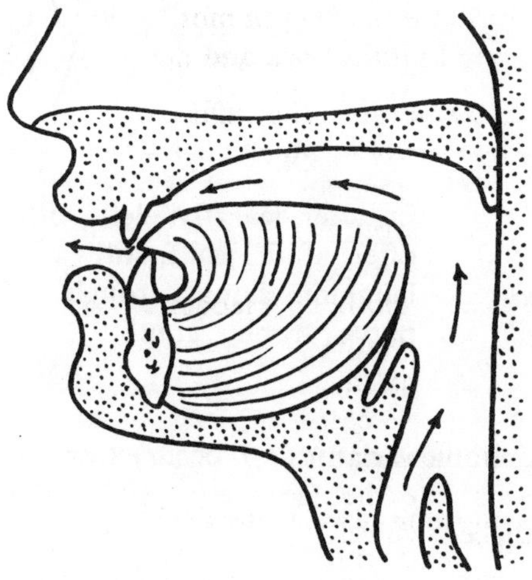

Fig. 37 /θ, ð/

SPELLING /θ/ is always spelt *th* as in *thin*, *atheist*, *bath*.

Allophones of /θ/

No important allophonic variants of /θ/ occur except in respect of the lip position, which depends upon the lip position required by an adjacent vowel (see section 10.35).

OCCURRENCE /θ/ occurs in all the three positions in a word.

/ð/

DESCRIPTION /ð/ is articulated in the same way as /θ/, except that in the articulation of /ð/ the vocal cords vibrate. /ð/ is thus a *voiced dental fricative*.

SPELLING Like /θ/, /ð/ is also always spelt *th* as in *that*, *lather*, *booth*.

Allophones of /ð/

(i) *Partially voiced* /ð/ /ð/ is only partially voiced when it occurs initially (i e after silence) as in *therefore, then, though.*

(ii) *Devoiced* /ð/ /ð/ may be completely devoiced when it occurs finally (i e before silence) as in *bathe, wreathe, bequeath.*

Further, as in the case of /θ/, the lip position for /ð/ will depend upon the adjacent vowel (see section 10.35).

OCCURRENCE /ð/ occurs in all the three positions in a word.

The pronunciation of *th*

In a few proper names, *th* is pronounced /t/, e g *Thames* /temz/, *Thailand* /'taɪlənd/, *Thomas* /'tɒməs/, *Thomson* /'tɒmsn/. In all other cases, *th* is pronounced either /θ/ or /ð/, and in each case a learner must ascertain whether *th* is /θ/ or /ð/. The position is made even more difficult by the fact that *th* may be pronounced differently in inflections and derivations. Examples follow.

(i) *Inflections* In some cases, the suffix -(*e*)*s* changes /θ/ in the stem to /ð/:

/θ/	/ð/
mouth	mouths
youth	youths
path	paths
cloth /klɒθ/	clothes /kləʊðz/
truth	truths
oath	oaths
wreath	wreaths
sheath	sheaths

(ii) *Derivations* In some cases, while the stems are pronounced with /θ/, the derivatives are pronounced with /ð/:

/θ/	/ð/
north	northern
south	southern
cloth (n)	clothe (v)
bath (n)	bathe (v)
breath (n)	breathe (v)
heath	heathen
wreath (n)	wreathe (v)
sheath (n)	sheathe (v)
mouth (n)	mouth (v)

10.353 Alveolar fricatives /s, z/

/s/

DESCRIPTION For the articulation of /s/, the soft palate is raised to shut off the nasal passage of air; the tip and blade of the tongue make a light contact with the teeth ridge, the side rims of the tongue making, at the same time, a firm contact with the upper side teeth. The airstream escapes through a narrow groove along the centre of the tongue, causing audible friction between the tongue and the teeth ridge. The vocal cords are wide apart. Thus /s/ is a *voiceless alveolar fricative*.

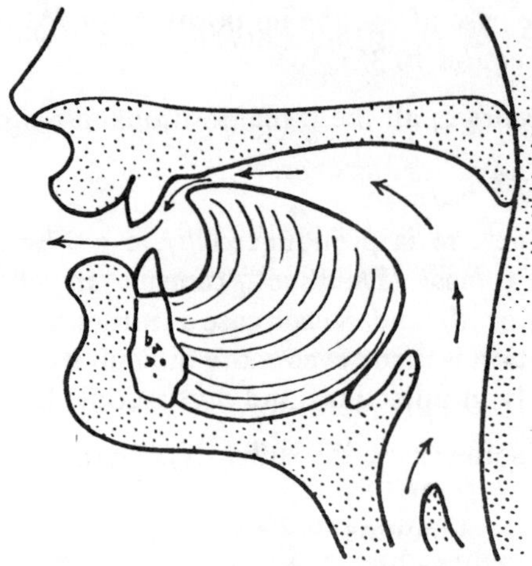

Fig. 38 /s, z/

SPELLING	*s*	see, fast, books
	ss	essay, loss, assess
	sc	scene, science, ascend
	c	cement, fancy, face
	x (pronounced /ks/)	extra, axe, lax

Allophones of /s/

There are no important allophonic variants of /s/, except in respect of the position of lips, which depends on the lip position required by an adjacent vowel (see section 10.35)

OCCURRENCE /s/ occurs in all the three positions in a word.

/z/

DESCRIPTION /z/ is articulated in the same way as /s/, except that for /z/ the vocal cords vibrate. /z/ is thus a *voiced alveolar fricative*.

SPELLING	*s*	cousin, please, bags
	ss	scissors, po*ss*ess, dessert
	z	zeal, crazy, amaze
	zz	dazzle, buzz
	x (pronounced /gz/	exact, examine

There are some words containing *x* where this letter can be pronounced either /ks/ or /gz/. Example are:

exit /'eksɪt/ or /'egzɪt/, *exile* /'eksaɪl/ or /'egzaɪl/, and *exigency* /'eksɪdʒənsɪ/ or /'egzɪdʒənsɪ/.

Allophones of /z/

(i) *Partially voiced /z/* /z/ is only partially voiced when it occurs initially (i e after silence) as in *zinc, zebra, zoo.*

(ii) *Devoiced /z/* /z/ may be completely devoiced when it occurs finally (i e before silence) as in *boys, lose, airlines.*

Further, as in the case of /s/, the position of lips during the articulation of /z/ depends on the position of lips required by an adjacent vowel (see section 10.35).

The pronunciation of the suffixes -(*e*)*s*, '*s*, *s*'

The suffix -*s* or -*es* used in the plural-formation of nouns or the third person singular present-tense formation of verbs, and the suffix '*s* or *s*' for the possessive-formation of nouns are pronounced in three different ways, depending upon the ending of the stem (i e the uninflected form of the noun or verb). They are pronounced in the following three ways:

(1) /ɪz/ after /s, z, ʃ, ʒ, tʃ, dʒ/:

horses	crosses	lass's	
roses	chooses	Dickens's	/'dɪkɪnzɪz/
bushes	rushes	witch's	/'wɪtʃɪz/
garages	massages	witches'	
benches	fetches	judge's	/'dʒʌdʒɪz/
hedges	budges	judges'	

Note: *house* /haʊs/; *houses* /'haʊzɪz/ (where the /s/ of the stem also changes to /z/).

(2) /z/ after a voiced sound (i e all vowels and voiced consonants) other than /z, ʒ, dʒ/:

boys	goes	man's
girls	stands	men's
airlines	shines	boy's
bags	loves	boys'
leaves	wears	officer's
buds	sings	officers'
		employee's
		employees'

(3) /s/ after a voiceless consonant other than /s, ʃ, tʃ/:

books	walks	priests'
taps	laughs	chief's
cats	sniffs	chap's
moths	stops	Dick's
cloths	fits	Ruth's

10.354 Palato-alveolar fricatives /ʃ, ʒ/

/ʃ/

DESCRIPTION The articulation of /ʃ/ resembles that of /s/ to a good extent: for both, the soft palate is raised to shut off the nasal passage; the tip and blade of the tongue make a light contact with the teeth ridge; and the side rims of the tongue make a firm contact with the upper side teeth. But this is where the similarity ends. For /ʃ/ (but not for /s/), the front of the tongue is also raised at the same time in the direction of the hard palate. As a result of this simultaneous raising of the front of the tongue, the narrowing between the tongue and the roof of the mouth is more diffuse: it spreads from the tip and blade to the front of the tongue. The air escapes through this narrow, but diffuse, gap with audible friction. The vocal cords are wide apart. /ʃ/ is thus a *voiceless palato-alveolar fricative*.

Some RP speakers use slight lip-rounding for /ʃ, ʒ/ in all positions; others do so only when a rounded vowel precedes or follows them.

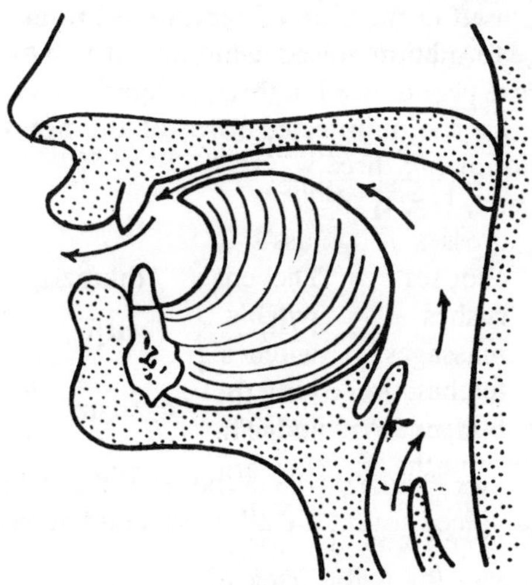

Fig. 39 /ʃ, ʒ/

SPELLING		
	sh	shell, marshal, harsh
	ch	chute, machine, moustache
	sch	schedule
	s (followed by *u*)	sure, sugar
	ss (followed by *u*)	assure
	ti	ration, initial, essential
	si	mansion, Asia
	ssi	mission, submission
	sci	conscious
	ci	special, official, electrician
	ce	ocean

Also note *x* pronounced /kʃ/ in *luxury*.

Allophones of /ʃ/

There are no allophonic variants of /ʃ/.

OCCURRENCE /ʃ/ occurs in all the three positions in a word.

/ʒ/

DESCRIPTION /ʒ/ is articulated in the same way as /ʃ/ with the only difference that for /ʒ/ the vocal cords vibrate. /ʒ/ is thus a *voiced palato-alveolar fricative*.

SPELLING	*si*	decision, vision, revision
	s (followed by *u*)	measure, treasure, leisure, usual
	z (followed by *u*)	azure, seizure
	ge (in French loan words)	garage, espionage, sabotage, rouge

Allophones of /ʒ/

Devoiced /ʒ/ /ʒ/ may be devoiced when it occurs finally as in *prestige*, *barrage*, *beige*.

OCCURRENCE /ʒ/ does not occur initially, except in *genre* /ʒɑ̃:r/, a French loan word sometimes used in English studies.

10.355 Glottal fricative

/h/

DESCRIPTION For the articulation of /h/, the air from the lungs escapes through a narrow glottis with audible friction. The soft palate is raised. As for the positions of the tongue and the lips, they are determined by the vowel following /h/. Thus, for the articulation of /h/ in *he* /hi:/, the front of the tongue is raised to the close position of vowels and the lips are spread. As against this, for the articulation of /h/ in *who* /hu:/, the back of the tongue is raised to the close position and the lips are rounded. What is common to all such types of English /h/ is, however, the passage of a strong, voiceless airstream through the open glottis. /h/ is therefore referred to as a *voiceless glottal fricative*.

SPELLING	*h*	he, hat, heed, hard, behave
	wh	who, whose, whom

The letter *h* is silent in words such as *hour*, *honest*, and *heir*. It is also silent in the sequence *gh* in *ghost* /gəʊst/, *aghast* /ə'gɑ:st/, *ghastly* /'gɑ:stlɪ/.

Allophones of /h/

Voiced /h/ Between voiced sounds, /h/ is realised as a voiced glottal fricative as in *behind*, *behave*, *aha*.

OCCURRENCE /h/ occurs in syllable-initial positions only. It does not occur in any consonant clusters, i e in groups of two or more consonants without any vowel(s) between them.

10.36 Frictionless Continuant

/r/

In RP, there are many varieties of /r/ (see under *Allophones of* /r/). The one we are choosing for description here is the commonest variety, the post-alveolar frictionless continuant [ɹ].

DESCRIPTION The soft palate being raised, and therefore the nasal passage shut off, the tip of the tongue is held near to the rear part of the teeth ridge, the rims of the tongue touching the upper side teeth. The gap between the tongue and the roof of the mouth is still wide enough for the airstream to escape through freely, without causing any audible friction. The vocal cords vibrate. This variety of /r/ is therefore a *voiced post-alveolar frictionless continuant* (Fig. 40).

The lip position is determined largely by the following vowel, e g the /r/ in *read* is said with spread lips, and that in *rude* with rounded lips.

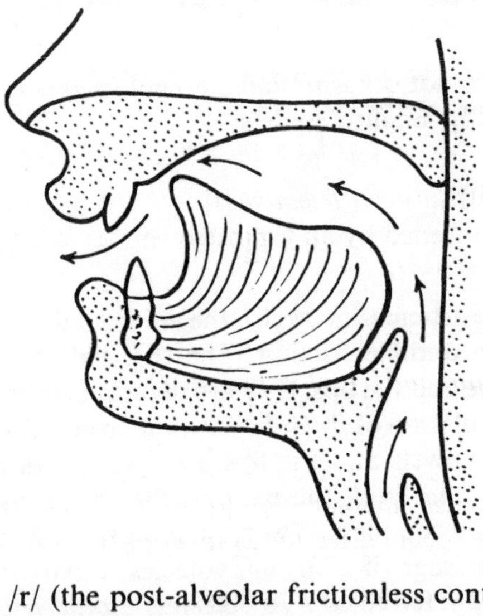

Fig. 40 /r/ (the post-alveolar frictionless continuant)

SPELLING	*r*	race, arouse, drive
	rr	'worry, sorry, carry
	rh	rhyme, rhythm
	wr	write, wreath, wrap

Pronunciation of the letter *r*

In RP, the letter *r* is pronounced only when it occurs immediately before vowels; elsewhere it is silent. Thus it is silent before consonants and word-finally, unless the word is immediately followed by another, beginning with a vowel. Such words as *art*, *curl*, *heart* are therefore pronounced without /r/ as /ɑːt, kɜːl, hɑːt/. Also such words as *car*, *father*, *here* are pronounced without /r/ if they are (i) followed by silence as in:

a car	/ə 'kɑː/
my father	/maɪ 'fɑːðə/
come here	/'kʌm 'hɪə/

or (ii) followed by a consonant as in:

a car mechanic	/ə 'kɑː mɪ'kænɪk/
my father came	/maɪ 'fɑːðə 'keɪm/
come here now	/'kʌm hɪə 'naʊ/

But, they are pronounced *with* /r/, if they are followed by another word beginning with a vowel. For example,

a car arrived	/ə 'kɑːr ə'raɪvd/
my father entered the room	/maɪ 'fɑːðər 'entəd ðə 'ruːm/
come here at once	/'kʌm 'hɪər ət 'wʌns/.

Allophones of /r/: Post-alveolar fricative

(i) *Voiced post-alveolar fricative* [ɹ̝] /r/ is realized as a voiced post-alveolar fricative when it is preceded by /d/ as in *dry*, *drain*, *drift*, *bedroom*, *good rain*.

(ii) *Partially devoiced post-alveolar fricative* [ɹ̝̊] /r/ becomes a partially devoiced post-alveolar fricative when it is preceded by voiceless consonants other than the aspirated /p, t, k/, and /θ/, e g in *free*, *shrimp*, *apron*, *spring*, *strong*, *screw*.

(iii) *Devoiced post-alveolar fricative* [ɹ̝̊] /r/ becomes a devoiced post-alveolar fricative when it is preceded by an aspirated /p/, /t/, or /k/, as in *print*, *apprise*, *tree*, *betray*, *crowd*, *decry*.

Allophones of /r/: Alveolar tap

(i) *Voiced alveolar tap* [ɾ] /r/ is realized as a voiced alveolar tap when it occurs between two vowels as in *bury*, *merry*, *sharing*, *sure enough*; and after /ð/ as in *with respect*.

(ii) *Partially devoiced alveolar tap* [ɾ̥] /r/ is realized as partially devoiced alveolar tap when it occurs after /θ/ as in *three*, *threat*, *thrive*, *forthright*.

Thus we see that, in quite a few contexts, a variety of /r/ other than the one described here (viz voiced post-alveolar frictionless continuant [ɹ]) occurs. Nevertheless, the variety of /r/ described here still remains the most frequent variety in RP because the contexts in which it occurs are the most frequent. These contexts are:

(1) Initially before vowels as in *rain*, *red*, *root*

(2) After voiced consonants other than /d/ as in *brain*, *great*, *all right*

(3) In the word-final positions when followed by another word beginning with a vowel as in *mother is*, *far off*, *butter and jam*.

OCCURRENCE In words said in isolation, /r/ occurs only in the initial and medial positions, in both cases immediately before vowels. Across word boundaries, it occurs only when a word ending in *r* or *re* is followed by another beginning with a vowel. (For details, see *Pronunciation of the letter r* discussed above.)

10.37 Semi-vowels

Semi-vowels are rapid vowel glides within the same syllable in much the same way as diphthongs are. The glide in the case of semi-vowels is from a less prominent to a more prominent sound in the same syllable. Therefore semi-vowels closely resemble rising diphthongs (see under /ɪə/, section 9.323). Nevertheless, they are treated as consonants because, in English, they function as consonants. This is illustrated by the fact that we use *a*, not *an*, before the words beginning with the semi-vowels /j, w/, e g *a yacht, a yard; a wedding-hall, a wasp.*

English has two semi-vowels: /w/ and /j/.

10.371 Labio-velar semi-vowel

/w/

DESCRIPTION /w/ is articulated by the back of the tongue assuming the position for a back half-close to close vowel (depending upon the degree of openness of the following vowel) and then moving away immediately to the position of the following sound. The lips are rounded—more so when followed by a rounded vowel than otherwise. There is thus a much greater lip-rounding in words like *woo, wool,* and *war* than in words such as *we, well,* and *wait.* The soft palate is raised to shut off the nasal passage, and the vocal cords vibrate. /w/ is thus a *voiced labio-velar semi-vowel.*

SPELLING		
	w	west, awake, sweet
	wh	which, where, when
	u (after *g*)	language, linguist
	u (after *q*)	queen, quality, request

Also note /w/ in *one* /wʌn/, *choir* /ˈkwaɪə/, *suite* /swiːt/.

The letter *w* is silent in the word-final and certain medial positions as in *saw, draw; awful, awkward* (the first *w*).

Allophones of /w/

(i) *Devoiced /w/* After aspirated /t, k/, /w/ is devoiced [ʍ] as in *twice, tweed quite, queen.* (/w/ does not occur after /p/.) The devoiced /w/ becomes a *voiceless labio-velar fricative.*

(ii) *Partially devoiced /w/* After unaspirated /t, k/ and other voiceless consonants, /w/ is partially devoiced as in *at once* /ət ˈwʌns/, *squeeze* /skwiːz/, *thwart, sweet.*

OCCURRENCE /w/ occurs only initially and medially in words.

10.372 Palatal semi-vowel

/j/

DESCRIPTION /j/ is articulated by the front of the tongue assuming the position for a front half-close to close vowel (depending on the degree of openness of the following vowel) and then moving away immediately to the position of the following sound. The lips are generally spread or neutral, but may become rounded if a rounded vowel follows as in *use*, *yacht*, *you*. The soft palate is raised to shut off the nasal passage, and the vocal cords vibrate. /j/ is thus a *voiced palatal semi-vowel.*

SPELLING			
	y		yet, yeast, beyond
	i		onion, bullion, spaniel
	eau	(pronounced /juː/)	beauty
	eu	(pronounced /juː/)	feud
	ew	(pronounced /juː/)	ewe, new, sewer
	iew	(pronounced /juː/)	view
	u	(pronounced /juː/)	unit, refuse, huge
	ue	(pronounced /juː/)	due, value, argue
	ui	(pronounced /juː/)	suit (*suit* is also pronounced /suːt/.)

Allophones of /j/

(i) *Voiceless palatal fricative /j/* /j/ is realized as a voiceless palatal fricative [ç] when it is preceded by aspirated, /p, t, k/ and /h/, and followed by /uː, ʊə/ as in *pupil, tube, cute, huge*; *pure, cure*.

(ii) *Partially devoiced /j/* /j/ is partially devoiced [j̊] when it is preceded by unaspirated /p, t, k/ as in *spurious, stew, skew*.

OCCURRENCE Like /w/, /j/ too does not occur word-finally. Also, it does not occur after the following:

(1) /tʃ, dʒ, r/. The words *chew*, *juice*, *rule* are pronounced /tʃuː/, /dʒuːs/, /ruːl/.

(2) /l/ preceded by a consonant. For example, *blue* /bluː/, flew /fluː/, *glue* /gluː/. But when /l/ is preceded by an accented vowel, /j/ regularly occurs as in *failure* /ˈfeɪljə/, *value* ˈvæljuː/.

After /s, z, θ/, /j/ occurs in the speech of some people, but more and more people are now using the forms without /j/. Thus *suit*, *presume*, *enthuse* are pronounced both with /j/ and without /j/, the latter forms being commoner now.

10.4 Summary

In RP, there are 24 consonants, which can be described in terms of (i) the presence or absence of voice, (ii) the place of articulation, and (iii) the manner of articulation. These are classified, according to the place of articulation, as bilabial: /p, b, m, w/; labio-dental: /f, v/; dental: /θ, ð/; alveolar: /t, d, n, l, s, z/; post-alveolar: /r/; palato-alveolar: /tʃ, dʒ, ʃ, ʒ/; palatal: /j/; velar: /k, g, ŋ/; and glottal: /h/. According to the manner of articulation, these are classified as plosives: /p, b, t, d, k, g/; affricates: /tʃ, dʒ/; nasals: /m, n, ŋ/; lateral: /l/; fricatives /f, v, θ, ð, s, z, ʃ, ʒ, h/; frictionless continuant: /r/; and semi-vowels: /w, j/. The plosives, affricates, and nasals require, for a short duration, a complete closure at some point in the mouth while the lateral requires a closure only in the centre of the oral passage. The fricatives are produced with a fair degree of narrowing in the mouth, while the frictionless continuant and semi-vowels are produced, like vowels, with a fair degree of opening in the mouth.

With regard to voice, the following constitute pairs of voiceless-voiced consonants: /p, b/, /t, d/, /k, g/, /tʃ, dʒ/, /f, v/, /θ, ð/, /s, z/, and /ʃ, ʒ/; /h/ is voiceless and the rest are all voiced. The voicing of consonants is, however, subject to certain modifications. All voiced consonants, except /ŋ/, become devoiced, or partially devoiced, in certain specifiable contexts: the plosives /b, d, g/, the affricate /dʒ/, and the fricatives /v, ð, z, ʒ/ word-initially and finally; and /m, n, l, r, w, j/ after voiceless consonants that can precede them (i.e. /m/ after /s/; /n/ after /s, t/; /l/ after /p, k, f, θ, s, ʃ/; /r/ after /p, t, k, θ/; /w/ after /t, k, θ, s/; and /j/ after /p, t, k, h/). (/ŋ/ does not occur in consonant clusters.) As against such devoicing of voiced consonants, the glottal fricative /h/ becomes voiced when it occurs between vowels.

The voiceless plosives /p, t, k/ are aspirated when they occur initially in accented syllables.

Most of the consonants have allophones. These may be arranged along the following parameters:

(1) Aspiration in /p, t, k/
(2) The nature of release affecting all plosives
(3) (Partial) devoicing of all voiced consonants except /ŋ/, and the voicing of /h/
(4) Retractedness or 'advancedness' affecting /t, d, k, g, m, n, l/ according to the place of articulation of a neighbouring consonant
(5) Syllabicity in /m, n, l/ (i e their becoming syllabic)
(6) Velarization of /l/, turning it into dark /l/ pre-consonantally and word-finally
(7) The lip position in the fricatives determined by an adjacent vowel.

The case of /r/ is rather peculiar: in addition to its commonest variety—the voiced post-alveolar frictionless continuant [ɹ]—there also occur the voiced post-alveolar fricative [ɹ̝] and the alveolar flap [ɾ], both of which may become (partially) devoiced in certain contexts.

In regard to occurrence, with the exception of /ŋ, ʒ, h, r, j, w/, all consonants occur initially, medially, and finally in words. /ŋ, ʒ/ do not occur word-initially (except in loan-words) and /h, r, j, w/ do not occur word-finally.

As in vowels, the relationship between sound and spelling is poor in consonants, although in most cases it is possible to name one or two letters that represent a given consonant most regularly. The pronunciations of suffixes -*(e)s* (as also of -*'s* and -*s'*) and -*(e)d* are governed by regular rules. So too is the pronunciation of the medial *ng*. The letter *r* is silent except when followed by a vowel in the same word or the next word.

EXERCISES

I Which of the following statements are true:

1 Plosives in any language can be articulated only at the following points: the lips, the teeth ridge, the soft palate.

2 In RP, the voiceless plosives /p, t, k/ are aspirated.

3 In RP, [pʰ] and [f] belong to two different phonemes.

4 A voiced consonant is generally devoiced when it occurs before silence.

5 The **k**-sound in the English word *coal* is more like the Hindi ख-sound [kh] than the Hindi क-sound [k].

6 The initial *p* in the word *prepare* (which is accented on the second syllable) is aspirated.

7 The suffix -*ed* in the word *sagged* is pronounced /d/.

8 For the articulation of unaspirated consonants the vocal cords do not vibrate.

9 The letter *g* is silent when it occurs before *n*.

10 The English affricates /tʃ, dʒ/ consist of two phonemes each.

11 The letters *ng* are pronounced [ŋ] when they occur finally in a word.

12 The nasal /m/ is always articulated with the two lips, no matter in what context it occurs.

13 The letter *l* in each of the words *milk* and *fool* represents a dark [ɫ].

14 To produce the fricatives of English there must be sufficient narrowing, but no closure, in the mouth.

15 The initial sounds in the words *vine* and *wine* are allophones of the same English phoneme.

16 While the Hindi थ [t̪h] is a dental plosive, the English /θ/ is a dental fricative.

17 The last sound in the word *airlines* is /z/, not /s/.

18 The letter *r* is silent in RP.

19 The semi-vowels /j, w/ are regarded as consonants in English because they function as consonants in this language.

20 All consonants of English require the pulmonic egressive airstream mechanism for their production.

II Give two examples for each of the following:

1 *ss* pronounced /z/

2 /ʃ/ represented by *si*

3 /θ/ becoming /ð/ in the process of pluralization

4 /p/ realized as unaspirated [p]

5 The past suffix pronounced /ɪd/

6 The possessive suffix -*'s* pronounced /z/

7 The letter *l* being silent
8 The letter *b* being silent
9 *ch* pronounced /ʃ/
10 The letter *r* pronounced at the end of a word
11 A voiced glottal fricative in the middle of words
12 A nasally released /t/
13 A laterally released /d/
14 An inaudibly released /p/
15 /j/ spelt with the help of the letter *u*
16 /w/ occurring in words containing no *w* in the spelling
17 The silent *w*
18 A devoiced /d/
19 Pairs of words distinguished *only* by the presence or absence of voice in the initial position
20 The post-alveolar fricative [ɹ̣].

III Give a three-term label for each of the consonants in the following words:
division, psychology, heart, womb

IV Give two pairs of words to distinguish between each of the following:
/z/, /dʒ/
/s/, /ʃ/
/v/, /w/
/b/, /v/
/s/, /tʃ/

V From the following, pick out the words containing /z/ and say them three times each:

False, clubs, possess, Charles, judges, scissors, tickets, falls, husband, house, release, houses, practise, use (n), bruise, loose, grows, cease, chase, seize, phase, tens, tense, preside, disallow, desire, airlines.

VI Group the following words according to the pronunciation of the suffix -(*e*)*s*:

Races, books, judges, plays, ladies, mats, materials, maths, garages, societies, churches, cars, purchases, sweaters.

VII Group the following words according to the pronunciation of the suffix -(*e*)*d*:

Raced, seized, chased, hated, beheaded, loosened, harmed, packed, heaped, tested, tried, played, cawed, bombed, lapsed, practised, presided, obeyed.

VIII The teacher will dictate the following sentences, choosing, at a time, one word from those given in the curly brackets. Each sentence will be said only once. Write it down as you hear it.

1 The boy was {racing / raising} the bicycle to the top of the hill.

2 My {niece / knees} got hurt in an accident.

3 The {pines / fines} were much bigger this time.

4 Our {vines / wines} are very good this year.

5 There are lots of {Jews / zoos} in that country.

6 He is a very {zealous / jealous} character.

7 The {ledger / leisure} we got was quite satisfactory.

8 The {composer / composure} was quite remarkable.

9 Are there enough {clothes / cloves} now?

10 His {jest / zest} was quite annoying.

IX Repeat the following words in pairs after the teacher:

ton	tongue	vie	why
kin	king	vie	buy
run	rung	vowels	bowels
sin	thin	very	berry
worse	worth	verse	worse
truce	truth	visor	wiser
bays	bathe	veal	wheel
tense	tens	yet	jet
seal	zeal	yacht	jot
fierce	fears	faced	phased
ceased	seized	house	houses
priced	prized	path	paths
partial	parcel	oath	oaths
person	Persian	truth	truths
fist	fished	mouth (n)	mouth (v)

X Look up the pronunciation of the following words in the dictionary, and say them correctly three times each:

quay	ghost	debut
lamb	exhibit	debris
comb	exhibition	liaison

rumour	booth	facade
mass	octroi	chasm
vase	vehicle	chaos
target	vehicular	cadre
epoch	nephew	moustache
asthma	healthy	laughed
rapport	wealthy	pleasure
sugar	suggestion	represent
tomb	chew	advertisement
loose	sandwich	mature
blue	gigantic	digestion
cupboard	dessert	glue
iron	adjust	indict

11 Phoneme Sequences and Consonant Clusters in English

11.1 Introduction

In the last two chapters, we studied in detail the phonemes of English, which combine with one another to form words. However, English does not exploit all the possible combinations of its phonemes in the word and the syllable. For example, the vowel phonemes /e, æ/ and consonant phonemes /h, j/ do not occur finally; long vowels and diphthongs do not occur before the phoneme /ŋ/; the types of *consonant clusters* permitted are subject to certain constraints, some of which are:

(1) In the initial position, /tʃ, dʒ, ð, z/ do not combine with any consonant
(2) /r, j, w/ can occur in clusters only as the final element
(3) In the final position, consonant clusters such as /pf, td, lzd, ʒbd/ are not possible.

In this chapter, we shall study the combinatorial possibilities of the phonemes of English.

11.2 Word-initial and Word-final Vowel Phonemes

The following vowel phonemes constitute monosyllabic words by themselves:

/ə/ (weak form)	a
/ɑː/	are
/ɔː/	or
/ɜː/	err
/eɪ/ (strong form)	a
/eɪ/	eh, A (a letter of the Roman alphabet)
/aɪ/	I, aye (yes)
/əʊ/	owe, oh
/ɪə/	ear
/eə/	air, heir

With the exception of /ʊ/ and /ʊə/, all vowel phonemes occur word-initially.

The vowel phonemes /e, æ, ʌ, ɒ, ʊ/ cannot occur word-finally (though they occur syllable-finally).

11.3 Syllable-initial and Syllable-final Consonant Phonemes and Consonant Clusters

11.31 Initial and Final Consonant Phonemes (CV-)

/ŋ/ does not occur in the initial position at all. In that position, /ʒ/ occurs only before /ɑː/, /ɪ/, and /iː/, and that too in such foreign borrowings as *genre* /ʒɑ̃ːr/, *gigolo* /ˈʒɪgələʊ/, *gigue* /ʒiːg/. The remaining 22 consonants generally occur before all vowels.

/r, h, j, w/ do not occur finally.

11.32 Consonant Clusters (see Section 7.5)

11.321 Initial two-consonant clusters (CC-)

	Consonant Cluster	*Examples*
/p/ as the first consonant	/pl-/	plan, plot
	/pr-/	prime, pram
	/pj-/	pupil, purify
/t/ as the first consonant	/tr-/	train, try
	/tj-/	tunic, tune
	/tw-/	twice, twelve
/k/ as the first consonant	/kl-/	clean, club
	/kr-/	create, cross
	/kj-/	cure, cute
	/kw-/	quite, question
/b/ as the first consonant	/bl-/	blame, block
	/br-/	brick, brim
	/bj-/	beauty, bugle
/d/ as the first consonant	/dr-/	draw, dress
	/dj-/	duty, during, dual, due
	/dw-/	dwarf, dwell
/g/ as the first consonant	/gl-/	glum, glow
	/gr-/	grass, green
	/gj-/	gules
	/gw-/	Gwen
/f/ as the first consonant	/fl-/	flash, flee
	/fr-/	fresh, frisk
	/fj-/	feud, few
/θ/ as the first consonant	/θr-/	thrice, thrash
	/θj-/	Thucydides
	/θw-/	thwart
/s/ as the first consonant	/sl-/	slim, slice
	/sj-/	suicide, sewerage
	/sw-/	sweep, swell
	/sp-/	spit, speak

	Consonant Cluster	Examples
	/st-/	store, steal
	/sk-/	sky, skin
	/sm-/	small, smoke
	/sn-/	snack, snore
/ʃ/ as the first consonant	/ʃr-/	shrine, shrink
/h/ as the first consonant	/hj-/	huge, hue
/v/ as the first consonant	/vj-/	view, (ne)*phew*
/m/ as the first consonant	/mj-/	mule, music
/n/ as the first consonant	/nj-/	news, nude
/l/ as the first consonant	/lj-/	lure, lurid

11.322 Initial three-consonant clusters (CCC-)

When three consonants form an initial cluster in English, the first consonant is invariably /s/, the second one of the three voiceless plosives /p, t, k/, and the last one of these: /l, r, j, w/. The possible clusters with examples are listed below.

Consonant Cluster	Examples
/spl-/	splash, spleen, split
/spr-/	spring, sprain, spray
/spj-/	spurious
/str-/	strain, strike, street
/stj-/	stupid, studio, student
/skl-/	sclerosis
/skr-/	screen, scream, scratch
/skw-/	squash, square, squint

11.323 Final two-consonant clusters (-CC)

	Consonant Cluster	Examples
/p/ as the first consonant	/-pt/	stopped, wept
	/-pθ/	depth
	/-ps/	taps, caps
/t/ as the first consonant	/-tθ/	eighth
	/-ts/	cuts, mats
/k/ as the first consonant	/-kt/	worked, talked
	/-ks/	talks, works
/b/ as the first consonant	/-bd/	robbed, rubbed
	/-bz/	herbs, cubs
/d/ as the first consonant	/-dz/	roads, woods
/g/ as the first consonant	/-gd/	mugged, begged
	/-gz/	rogues, bags
/tʃ/ as the first consonant	/-tʃt/	watched, hatched
/dʒ/ as the first consonant	/-dʒd/	judged, bridged
/f/ as the first consonant	/-ft/	laughed, craft

	Consonant Cluster	Examples
	/-fθ/	fifth
	/-fs/	sniffs, coughs
/θ/ as the first consonant	/-θt/	breathed /breθt/ (a phonetic term)
	/-θs/	myths, heaths
/s/ as the first consonant	/-sp/	wasp, crisp
	/-st/	last, most
	/-sk/	ask, task
/ʃ/ as the first consonant	/-ʃt/	washed, rushed
/v/ as the first consonant	/-vd/	halved, saved
	/-vz/	knives, leaves
/ð/ as the first consonant	/-ðd/	writhed
	/-ðz/	wreaths, breathes
/z/ as the first consonant	/-zd/	(sur)prised, (ad)vised
/ʒ/ as the first consonant	/-ʒd/	rouged
/m/ as the first consonant	/-mp/	camp, jump
	/-md/	damned, summed
	/-mf/	nymph
	/-mθ/	warmth
	/-mz/	bombs, combs
/n/ as the first consonant	/-nt/	want, sent
	/-ntʃ/	munch, bench
	/-ndʒ/	(re)venge, hinge
	/-nθ/	tenth, month
	/-ns/	dance, hence
	/-nz/	lens, nuns
/ŋ/ as the first consonant	/-ŋk/	bank, think
	/-ŋd/	banged, wronged
	/-ŋz/	sings, rings
/l/ as the first consonant	/-lp/	pulp, help
	/-lt/	knelt, spelt
	/-lk/	bulk, silk
	/-lb/	bulb
	/-ld/	world, sold
	/-ltʃ/	belch, milch
	/-ldʒ/	bulge, (di)vulge
	/-lm/	helm
	/-ln/	kiln
	/-lf/	pelf, self
	/-lv/	valve, solve
	/-lθ/	health, wealth
	/-ls/	false, else
	/-lz/	hills, mills

11.324 Final three-consonant clusters (-CCC)

In all the consonant clusters listed below, /s/ is the last consonant, which usually represents the suffixes -*(e)s*, -'*s*, and -*s*':

Consonant Cluster	*Example(s)*
/-pts/	(a)dopts
/-pθs/	depths
/-tθs/	eighths
/-kts/	acts
/-mps/	lamps
/-mfs/	nymphs, nymph's
/-nts/	tents
/-nθs/	tenths
/-ŋks/	links
/-lps/	helps
/-lts/	belts
/-lks/	hulks, silks
/-lfs/	gulfs
/-lθs/	healths
/-fts/	lifts
/-fθs/	fifths
/-sps/	wasps, grasps
/-sts/	toasts
/-sks/	asks

/z/ is the final consonant in the clusters listed below; it usually represents the suffixes -*(e)s*, -'*s*, -*s*':

Consonant Cluster	*Example*
/-ndz/	sands
/-lbz/	bulbs
/-ldz/	holds
/-lmz/	elms
/-lnz/	kilns
/-lvz/	wolves

/t/ is the last consonant in the clusters listed below, which usually represents the past suffix -*(e)d*:

Consonant Cluster	*Example(s)*
/-pst/	lapsed
/-kst/	next, fixed
/-dst/	midst
/-mpt/	pumped
/-nst/	danced
/-ntʃt/	launched, clinched
/-ŋkt/	linked
/-lpt/	helped
/-lkt/	milked
/-ltʃt/	belched

Consonant Cluster	*Example(s)*
/-lst/	(re)pulsed
/-spt/	lisped
/-skt/	asked

/d/ is the final consonant in all the clusters given below, which usually represents the past suffix -(*e*)*d*:

Consonant Cluster	*Example*
/-ndʒd/	lunged
/-nzd/	cleansed
/-ldʒd/	bulged
/-lmd/	(over)whelmed
/-lvd/	solved

/θ/ is the final element in all the clusters listed below:

Consonant Cluster	*Example*
/-ksθ/	sixth
/-ŋkθ/	length
/-lfθ/	twelfth

11.325 Final four-consonant clusters (-CCCC)

/s/ or /t/ is the final element in all the consonant clusters listed below; it invariably represents the suffix -(*e*)*s* or the past suffix -(*e*)*d*:

Consonant Cluster	*Example(s)*
/-mpts/	prompts, (ex)empts
/-mpst/	glimpsed
/-lkts/	mulcts
/-lpts/	sculpts
/-lfθs/	twelfths
/-ksts/	texts
/-ksθs/	sixths

11.4 Summary

English does not use all the combinatorial possibilities (i e the potential combinations) of its phonemes in the word and the syllable. Not all the vowel and consonant phonemes occur initially or finally. /ʊ, ʊə/ and /ŋ/ do not occur word-initially; /e, æ, ʌ, ɒ, ʊ/ do not occur word-finally, and /h, r, j, w/ word- or syllable-finally. Morever, the types of consonant clusters permitted are subject to a number of constraints: In initial CC clusters, /tʃ, dʒ, ð, z/ do not participate at all, and /l, r, w/ cannot occur as the initial element. In initial CCC clusters, the first consonant is always /s/, the second one of the three voiceless plosives /p, t, k/, and the last /l/, /r/, /j/ or /w/. As for the final consonant clusters, CC clusters do not admit of any combinations with /r, h, j, w/; in CCC clusters, /s/, /z/, /t/, or /d/ is usually the last element, which generally represents the suffixes -(*e*)*s*, -'*s*, -*s*', and -(*e*)*d*; in CCCC clusters, /s/ or /t/ occurs as the last consonant, which always represents the suffix -(*e*)*s* or the past suffix -(*e*)*d*.

EXERCISES

I Write the following words in phonemic transcription and point out the initial and/or final consonant clusters as in the given examples:

EXAMPLES

texts: /teksts/	Final cluster: /-ksts/
grasped: /grɑːspt/	Initial cluster: /gr-/
	Final cluster: /-spt/

1 glimpsed	9 burns	17 twelfth
2 strength	10 sculpts	18 hinge
3 bats	11 splashed	19 toasts
4 gulfs	12 news	20 eighths
5 trapped	13 scratch	21 asked
6 strap	14 judged	22 grasps
7 bless	15 lisped	23 lists
8 cute	16 cursed	24 prompts
		25 sprung

II Supply three words to illustrate each of the following types of consonant cluster:

(1) Final cluster with 3 consonants
(2) Final cluster with 2 consonants
(3) Initial cluster with 3 consonants
(4) Initial cluster with 2 consonants
(5) Final cluster with 4 consonants

III Give two examples each of the following types of syllable:

(1) CVCCC
(2) CCVCCC
(3) CCCVCC
(4) CVCCCC
(5) CCVCCCC
(6) CCCVCCC

IV Three-consonant final clusters in English with /θ/ as the final element pattern as follows:

$$\left.\begin{matrix} k+s \\ ŋ+k \\ l+f \end{matrix}\right\} +θ$$

Supply words to illustrate these clusters.

V List the initial consonant clusters with /j/ as their final element. Give words to illustrate them.

VI Write down the following words in phonemic transcription and divide them into their constituent syllables, indicating the syllable division with hyphens. After you have done that, indicate the structure of each syllable in terms of C and V. Look at the example first:

EXAMPLE

sympathetic /sɪm-pə-θe-tɪk/
CVC.CV.CV.CVC

Fantastic, marriage, generation, benevolence, English, intonation, exercise, button, comprehend, institute, credibility, territorial, cattle, rhetorical, archaic, customary, indescribable, indict, mystique, shortcoming.

12
Word Accent

12.1 Introduction

We examined the nature of the syllable in Chapter 7, and know that the word consists of one or more syllables. Now, a word of more than one syllable is not just a simple addition of the syllables that constitute it; it combines them into a certain relationship of interdependence. That is to say, the syllables so combined are said with varying degrees of *prominence*. In English, for instance, in words of more than one syllable, one syllable or occasionally two syllables stand out from the remainder. The syllable or syllables which stand out, or are prominent, are said to be *accented*, or to receive the *accent*. For example, in the English words ***pro**-mi-nent* and *per-**ceive***, the first and second syllables respectively are accented. In the word ***in**-ca-**pa**-ci-tate*, the first and the third, and in the word *pro-**nun**-ci-**a**-tion*, the second and the fourth syllables are accented.

Word accent is thus the relative degree of prominence with which the different syllables of a word are pronounced. In this sense, monosvllabic words said in isolation (i e not in connected speech) can be said to have 'no accent'. That is why accent on monosyllabic words is not marked in dictionaries.

12.11

The prominence of a particular syllable in a word may occasionally be due to stress, i e greater breath effort, or greater muscular energy, expended on the articulation of this syllable than on the articulation of the other syllables in that word. But more often, it is not due to stress alone, but to any or all of the following four factors—the *stress* and the *pitch change* on that syllable, and *length* and the *quality* of the vowel in that syllable. It is for this reason that the term 'word accent' is sometimes preferred to 'word stress'.

12.12

Word accent is an essential part of the word shape. Every word in English, for example, has a certain characteristic accentual pattern shared by the speaker and the listener alike. Any arbitrary change in this pattern, as we may find in a non-native speaker's pronunciation of that word, may deform the word beyond recognition. As a matter of fact, this characteristic pattern is as much a part of the word's identity as its sound (vowel and consonant) sequence. It follows that no one can learn the pronunciation of an English word (of more than one syllable) without learning its accent, or accentual pattern.

12.2 Degrees of Word Accent

In a large number of polysyllabic English words, more than one syllable is accented. For example, the English word *organization* /ɔː-gə-naɪ-zeɪ-ʃn/ has the highest degree of accent on the fourth syllable. The first syllable receives the next degree of accent. Next in order of the degree of accent it receives is the third syllable, and so on. In practice, however, only two degrees of accent are generally recognized, since it serves no useful purpose to go beyond the second degree. In the word *organization*, therefore, the fourth syllable would be said to carry the *primary accent*, and the first syllable the *secondary accent*. The remaining three syllables would be grouped together and described as *weak* or *unaccented*. The primary accent may be marked with a vertical stroke above and in front of the syllable in question, and the secondary accent with a vertical stroke below and in front of the syllable. Thus the word *organization* will be marked in this way: /ˌɔːgənaɪˈzeɪʃn/. This is the practice generally followed in modern books on phonetics and linguistics. But it is by no means a universal practice. Therefore, while looking up the pronunciation of a word in a dictionary, the student is advised to refer to the *note* on signs and symbols used in that dictionary and then decide where the primary and secondary accents are marked on that word.

12.3 Placement of Word Accent

It cannot be denied that the learning of word accent in English presents a number of difficulties to a non-native speaker. There is no easy 'formula' which he can master in order to place the accent on the right syllable. In some languages, the incidence of word accent is 'fixed' as, for example, in Czech and Finnish in which words are accented on their initial syllable, or in Polish in which words are accented on their last but one syllable. In some other languages, such as Spanish and Italian, rules governing the placement of accent in the majority of words can be formulated. In English, however, no simple rules of this kind can be given. The reason is that word accent in English is not fixed in the sense in which it is fixed in the case of Czech or Polish; it is 'fixed' only in the limited sense that every word (with certain exceptions, which will be dealt with in Chapter 13) has its own fixed accentual pattern. It is 'free' in that some words in English are accented on the first syllable, some on the second syllable, others on the third syllable, and so on. Some examples of polysyllabic words with their primary accent on different syllables are given below.

Three-syllable word	*Primary accent on the first syllable*
recognize	/ˈre-kəg-naɪz/
absolute	/ˈæb-sə-ljuːt/
accident	/ˈæk-sɪ-dənt/
	Primary accent on the second syllable
exception	/ɪk-ˈsep-ʃən/
contrastive	/kən-ˈtrɑːs-tɪv/

production	/prə-'dʌk-ʃən/
	Primary accent on the third syllable
guarantee	/gæ-rən-'tiː/
cigarette	/sɪ-gə-'ret/
reminisce	/re-mɪ-'nɪs/
Four-syllable word	*Primary accent on the first syllable*
territory	/'te-rɪ-tə-rɪ/
purchasable	/'pɜː-tʃə-sə-bl/
purgatory	/'pɜː-gə-tə-rɪ/
	Primary accent on the second syllable
participate	/pɑː-'tɪ-sə-peɪt/
appreciate	/ə-'priː-ʃɪ-eɪt/
ridiculous	/rɪ-'dɪ-kjʊ-ləs/
	Primary accent on the third syllable
appelation	/æ-pə-'leɪ-ʃən/
application	/æ-plɪ-'keɪ-ʃən/
apposition	/æ-pə-'zɪ-ʃən/
apparatus	/æ-pə-'reɪ-təs/
	Primary accent on the fourth syllable
dedicatee	/de-dɪ-kə-'tiː/
corroboree	/kə-rɒ-bə-'riː/
Five-syllable word	*Primary accent on the first syllable*
cannibalism	/'kæ-nɪ-bə-lɪ-zəm/
secularism	/'se-kjʊ-lə-rɪ-zəm/
	Primary accent on the second syllable
conservatism	/kən-'sɜː-və-tɪ-zəm/
Americanize	/ə-'me-rɪ-kə-naɪz/
irrefutable	/ɪ-'re-fjʊ-tə-bl/
	Primary accent on the third syllable
irreproachable	/ɪ-rɪ-'prəʊ-tʃə-bl/
irrepressible	/ɪ-rɪ-'pre-sə-bl/
irresponsible	/ɪ-rɪ-'spɒn-sə-bl/
electricity	/ɪ-lek-'trɪ-sə-tɪ/
	Primary accent on the fourth syllable
civilization	/sɪ-vɪ-laɪ-'zeɪ-ʃən/
mechanization	/me-kə-naɪ-'zeɪ-ʃən/
participation	/pɑː-tɪ-sə-'peɪ-ʃən/

12.4 Functions of Word Accent in English

In the preceding sections, we saw that word accent is an indispensable part of the word *form* (that is, the word is constituted from the relative degree of prominence of its syllables as well as from the sequence of its vowels and consonants). In the following sections, we shall see that word accent also sometimes contributes to the word *function* in the sense that it tends to determine, among other things, whether a particular word is a noun/adjective or verb.

12.41

First of all, word accent underlies grammatical relationships between words. There are a good many noun/adjective-verb oppositions in English, such as '*increase* (n) and *in'crease* (v), and '*absent* (adj) and *ab'sent* (v), in which the noun and adjective are nearly always accented on the *first* syllable and the verb is accented on the *second*. To illustrate this, we give below some of the more important pairs of such words:

Word	*Noun/Adjective*	*Verb*
absent	/'æbsənt/	/əb'sent/
accent	/'æksənt/	/ək'sent/
addict	/'ædɪkt/	/ə'dɪkt/
compound	/'kɒmpaʊnd/	/kəm'paʊnd/
conduct	/'kɒndəkt/	/kən'dʌkt/
conflict	/'kɒnflɪkt/	/kən'flɪkt/
contract	/'kɒntrækt/	/kən'trækt/
contrast	/'kɒntrɑːst/	/kən'trɑːst/
convict	/'kɒnvɪkt/	/kən'vɪkt/
decrease	/'diːkriːs/	/diː'kriːs/
desert	/'dezət/	/dɪ'zɜːt/
export	/'ekspɔːt/	/ɪk'spɔːt/
frequent	/'friːkwənt/	/frɪ'kwent/
import	/'ɪmpɔːt/	/ɪm'pɔːt/
increase	/'ɪnkriːs/	/ɪn'kriːs/
object	/'ɒbdʒɪkt/	/əb'dʒekt/
perfect	/'pɜːfɪkt/	/pə'fekt/
permit	/'pɜːmɪt/	/pə'mɪt/
present	/'prezənt/	/prɪ'zent/
project	/'prɒdʒɪkt/	/prə'dʒekt/
protest	/'prəʊtest/	/prə'test/
rebel	/'rebəl/	/rɪ'bel/
record	/'rekɔːd/	/rɪ'kɔːd/

EXAMPLE

His 'conduct was satisfactory.
He con'ducted himself very well.

12.42

Sometimes variations in word accent in English are associated with the morphological structure of words (i e the way words are constituted from their stems, prefixes, and suffixes). Accent shifts from the first syllable to the second, the third, or the fourth syllable as longer words are derived from smaller words, or as, to put it differently, words change their grammatical forms. Given below is a list of grammatically (or derivationally) related words with the primary accent marked on each word:

'democrat	de'mocracy	demo'cratic	
'diplomat	di'plomacy	diplo'matic	
'politics	po'litical	poli'tician	
'photograph	pho'tographer pho'tography	photo'graphic/al	
'mechanism	me'chanical	mecha'nician	mechani'zation
'meteor		mete'oric meteo'rology	meteoro'logical
'family	fa'miliar		famili'arity
'telephone	te'lephony	tele'phonic	
'hypocrite	hy'pocrisy	hypo'critical	
'monotone	mo'notony mo'notonous	mono'tonic	

12.43

Word accent also sometimes helps distinguish certain compound words from related noun phrases (adj + n, n + n) and verb-plus-adverbial collocations, as in the following sets of words:

Compound	*Noun Phrase, etc.*
'blackbird	'black 'bird
'copperplate	'copper 'plate
'crossword	'cross 'word
'dropout	'drop 'out
'grandmother	'grand 'mother
'greenfly	'green 'fly
'lightship	'light 'ship
'pushover	'push 'over
'put-on	'put 'on
'walkout	'walk 'out

12.5 Regularities in Word Accentual Patterns (Primary Accent)

We have seen that word accent in English is 'free': given a polysyllabic word, it is by no means easy to predict where the accent is to be placed. It can be anywhere from the first to the last syllable. It is fixed only in the limited sense that a given word is nearly always accented on the same syllable. This might give the impression that one has to learn the accentual pattern of each and every English word separately. But things are really not as bad as they might seem. Studies have been made and quite a number of regularities in word accentual patterns in English have been observed. And these regularities (or generalizations) are sometimes subject to so few exceptions that they can be safely called 'rules' of word accent. We shall now examine some of the more important of these rules,

and the student will find them extremely helpful. They are generally based on the kinds of prefixes or suffixes (or endings) these words contain.

12.51 Rules Related to Prefixes

Generally speaking, prefixes do not have any regular and predictable effect on the location of word accent. There is, however, one prefix, *re-*, which deserves some attention because it sometimes carries the secondary accent in a somewhat regular and predictable fashion:

(i) It carries the secondary accent when it adds the sense of 'again' to the word to which it is prefixed. In such situations, it is pronounced /ri:/.

EXAMPLES

re-tell, re-furnish, re-issue, re-set, re-number, re-sell, re-count, re-marry, re-collect (collect again), re-surface.

(ii) It is not accented, and is pronounced /rɪ/, when it does not add the sense of 'again'.

EXAMPLES

remove, remember, recall, resource, research, report, recount, review, recoil.

In certain pairs of words, the presence or absence of accent on the prefix may determine their meanings.

EXAMPLES

ˌre-ˈcover (=to cover again)	reˈcover (=to get well)
ˌre-ˈcall (=to call again)	reˈcall (=to remember)
ˌre-ˈpay (=to pay again)	reˈpay (=to pay back)
ˌre-ˈform (=to form again)	reˈform (=to make better)

12.52 Rules Related to Suffixes or Endings

12.521 Inflexional suffixes

Inflexional suffixes are those which when affixed to words do not change their grammatical status (i.e. their part of speech). Such suffixes do not affect the accent of the words either.

EXAMPLES

ˈtable	ˈtables		
ˈstudent	ˈstudents	ˈstudent's	ˈstudents'
ˈenter	ˈenters	ˈentering	ˈentered
ˈrealize	ˈrealizes	ˈrealizing	ˈrealized
ˈsimple	ˈsimpler	ˈsimplest	

12.522 Derivational Suffixes

Derivational suffixes are those which when affixed to words change their grammatical status (i.e. their part of speech). They fall into two classes: (a) those which do not affect word accent and (b) those which do.

(a) The suffixes listed below, with their pronunciation, do not affect word accent. Examples are given against each suffix.

-ance /əns/	'utter	'utterance
-age /ɪdʒ/	'person	'personage
-ant /ənt/	re'sist	re'sistant
-ence /əns/	'differ	'difference*
-ent /ənt/	de'ter	de'terrent
-en /ən/	light	'lighten
-er /-or/ə(r)/	'supervise	'supervisor
	de'bate	de'bater
-ess /ɪs/	'tiger	'tigress
/es/	'lion	'lioness
-ful /fl/	'beauty	'beautiful
-fy /faɪ/	'beauty	'beautify
-hood /hʊd/	'woman	'womanhood
-ice /ɪs/	'coward	'cowardice
-ish /ɪʃ/	'yellow	'yellowish
-ism /ɪzəm/	'Indian	'Indianism
-ive /ɪv/	at'tract	at'tractive
-less /lɪs/	'manner	'mannerless
-ly /lɪ/	'boyish	'boyishly
-ment /mənt/	enter'tain	enter'tainment
-ness /nɪs/	'sloppy	'sloppiness
-ship /ʃɪp/	'fellow	'fellowship
-ter /tə/	laugh	'laughter
-ure /ə/ or /jə/	en'close	en'closure
	fail	'failure
-zen /zn/	'city	'citizen

*But note:

re'fer	'reference	de'fer	'deference
pre'fer	'preference	in'fer	'inference

(b) The suffixes or endings that do affect word accent are discussed below individually. Also given in each case is the rule to determine the primary word accent. This is followed by a number of examples for illustration and practice.

(i) *-aire*, *-eer/-ier*, *-ee*

The syllable containing the suffix (i.e. the *last* syllable) is accented.

millio'naire	engi'neer	addres'see
question'naire	gazet'teer	guaran'tee
doctri'naire	profi'teer	pay'ee
opinio'naire	ve'neer	employ'ee
	marke'teer	les'see

briga'dier	draw'ee
cava'lier	ru'pee
	trus'tee

(ii) *-ate*

(1) *In verbs*

Verbs ending in *-ate* are accented (a) on the *last* syllable if they consist of two syllables only, and (b) on the *third* syllable from the end if they consist of three or more syllables.

(a)	(b)
nar'rate	ar'ticulate
cre'ate	'educate
trans'late	'abdicate
mi'grate	'cultivate
re'late	'liberate
pro'strate	par'ticipate
dic'tate	re'patriate
con'flate	reca'pitulate
col'late	'generate
	'fabricate

(2) *In adjectives and nouns*

Adjectives and nouns consisting of more than two syllables and ending in *-ate* are accented on the *third* syllable from the end.

Adjectives	*Nouns*
'adequate	'surrogate
'obdurate	'consulate
'passionate	'correlate
'surrogate	

(iii) *-ize* (or *-ise*)

Verbs ending in *-ize* (or *-ise*) are generally accented in accordance with the following rules:

(a) Disyllabic verbs are usually accented on the *ending* itself.

bap'tize, cap'size, de'vise, re'vise (an important exception being *'realize*).

(b) Verbs consisting of three or four syllables are generally accented on the *third* syllable from the end.

'agonize, 'cauterize, 'criticize, ac'climatize, a'natomize (two important exceptions being *i'dealize* and *'characterize*).

(c) Verbs of five or six syllables generally carry the primary accent on the *fourth* syllable from the end.

A'mericanize, cosmo'politanize, le'gitimatize (an important exception being *atti'tudinize*).

(iv) *-ental*

The *second* syllable from the end is accented.

'dental	govern'mental
pa'rental	instru'mental

acci'dental	orna'mental
funda'mental	tempera'mental

(v) *-graphy, -logy, -metry, -sophy, -cracy/-crisy, -gamy, -nomy, -phony.* The syllable *preceding the suffix* is accented.

bi'ography	bi'ology	bi'ometry	phi'losophy
bibli'ography	ge'ology	ge'ometry	the'osophy
ge'ography	psy'chology	trigo'nometry	
ocea'nography	physi'ology	psy'chometry	
pho'tography	zo'ology		
te'legraphy			

de'mocracy	'bigamy	a'stronomy	te'lephony
hy'pocrisy	mo'nogamy	a'gronomy	'euphony
bu'reaucracy	po'lygamy	e'conomy	
au'tocracy		physi'ognomy	

The nouns formed with the suffixes *-grapher, -logist, -sopher/-sophist, -nomer/ -nomist* are also accented on the syllable *preceding the suffix.*

bi'ographer	bi'ologist	phi'losopher	a'stronomer
ge'ographer	ge'ologist	the'osophist	e'conomist
ocea'nographer	physi'ologist		physi'ognomist
pho'tographer	psy'chologist		
	zo'ologist		

(vi) *-ial, -ian, -ion*

The syllable *preceding the suffix* (i.e. the second syllable from the end) is accented.

cere'monial	elec'trician	ad'mission
me'morial	ma'gician	per'mission
re'medial	mu'sician	di'vision
testi'monial	phy'sician	re'vision
com'mercial	stati'stician	compe'tition
confi'dential	poli'tician	occu'pation
dicta'torial	ci'vilian	civili'zation
terri'torial	co'median	exami'nation
tu'torial		

(vii) *-ic, -ics*

The syllable *preceding the suffix* (i.e. the second syllable from the end) is accented.

aca'demic	eco'nomic	dia'lectics
ar'tistic	ro'mantic	eco'nomics
dra'matic	scien'tific	lin'guistics
ge'neric	syste'matic	mathe'matics
philo'sophic	typo'graphic	pho'netics
photo'graphic		'ethics

EXCEPTIONS: 'Arabic, a'rithmetic(n), 'catholic, 'lunatic, ma'tric, 'politics, 'rhetoric(s), 'turmeric, 'heretic.

The addition of the suffixes *-al* and *-ally* to the *ic*-ending words (wherever such addition is possible) does not affect the accent. Thus words ending in *-ical* and *-ically* are accented on the *syllable immediately preceding the endings.*

geo'metric	geo'metrical	geo'metrically
dia'lectic	dia'lectical	dia'lectically
geo'graphic	geo'graphical	geo'graphically
po'etic	po'etical	po'etically
philo'sophic	philo'sophical	philo'sophically
photo'graphic	photo'graphical	photo'graphically
scien'tific		scien'tifically
syste'matic		syste'matically
eco'nomic	eco'nomical	eco'nomically

Notice also that words such as *heretic* and *politics*, which fall under exceptions to the rule for *ic(s)*-ending words, become regular in regard to accentuation when *-al* and *-ally* are added to them:

'heretic but *he'retical* and *he'retically*; *'politics* but *po'litical* and *po'litically*

(viii) *-ious*

The syllable *preceding the ending* (i.e. the second syllable from the end) is accented.

a'trocious	de'licious
ju'dicious	hi'larious
no'torious	fal'lacious

(ix) *-ity*

The syllable *preceding the ending* (i.e. the third syllable from the end) is accented.

'quality	fa'cility	pub'licity
ambi'guity	fu'tility	sa'gacity
ano'nymity	magna'nimity	sponta'neity
'deity	oppor'tunity	suita'bility
dura'bility	popu'larity	una'nimity
elec'tricity	possi'bility	uni'versity

12.6 Placement of Secondary Accent

The rules of word accent given in section 12.522 can be applied to determine only the primary accent. But a large number of English words, especially those consisting of more than three syllables, have a secondary accent as well (see Section 12.2), rules for which can be formulated. However, before formulating such rules, it will be essential to state a general principle of accentuation in English.

All English words of more than two syllables have (a) either the *primary* accent or (b) the *secondary* accent on the *first* syllable or the *second* syllable. Look at the following examples:

(a) 'analyse, a'nalysis, 'circumstance, 'classify, cli'matic, al'leviate, ex'tremity, 'generalize, ge'netic, 'shortage, 'college, gra'phology, 'aptitude, ef'ficient, 'positive, 'dynamism.

(b) ˌclassifi'cation, ˌcircum'stantial, ˌinfor'mation, ˌhuma'nistic, ˌcruci'fixion, ˌcrimi'nality, diˌscrimi'nation, ˌdemo'cratic, ˌambi'guity, parˌticulari'zation, reˌduci'bility.

In (a) above, the words have only the primary accent, and this is placed either on the first or the second syllable. In (b), the words have both the primary and secondary accents. Since in all these words the primary accent is on the third syllable or later, they have a secondary accent as well, and this is placed either on the first or the second syllable. The above formulation about the first or the second syllable in English carrying some accent—secondary, if not the primary—is extremely helpful in locating the syllable for the placement of the secondary accent. Once the syllable for the placement of the primary accent has been identified, the following rules will help locate the syllable which should receive the secondary accent.

(1) In all *simple* (not *compound*) words, the secondary accent is located on the left of the primary accent.

EXAMPLES

acˌcentu'ation ˌguaran'tee
ˌindi'vidual ˌbio'graphical
ˌsponta'neity

(2) When the primary accent is on the third or a later syllable, the secondary accent will be on the first or the second syllable.

EXAMPLES

ˌphilo'sophical, ˌcharacteri'zation, eˌxami'nation.

(3) The secondary accent cannot be on a syllable immediately preceding the primary accent.

EXAMPLES

aˌdjudi'cation, ˌado'lescence, ˌcrea'tivity.

(4) In derived words, when the primary accent is on the fourth or a later syllable and it is not clear whether the secondary accent should be on the first or the second syllable, the accentual pattern of the word before its derivation into the present form comes to help: the syllable carrying the primary accent before the process of derivation will now carry the secondary accent.

EXAMPLES

Before derivation	*After derivation*
e'xaggerate	eˌxagge'ration
i'dentify	iˌdentifi'cation
ar'ticulate	arˌticu'lation
im'ponderable	imˌpondera'bility

Note this exception:

cre'ative ˌcrea'tivity

But also note that this exception is covered under Rule (3) above and that when there is a clash between Rule (3) and Rule (4), Rule (3) applies *first*.

12.7 Summary

Word accent is the relative degree of prominence with which the different syllables of a word are pronounced. In this sense, a monosyllabic word said in isolation can be said to have 'no accent'. The prominence of a particular syllable in a word is quite often due to any or all of the following four factors—stress, pitch change, quality, and quantity (length). That is why the term 'word accent' is generally preferred to the term 'word stress'.

Word accent is an essential part of the word form. The word is constituted as much from the relative prominence of its syllables as from vowels and consonants. Every word of more than one syllable in English, for example, has its own characteristic accentual pattern. To learn the pronunciation of an English word, it is absolutely necessary to learn its accentual pattern, apart from the vowel and consonant sounds constituting it. Wrong accentuation may deform a word beyond recognition and impair its intelligibility in a very serious way.

While word accent in a number of languages, such as Czech, Finnish, and French, is fixed, it is free in English in the sense that there is no easy way to predict where the accent would be on a given disyllabic or polysyllabic word. Nevertheless, some rules of word accent have been formulated on the basis of prefixes and word endings, and they are extremely useful for learning the pronunciation of English words.

EXERCISES

A Listen and Repeat

I Two-syllable words with the primary accent on the *first* syllable

Listen to the teacher's (recorded) pronunciations of the following words and repeat them side by side:

1 'absent	6 'borrow	11 'getting
2 'action	7 'burden	12 'honest
3 'also	8 'follow	13 'carrot
4 'answer	9 'future	14 'lesson
5 'angle	10 'feeling	15 'moment

II Two-syllable words with the primary accent on the *second* syllable

Listen to the teacher's (recorded) pronunciations of the following words and repeat them side by side:

1 a'gain	7 be'hind	13 se'lect
2 a'lone	8 be'tween	14 sur'round
3 a'long	9 cre'ate	15 to'wards
4 a'loud	10 de'cide	16 be'gin
5 at'tend	11 de'lay	17 to'day
6 be'fore	12 re'late	

III Three-syllable words with the primary accent on the *first* syllable

Listen to and repeat the following words:

1 'absolute
2 'adequate
3 'anything
4 'beautiful
5 'betterment
6 'coverage
7 'culminate
8 'decorate
9 'delicate
10 'deviate
11 'discipline
12 'elevate
13 'eminent
14 'excellent
15 'gardening
16 'memory
17 'minister

IV Three-syllable words with the primary accent on the *second* syllable

Listen to and repeat the following words:

1 ad'vantage
2 al'ready
3 a'nother
4 at'tention
5 be'haviour
6 con'ception
7 con'dition
8 cor'rection
9 de'cision
10 de'termine
11 di'vision
12 ex'ample
13 ex'cessive
14 ex'pression
15 im'portant
16 in'fection

V Three-syllable words with the primary accent on the *third* syllable

Listen to and repeat the following words:

1 addres'see
2 compre'hend
3 consig'nee
4 disap'pear
5 domi'neer
6 employ'ee
7 engi'neer
8 intro'duce
9 refe'ree
10 repar'tee
11 repre'sent
12 repro'duce
13 under'stand

VI Four-syllable words with the primary accent on the *first* syllable

Listen to and repeat the following words:

1 'capitalize
2 'constipated
3 'criticism
4 'educated
5 'helicopter
6 'melancholy
7 'prophesying
8 'commentary
9 'counterattack
10 'pessimism
11 'optimism
12 'hospitable
13 'kilometre
14 'applicable
15 'controversy

VII Four- and five-syllable words with the primary accent on the *second* syllable

Listen to and repeat the following words:

1 a'natomize
2 bo'tanical
3 ca'tastrophe
4 de'mocracy
5 gram'matical
6 hy'pocrisy
7 in'telligence
8 in'telligible
9 le'gitimatize
10 ma'nipulate
11 me'chanical
12 par'ticular
13 par'ticularize
14 phi'losophy
15 ther'mometre

VIII Four- and five-syllable words with the primary accent on the *third* syllable

Listen to and repeat the following words:

1 advan'tageous
2 libe'rality
3 cancel'lation
4 compre'hension
5 contra'diction
6 diso'bedient
7 elec'tricity
8 emi'gration
9 inde'pendent
10 instru'mental
11 inter'national
12 monu'mental
13 rela'tivity
14 seni'ority
15 under'standing

IX Five- and six-syllable words with the primary accent on the *fourth* syllable

Listen to and repeat the following words:

1 accommo'dation
2 aristo'cratic
3 autobi'ography
4 characte'ristic
5 civili'zation
6 evalu'ation
7 exami'nation
8 intelli'gentsia
9 meteoro'logical
10 partici'pation
11 particu'larity
12 peculi'arity
13 qualifi'cation
14 recommen'dation
15 instrumentation

B Recognition

I Listen to the pronunciations of the following disyllabic words and say whether the accent is on the first syllable or the second syllable:

1 allow
2 gainer
3 translate
4 beauty
5 nation
6 propose
7 anything
8 complete
9 certain
10 invite
11 station
12 besides
13 booking
14 human
15 woman
16 manner
17 receive
18 reply
19 wisdom
20 goodness
21 without

II Listen to the pronunciations of the following words and locate the primary and the secondary accent:

1 alphabetic
2 altruistic
3 archaeological
4 arbitration
5 camaraderie
6 centenarian
7 Christianity
8 cinematography
9 demilitarize
10 denominational
11 disproportionate
12 disqualification
13 escalation
14 geophysical
15 hippopotamus
16 ignoramus

III Listen to the pronunciations of the following words and say whether a particular word is a noun or a verb:

1 export
2 increase
3 record
4 record
5 produce
6 protest
7 rebel
8 dictate
9 incline
10 accent
11 refuse
12 survey
13 subject
14 contest
15 combine

IV Listen to the pronunciations of the following words and say whether a particular word is a noun/adjective, or a verb:

1 August	6 envelope
2 absent	7 invalid
3 frequent	8 insult
4 perfect	9 conduct
5 alternate	10 content

C Production

I Mark the primary accent on the following words and say them correctly:

1 enough	11 decrease (n)	21 homeless
2 unless	12 deceive	22 performance
3 until	13 reception	23 threaten
4 before	14 development	24 therefore
5 hotel	15 decoration	25 proverb
6 provision	16 discuss	26 psychology
7 determine	17 describe	27 component
8 refusal	18 demonstrate	28 opponent
9 extremity	19 translation	29 debator
10 extinguish	20 appropriate	30 opposition

II (a) Bearing in mind the rules of word accent we have discussed in the foregoing sections, mark the primary accent in the following groups of words and say them correctly:

(1) Simplification, realization, supposition, dimension, collection, articulation.

(2) Possibility, veracity, capacity, hostility, ability, electricity.

(3) Specific, mechanic, energetic, dramatic, academic, alcoholic.

(4) Medial, congenial, commercial, trivial, cordial, remedial, industrial.

(5) Ornamental, elemental, instrumental, experimental.

(6) Magician, optician, musician.

(7) Locate, vacate, contemplate, deliberate, authorize, colonize, dehumanize, economize.

(8) Biology, photography, geometry, economy, autocracy, zoology.

II (b) Mark the primary and the secondary accent in the following words and say them correctly:

1 invalidation	7 maladjustment
2 isolation	8 masculinity
3 jurisdiction	9 mediaeval
4 lackadaisical	10 musicologist
5 logarithmic	11 matrimonial
6 machination	12 nevertheless

II (c) Divide the following words into syllables and, by the application of accent rules, mark the primary accent in each word:

EXAMPLE

hostility ho-'sti-li-ty

Optical, reduction, synthetic, generic, unanimity, university, pilgrimage, remedial, participation, rhetorical, phonetics, democracy.

III Mark the primary accent on the following sets of compound words and say them with the correct accentual patterns:

(a)

1 airport
2 bedtime
3 lipstick
4 schoolmaster
5 shipwreck
6 stateboat
7 storeroom
8 teacup
9 tinsmith
10 watercolour

(b)

1 alms-giving
2 fault-finding
3 fox-hunting
4 fellow-feeling
5 mass-meeting
6 thanks-giving
7 craftsman
8 foolscap
9 salesman
10 statesman

IV Pronounce the following noun-adjective pairs with the correct accentuation:

1 rhetoric, rhetorical
2 politics, political
3 benefit, beneficient
4 geology, geological
5 economy, economical
6 telegraph, telegraphic
7 democrat, democratic
8 mechanism, mechanical

V Look up the dictionary and say the following words with the primary accent on the right syllable:

1 selfish
2 personify
3 kingdom
4 courtship
5 aimless
6 appointment
7 development
8 beginning
9 womanhood
10 clearance
11 cowardice
12 graceful
13 gracefulness
14 broaden
15 exposure

VI Give five examples each of the words having the same accentual patterns as the following words. But look at the following three examples before answering this question.

EXAMPLES

Word	*Accentual Pattern*
ˈcivilize	– ⌣ ⌣
conˈcerning	⌣ – ⌣
ˌrefeˈree	– ⌣ –

1 introduce
2 refinement
3 namely
4 correct
5 prohibition
6 recently
7 civilization
8 possibility
9 reliable
10 guarantee

VII Given below is a list of words consisting of two, three, four, or five syllables and having varied accentual patterns. Look up your dictionary and group them together according to their accentual patterns—i.e. identify, and group together, words of the same number of syllables and the same accentual pattern:

> Identity, mechanise, celebrate, behave, hostility, beginning, waiting, laziness, credit, writing, reduction, beautiful, celebrity, organization, hatred, union, government, method, decision, listless, answer, reply, correspondence, regular, adolescence, comprehension, meanness, employment, regularity, cohesion, versatility, examination, blockage, nuclear, readiness, realize, perhaps, nowhere, narrate, sympathetic, carelessness, remember, heresy.

13
Accent and Rhythm in Connected Speech

13.1 Introduction

We studied the accentual patterns of English words in Chapter 12 and found that, in all disyllabic and polysyllabic words, one syllable always stands out from its neighbouring syllable or syllables, i e one syllable is always most prominent. In much the same way, some words always stand out from the rest in an utterance comprising two or more words. They are more prominent than others. Their relative prominence is studied under the accentual features of connected speech, and this forms the subject-matter of this chapter.

13.2 Words Generally Accented

As we said in Section 13.1, not all words in connected speech receive equal prominence. Some words (or, more precisely, certain syllables, especially in words of more than one syllable) are more prominent than others. Such words are said to be accented. By way of illustration, we shall look at the following examples, in which the words, or the syllables in other than the monosyllabic words, that are accented are marked with a stroke placed before them:

1 I've 'found my 'book.
2 It's 'kind of you to 'ask me.
3 'Mohan and 'Sohan are 'brothers.
4 He 'wants us to 'take it a'way.
5 He 'promised he'd ac'cept the invi'tation.
6 'That's the 'house we 'bought 'yesterday.
7 It's 'no 'trouble at 'all.
8 I 'couldn't 'see the 'house.
9 'Don't 'bother.
10 'Have you 'heard the 'latest 'news?
11 'Can you 'come to 'lunch to'morrow?
12 Did 'anyone re'member to 'lock the 'door?
13 'Yes, he 'will.
14 'No, 'thanks.
15 'Would you 'like it 'painted 'red?

16 'Where are you 'going on 'Monday?
17 He 'doesn't want to 'come 'here.
18 Oh, I 'haven't got an i'dea.
19 You 'ought to 'know the 'place by 'now.
20 He 'used to 'come on 'Sundays.

A close examination of the above sentences shows that the words which are generally accented in connected speech are those that are more important than others in conveying meaning. Now, the most important words, from the point of view of meaning, are usually the nouns, main verbs, adjectives, adverbs, demonstrative and interrogative pronouns, and the words *yes* and *no*: therefore they are the ones generally accented in sentences. To put it in another way, it is, by and large, the *content*, or *lexical*, words that receive the accent.

We also notice, from a study of the same sentences, that the words that are generally not accented are personal pronouns, prepositions, auxiliary verbs, articles, and conjunctions—that is, words which, by and large, perform a grammatical function and are called *grammatical*, or *form*, or *structure*, words.

There are, however, some notable exceptions to the general rule stated in the above paragraphs. These are discussed below in sections 13.21 and 13.22.

13.21 Content Words Not Accented

Content words are not accented in the following situations:

(1) When they are repeated in a context as in: You 'want me to 'come? I 'won't *come*.

(2) When words in their neighbourhood are emphasized as in sentence 18: Oh, I 'haven't *got* an i'dea.

(3) When the rhythmic pattern (to be discussed in Section 13.5) of a sentence demands that these words be left unaccented as *went* in: 'Ram *went* a'way. (Contrast this sentence with: He 'went a'way.)

Here we may add that when a learner is in doubt as to whether or not a content word should lose the accent *on account of rhythm*, it is safer for him to retain the accent.

(4) When one word in a sequence of two content words is habitually contrasted with some other word, that word alone is accented. Examples: *a'cute angle* (*Angle* not accented; *acute* accented even when no contrast with *obtuse* is intended.) Similarly, *'bus journey*, *'pleasure trip*, *'safety razor*.

(5) When the main verbs *be*, and *have* in the sense of *possess*, occur medially in a sentence as *are* in sentence 3 above: 'Mohan and 'Sohan are 'brothers (.) and *have* in the sentence: I have a 'new 'dictionary at 'home.

(6) When the demonstrative pronouns *this*, *that*, *these*, and *those* are used more or less like the definite article *the*, carrying no force of demonstrativeness as in: I 'don't 'like this 'other one; that 'book I was 'talking about ...; these ins'tructions in the 'leaflet are im'portant; those 'people we were 'speaking to...

13.22 Form Words Accented

Form words are accented in the following situations:

(1) When they contrast as in: *'My* 'bicycle is 'nicer than *'yours*.

(2) When they are polysyllabic prepositions occurring before pronouns as in: Tell me something 'more *a'bout* it.

(3) When they are emphasized as in: (I don't think he'll come.) But he *'is* coming. You can take 'this *'or* 'that (meaning: You can't take both.)

While rules 1 and 3 above apply to auxiliaries just as they apply to other form words, the former (auxiliaries) are accented in certain other situations as well. These are discussed below.

(i) When they are attached to *n't* as in sentence 17: He *'doesn't* want to 'come 'here. (Contrast with: He does 'not want to 'come 'here.)

(ii) When they occur at the end of a sentence as in sentence 13: 'Yes, he *'will*. (This rule applies equally to the main verb *be* as well, which is ordinarily not accented.)

(iii) When they occur at the beginning of a sentence as in sentence 11: *'Can* you 'come to 'lunch to'morrow? In this case, however, accenting the auxiliary is optional: we have no accent on the auxiliary at the beginning of sentence 12, for example: *Did* 'anyone re'member to 'lock the 'door?

13.3 Location of Accent

It must be noted that when words of more than one syllable are accented in an utterance, only those syllables are accented which receive the accent when the words are said in isolation. This will be clear from an examination of sentences 5, 7, and 11, in which the words *'promised*, *ac'cept*, *invi'tation*, *'trouble*, and *to'morrow* receive the accent only on the syllables which receive the accent when these words are said in isolation. The following examples further illustrate this statement:

21 'How much 'practice shall I 'do?
22 It's 'very 'difficult.
23 'Do you re'member that 'party?
24 He's 'just made an'other ap'pointment.
25 'Read the be'ginning of the 'paragraph.

The words *practice*, *very*, *difficult*, *remember*, *party*, *another*, *appointment*, *beginning*, and *paragraph* in these sentences are apparently accented on the syllables that would receive the accent even if the words were said in isolation. There are, however, words of variable accentual patterns in English like *sixteen*, and some compounds, such as *downstairs* and *off-hand*, which are accented on the first or the second syllable depending on their position in an utterance. Such words, and some other words of variable grammatical functions, like *one*, *some*, *more*, *most*, and *there*, will be dealt with in the following two sections.

13.4 Miscellaneous Accentual Patterns

13.41 Words with Two Strong Accents

There are a number of words in English, mostly compounds, which take two strong accents, one primary and the other secondary. When used in connected speech, they invariably lose one of the accents, under the force of rhythm (see Section 13.5), according to the following pattern:

(1) The word loses its first accent when it occurs in the final position in a sentence and is immediately preceded by a word containing an accented syllable.

(2) The word loses its second accent when it occurs non-finally and is immediately followed by an accented syllable, or a word containing an accented syllable.

The following pairs of examples will make the point clear:

26a He's 'just fif'teen.
26b It's 'fifteen 'kilometers.
27a We 'go to see a 'movie almost 'every after'noon.
27b 'Where shall we 'take the 'afternoon 'tea?
28a I 'can't tell you 'anything off-'hand.
28b He 'gave me an 'off-hand 'answer.
29a Your 'friend is 'waiting down'stairs.
29b He 'lives in the 'downstairs 'room.
30a The 'cheque he 'gave me was 'not post-'dated.
30b He 'gave me a 'post-dated 'cheque.
31a They 'come to me 'every week-'end.
31b He has a 'week-end re'sort at 'Ooty.
32a I 'always 'go second-'class.
32b 'Buy me a 'second-class 'ticket.

13.42

In this section we shall consider words such as *one*, *body*, *things*, and *business*. These words would normally be classified as content words and therefore accented. But sometimes when they function as what might be called *prop-words*, in that they stand for something that has already been said, they remain unaccented. Note the following examples:

33 He 'asked for 'those *ones*.
34 'Every*one* was 'trying to 'help them.
35 'No-*one* 'came to my 'help.
36 'Every*body* 'present 'there 'interested me.
37 'Let's 'talk *things* 'over.
38 It's 'no *business* of 'yours.

13.43

The case of the reflexive pronouns is slightly different in the sense that their grammatical function is always that of pronouns. They are accented according to the following rule:

(i) *Used as object* They are not accented when they occur sentence-medially:
39 He 'killed himself 'yesterday.
40 She 'never for'gave herself for her 'act of o'mission.
They are accented when they occur sentence-finally:
41 He 'killed him'self.
42 'Help your'selves.

(ii) *Used as subject intensifier* (for emphasis) They are always accented:
43 He 'gave it to me him'self.
44 She her'self 'told me the 'story.

13.44

It might also be helpful to examine in this context certain words like *more*, *most*, *some*, and *there*, which are used almost as often as *form* words as *content* words. As expected, when they function as form words, they are normally not accented, whereas when they function as content words, they are usually accented.

When *more* and *most* are used to make comparative and superlative degrees of adjectives (i e when they are used as form words), they remain unaccented as in the following sentences:

45 'He's the most 'honest 'man I've ever 'met.
46 She's more 'beautiful than her 'sister.

But when they function as adjectives, they are usually accented as in the following examples:

47 'Most 'people are 'self-centred. (adjective)
48 We 'need 'more 'milk for the 'children. (adjective)

What is however of special interest here is that even when they function as pronouns (i e as form words), they retain the accent as in the following sentences:

49 'Most of us 'speak 'Hindi 'well. (pronoun)
50 'More of 'such in'difference will 'spell di'saster. (pronoun)

Equally interesting is the case with the words *some* and *there*. When *some* is used as an indefinite article (i e as a form word) like *a* and *an*, it does not take the accent and is pronounced as /səm/ or /sm/ as in the following examples:

51 'Pour him 'out some 'coffee.
52 'Give me some 'water to 'drink.

Also, when it is used as an indefinite pronoun or when it refers to something like 'one of a type', it is not accented though it is then pronounced as /sʌm/ as in the following sentences:

53 Re'serve some for me.
54 'Let me 'keep some for the 'boys.
55 I am 'looking for some 'woman to 'help me with 'cooking.

But when it functions as an adjective, or occurs in a structure like *some + prep. + NP*, it is almost always accented as in the following examples:

56 'Some people pre'fer 'tea to 'coffee.
57 'Some of 'those 'boys are 'here.

The case of *there* is much simpler. When used as an existential, or preparatory, subject, it is never accented; but when it functions as an adverb, it usually keeps the accent. Look at the following examples:

58 There's 'nothing in the 'room.
59 He 'put it 'there.

The case of *each* is slightly different in that it never functions as a form word. As a content word, it is not accented in the collocation *each other*:

59a Let's 'help each 'other.

13.5 Accent and Rhythm

Rhythm is a kind of periodicity, which would mean the recurrence of certain patterns of colour, design, or sound at regular (equal) intervals of space or time. Rhythm in a piece of drawing or embroidery refers to the even spacing of a certain motif or design. In music, a certain kind of beat or sound complex being repeated at equal intervals of time constitutes its rhythm. Rhythm in language likewise refers to the periodic recurrence of certain complexes or patterns of sound in utterances constituting a text.

13.51 Kinds of Rhythm

It has often been claimed that, in some languages of the world (e g French), syllables constituting utterances, whether accented or unaccented, tend to occur at equal time-intervals and that the time taken from one accented syllable to the next will be in proportion to the number of unaccented syllables between them. Such languages are said to have *syllable-timed rhythm.* It has been further claimed that some other languages of the world have *stress-timed rhythm.* In these languages, accented syllables have a tendency to occur at approximately equal intervals of time, irrespective of the number of unaccented syllables intervening between one accented syllable and the next.

According to this theory, which so far has neither been validated nor refuted beyond doubt, English belongs to the second category of languages and has *stress-timed rhythm*. This would mean that, in English utterances, accented syllables *tend* to occur at approximately equal intervals of time. The word *tend* suggests that accented syllables have quite often a tendency to be equally spaced in time, and that is all. English speech surely does not have the rhythmical structure of English verse, and the time-precision of a metronome in the recurrence of accented syllables is completely ruled out. Once this is understood, we might find the notion of *stress-timed rhythm* a useful tool in the learning and teaching of the rhythm of English.

13.52 Influence of Rhythm on Accent

In the foregoing sections we formulated a general 'rule' that content words are usually accented and form words are usually not. We also noted some of the more important exceptions to this rule and said in passing that accentuation in connected speech is in the final analysis governed by the principle of rhythm. Let us discuss this last point here in some detail.

If we carefully look at sentences 1–57 in this chapter and read them deliberately, we shall notice that the accented syllables do recur *somewhat* regularly, irrespective of the number of unaccented syllables between one accented syllable and the next. In fact it is mainly to ensure the regularity of recurrence of the accented syllables that the form words *ought to* and *used to* are accented in sentences 19–20. This regularity, or rhythm, is a very important feature of English connected speech, and to ignore it would be to neglect a vital aspect of English pronunciation.

When the number of unaccented syllables between any two accented syllables in a given utterance is more or less the same as between any other two accented syllables, the speaker smoothly hops over from one accented syllable to the next and maintains, without difficulty, the 'characteristic' stress-timed rhythm of the utterance. But when the number of unaccented syllables between successive accented syllables varies widely, it would not be easy to maintain the rhythm. What the speaker would, and perhaps should, achieve in such utterances is some degree of approximation to stress-timed rhythm. Let us consider in this connection the following sentences:

60 He 'did his 'best to 'save the 'man.
61 I 'always 'like a 'cup of 'coffee.
62 I 'told him to 'wait in the 'corridor.
63 'Tell him to 'go to the exami'nation 'hall.
64 'Do you 'know that they are in 'trouble?
65 He sug'gested that we all should 'go to 'church 'every 'Sunday.

In sentences 60 and 61, there is one unaccented syllable each between any two accented syllables, and in sentence 62, there are two unaccented syllables each between any two accented ones so that it will be quite easy for the speaker to say these three sentences in such a way that the accented syllables tend to occur at almost equal intervals of time. But in sentence 64, there is only one unaccented syllable between the first and the second accented syllable as against four between the second and the third. In sentence 65, the unaccented syllables are even more unevenly distributed. There are as many as five between the first and the second accented syllable as against one between the second and the third, none between the third and the fourth, and one between the fourth and the last.

Now, it will be difficult for the speaker to say these and other similar sentences in such a way that the accented syllables may occur at approximately equal time-intervals (unless he takes care to weaken considerably the pronunciations of certain words and prolong those of others). In order that in sentence 64, for instance, syllables *Do*, *know*, and *trou-* may be fairly equally spaced in time, it should take one more or less the same amount of time to say *you* as to say the whole stretch of four syllables *that they are in*. In other words, each of these four syllables must be said four times as fast as *you*. Similarly, each of the five syllables *-ted that we all should*, in sentence 65, must be said roughly five times as fast as the syllable *to*. But this is not done. If we beat the time as each accented syllable in these sentences is said by the native speaker of English, we may not perceive absolute regularity in their recurrence. But we will certainly perceive a marked tendency on his part to slur over *any number* of *unaccented syllables* and smoothly glide over to the next accented syllable. What follows from this is that unaccented syllables should be said very fast when several of them come together between accented syllables. This can be possible only if these unaccented syllables, most of which are form words, are considerably weakened. The use of the *weakened* pronunciations, or *weak forms*, is therefore very important.

13.53 Weak Forms

There are roughly 45 words in English, which have two or more pronunciations—one *strong* (or dictionary) pronunciation, and one or more than one *weak* pronunciation or *weak form*. Words of this kind will be called *weak form* words. The learning of weak forms is extremely necessary. Many non-native speakers of English, who generally use only strong forms of these words in their pronunciation, fail to approximate to the characteristic rhythm of English, thus reducing considerably the level of intelligibility of their pronunciation, especially in relation to native speakers of RP. And, more importantly, since almost all native speakers of RP use weak forms in their pronunciation, learners of RP will find it very difficult to understand what they hear unless they learn (or, at least, learn *about*) these weak forms themselves.

13.54 Use of Strong Forms of Grammatical Words

It will be noticed that practically all the words that have weak forms or pronunciations are form words, or *grammatical* words. These form words do, in certain circumstances, retain their strong forms, though generally they are pronounced in their weak forms. We shall now list the contexts or circumstances in which only strong forms are acceptable. (In all other cases, weak forms are the normal pronunciations of these words.)

(1) When weak form words, even when not accented, occur sentence-finally. For example, the words *from*, *for*, *at*, *to*, *of*, *can*, *was*, *have*, which have /frəm/, /fə(r)/, /ət/, /tə, tʊ/, /əv/, /kən/, /wəz/, /həv/ as their normal weakened pronunciations, are pronounced, in their strong forms, as /frɒm/, /fɔ:(r)/, /æt/, /tu:/, /ɒv/, /kæn/, wɒz/, /hæv/ when they occur at the end of a sentence. Examples are given below. Pronouns form an exception to this rule.

(i) Where are you coming *from*?
/'weər ə jʊ 'kʌmɪŋ frɒm/

(ii) Who are you waiting *for*?
/'hu: ə jʊ 'weɪtɪŋ fɔ:/

(iii) What's he looking *at*?
/'wɒts hɪ 'lʊkɪŋ æt/

(iv) Who are you sending it *to*?
/'hu: ə jʊ 'sendɪŋ ɪt tu:/

(v) What's it made *of*?
/'wɒts ɪt 'meɪd ɒv/

(vi) (Who can attempt this?) I *can*.
/'aɪ kæn/

(vii) (Were they all going?) No, but Rahul *was*.
/'nəʊ bət 'rɑ:hʊl wɒz/

(viii) (Have they won the game?) No, but we *have*.
/'nəʊ bət 'wi: hæv/

(2) When a weak form word is accented (see Section 13.2) for the purpose of contrast, coordination, emphasis, or citation. For example, the words *from*, *to*, *of*, *for*, *will*, *and*, and *that* will be pronounced in their strong forms when they are accented as in the following examples:

The journey *to* /tu:/ Delhi, and not *from* /frɑm/ Delhi. (contrast)
The government *of* /ɒv/ the people and *for* /fɔ:/ the people. (coordination)
He *will* /wɪl/ have his own way. (emphasis)
I said 'and' /ænd/, and not 'that' /ðæt/. (citation)

From the foregoing paragraphs, it follows that, while weak forms are never accented, strong forms may or may not be.

13.55 Most Common Form Words

In this section, we shall introduce the most common form words, along with their strong and weak pronunciations, or forms, and the contexts in which their different weak forms occur.

13.551 Auxiliary verbs

	Auxiliary verb	*Strong form*	*Weak form*	*Example*
1	am	/æm/	/əm/	Why am I here? /'waɪ əm aɪ 'hɪə/
2	are	/ɑ:/	/ə/	(before consonants) They're going. /ðeə 'gəʊɪŋ/
		/ɑ:r/	/ər/	(before vowels) They're honest. /ðeər 'ɒnɪst/

3 is	/ɪz/	/ɪz/	(after /s, z, tʃ, dʒ, ʃ, ʒ/) This watch is mine. /'ðɪs 'wɒtʃ ɪz 'maɪn/
		/z/	(after voiced sounds other than /z, dʒ, ʒ/) This dog's lovely. /ðɪs 'dɒgz 'lʌvlɪ/
		/s/	(after voiceless sounds other than /s, tʃ, ʃ/) But the cat's ugly. /bət ðə 'kæts 'ʌglɪ/
4 was	/wɒz/	/wəz/	I was there. /aɪ wəz 'ðeə/
5 were	/wɜː/	/wə/	(before consonants) We were late. /wɪ wə 'leɪt/
	/wɜːr/	/wər/	(before vowels) They were asleep. /ðeɪ wər ə'sliːp/
6 do	/duː/	/də/	(before consonants) How do they come? /'haʊ də ðeɪ 'kʌm/
		/dʊ/	(before vowels) What do I get? /'wɒt dʊ aɪ 'get/
7 does	/dʌz/	/dəz/	When does he go? /'wen dəz ɪ 'gəʊ/
8 had	/hæd/	/həd/	(initially in a sentence) Had he already gone? /həd ɪ ɔːl'redɪ 'gɒn/
		/d/	(after vowels) We'd never seen it. before. /wiːd 'nevə siːn ɪt bɪ'fɔː/
		/əd/	(elsewhere) The men had gone home. /ðə 'men əd 'gɒn 'həʊm/
9 has	/hæz/	/həz/	(initially in a sentence) Has he paid the bill? /həz ɪ'peɪd ðə 'bɪl/
		/əz/	(after /s, z, tʃ, dʒ, ʃ, ʒ/)

	Auxiliary verb	*Strong form*	*Weak form*	*Example*
				The rose has withered. /ðə 'rəʊz əz 'wɪðəd/
			/z/	(after voiced sounds minus /z, dʒ, ʒ/) The lion's died. /ðə 'laɪənz 'daɪd/
			/s/	(after voiceless sounds minus /s, tʃ, ʃ/) The milk's gone. sour. /ðə 'mɪlks 'gɒn 'saʊə/
10	have	/hæv/	/həv/	(in the initial position in a sentence) Have you done the work? /həv jʊ 'dʌn ðə 'wɜːk/
			/v/	(after personal pronouns) You've done that. /juːv 'dʌn 'ðæt/
			/əv/	(in all other positions) What have you seen? /'wɒt əv jʊ 'siːn/
11	can	/kæn/	/kən/(/kn/)	They can wait. /ðeɪ kən (or kn) 'weɪt/
12	could	/kʊd/	/kəd/	How could he do it? /'haʊ kəd ɪ 'duː ɪt/
13	shall	/ʃæl/	/ʃəl/(/ʃl/)	We shall need to run. /wɪ ʃəl (or ʃl) 'niːd tə 'rʌn/
14	should	/ʃʊd/	/ʃəd/	Why should he care for anybody? /'waɪ ʃəd ɪ 'keə fər 'enɪbɒdɪ/
15	must	/mʌst/	/məs/	(before consonants) You must try your best. /jʊ məs 'traɪ jɔː 'best/
			/məst/	(before vowels) He must eat well. /hɪ məst iːt 'wel/
16	will	/wɪl/	[l̩]	(after consonants, except [illegible])

			This watch'll do. /'ðɪs 'wɒtʃl̩ 'duː/
		/əl/	(after vowels, and /l/) The boy will lose and the girl will win. /ðə 'bɔɪ əl 'luːz ən ðə 'gɜːl əl 'wɪn/
		/l/	(after *I*, *he*, *she*, *we*, *you*, *they*) We'll come. /wiːl 'kʌm/ He'll go. /hiːl 'gəʊ/
17 would	/wʊd/	/wəd/	(sentence-initially) Would you come for a walk? /wəd jʊ 'kʌm fər ə 'wɔːk/
		/d/	(after *I*, *he*, *she*, *we*, *you*, *they*) He'd be happy. /hiːd bɪ 'hæpɪ/
		/əd/	(elsewhere) All would agree. /'ɔːl əd ə'griː/

13.552 Conjunctions

Conjunction	*Strong form*	*Weak form*	*Example*
18 and	/ænd/	/ən/	Come and sit down. /'kʌm ən 'sɪt 'daʊn/
		[n̩]	(sometimes after /t, d, s, z, ʃ/) Wash and wear /'wɒʃ n̩ 'weə/ Bread and butter /'bred n̩ 'bʌtə/
19 as	/æz/	/əz/	As soon as possible /əz 'suːn əz 'pɒsɪbl/

Note: Initial *as* is likely to be accented, which then takes its full form /æz/.

EXAMPLES

'As /æz/ a 'member of our 'party, he was an 'asset. 'As /æz/ he 'wasn't 'present, he 'missed the oppor'tunity.

In the special use illustrated in the following sentence, *as* is accented and takes its full form:

'As /æz/ for 'him, it is 'not 'possible to 'say 'anything at the 'moment.

	Conjunction	*Strong form*	*Weak form*	*Example*
20	than	/ðæn/	/ðən/(/ðn/)	This is better than that. /'ðɪs ɪz 'betə ðən (or ðn) 'ðæt/
21	that	/ðæt/	/ðət/	This is the method that works. /'ðɪs ɪz ðə 'meθəd ðət 'wɜːks/ He said that he was coming. /hɪ 'sed ðət ɪ wəz 'kʌmɪŋ/
22	but	/bʌt/	/bət/	But why not today? /bət 'waɪ nɒt tə'deɪ/

13.553 Pronouns

	Pronoun	*Strong form*	*Weak form*	*Example*
23	he	/hiː/	/hɪ/	(at the beginning of a sentence) He was very late. /hɪ wəz 'verɪ 'leɪt/
			/ɪ/	Why did he come back?/'waɪ dɪd ɪ 'kʌm 'bæk/
24	her	/hɜː/	/hə/	(at the beginning of a sentence) Her purse is missing. /hə 'pɜːs ɪz 'mɪsɪŋ/
			/ə/	Has her brother returned? /'hæz ə 'brʌðə rɪ'tɜːnd/ I've seen her. /aɪv 'siːn ə/
25	him	/hɪm/	/ɪm/	I've given him a pen. /aɪv 'gɪvən ɪm ə 'pen/ I've met him. /aɪv 'met ɪm/
26	his	/hɪz/	/hɪz/	(at the beginning of a sentence) His name was mentioned. /hɪz 'neɪm wəz 'menʃnd/
			/ɪz/	Give me his books. /'gɪv mɪ ɪz 'bʊks/

27 me	/miː/	/mɪ/	Bring me a chair. /'briŋ mɪ ə 'tʃeə/
28 she	/ʃiː/	/ʃɪ/	Where does she live? /'weə dəz ʃɪ 'lɪv/
29 them	/ðem/	/ðəm/(/ðm/)	Let them come. /'let ðəm (ðm) 'kʌm/
30 us	/ʌs/	/s/	(only in *let's*) Let's go there right now. /'lets 'gəʊ ðeə 'raɪt 'naʊ/
		/əs/	(elsewhere) He'll let us do it. /hiːl 'let əs 'duː ɪt/
31 we	/wiː/	wɪ/	We came here yesterday. /wɪ 'keɪm hɪə 'jestədeɪ/
32 who	/huː/	/hʊ/	Who do you want? /hʊ də jʊ 'wɒnt/
		/uː/	The man who is standing there . . . /ðə 'mæn uːz 'stændɪŋ ðeə . . ./
33 you	/juː/	/jʊ/	I'll tell you. everything. /aɪl 'tel jʊ 'evrɪθɪŋ/

13.554 Prepositions

Preposition	*Strong form*	*Weak form*	*Example*
34 at	/æt/	/ət/	He'll come at nine. /hiːl 'kʌm ət 'naɪn/
35 for	/fɔː/	/fə/	(before consonants) Come for coffee. /'kʌm fə 'kɒfɪ/
	/fɔːr/	/fər/	(before vowels) Come for a game of chess. /'kʌm fər ə 'geɪm əv 'tʃes/
36 from	/frɒm/	/frəm/	I've come from Delhi. /aɪv 'kʌm frəm 'delɪ/
37 of	/ɒv/	/əv/	He's a friend of my father. /hiːz ə 'frend əv maɪ 'fɑːðə/
38 to	/tuː/	/tə/	(before consonants) He's gone to take

Preposition	*Strong form*	*Weak form*	*Example*
			a test. /hiːz 'gɒn tə 'teɪk ə 'test/
		/tʊ/	(before vowels) Try to ask him over. /'traɪ tʊ 'ɑːsk ɪm 'əʊvə/

13.555 Articles

	Article	*Strong form*	*Weak form*	*Example*
39	a	/eɪ/	/ə/	(before consonants) I want a pen. /aɪ 'wɒnt ə 'pen/
40	an	/æn/	/ən/	(before vowels) Buy me an apple. /'baɪ mɪ ən 'æpl/
41	the	/ðiː/	/ðə/	(before consonants) The thief's escaped. /ðə 'θiːfs ɪ'skeɪpt/
			/ðɪ/	(before vowels) The apples are rotten. /ðɪ 'æplz ə 'rɒtn/
42	some	/sʌm/	/səm/(/sm/)	I want some tea. /aɪ 'wɒnt səm (or sm) 'tiː/

13.556 Miscellaneous words

	Word	*Strong form*	*Weak form*	*Example*
43	be	/biː/	/bɪ/	Don't be silly. /'dəʊnt bɪ 'sɪlɪ/.
44	been	/biːn/	/bɪn/	He hasn't been invited. /hɪ 'hæznt bɪn ɪn'vaɪtɪd/
45	there (existential, preparatory, subject)	/ðeə/	/ðə/	(before consonants) There was nobody in the room. /ðə wəz 'nəʊbədɪ ɪn ðə 'ruːm/
		/ðeər/	/ðər/	(before vowels) There're two books on the table. /ðərə 'tuː 'bʊks ɒn ðə 'teɪbl/

46 Sir	/sɜː/	/sə/	(before consonants) Sir William /sə 'wɪljəm/
	/sɜːr/	/sər/	(before vowels) Sir Anthony /sər 'æntənɪ/

If we carefully look again at the weak form words we have listed, we can draw the following conclusions, which should be extremely useful from the learner's point of view.

(1) All the words with initial /h/ (*he*, *his*, *him*, *her*, *who*, *had*, *has*, *have*) commonly lose their /h/, when they occur unaccented within a sentence. But they retain /h/, when they occur initially in a sentence, or when they are accented.

(2) In almost all the weak form words discussed above, weakening is effected by the replacement of a vowel phoneme by either /ə/, /ɪ/, or /ʊ/, according to the following pattern:

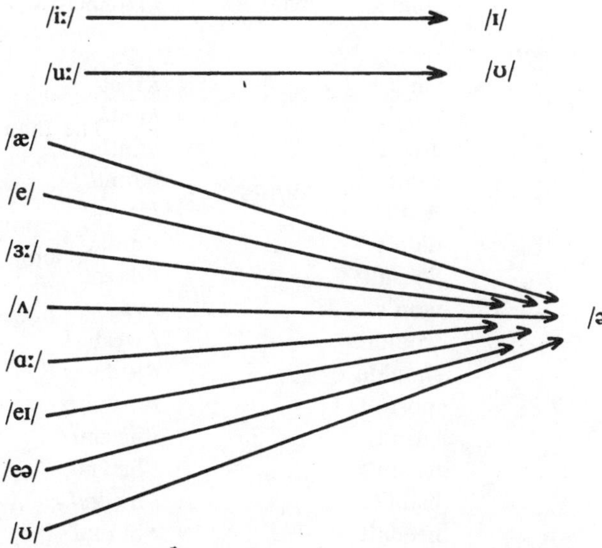

(3) In a few cases, even /ə/ disappears from the weakened pronunciations as, for example, in *for* /fr/ or *can* /kn/.

13.56 Contracted Forms

There are certain forms of words, in which either the severely reduced forms of auxiliary verbs, such as *is*, *are*, *have*, *has*, *had*, *will*, and *would*, are attached to the preceding subject, pronoun or noun (e.g. *he's* /hiːz/, *they're* /ðeə/, *we've* /wiːv/, and *John's* /dʒɒnz/) or the shortened form of *not* (i.e. *n't*) is attached to the preceding auxiliary verb (e.g. *doesn't* /'dʌznt/, *haven't* /'hævnt/ and *couldn't* /'kʊdnt/). Such forms of words are called *contracted forms*. A list of such words with their pronunciations is given below.

Personal pronoun/noun + auxiliary verb

I am	I'm	/aɪm/
I have	I've	/aɪv/
I had	I'd	/aɪd/
I would	I'd	/aɪd/
you are	you're	/jʊə(r)
you have	you've	/juːv/
you had	you'd	/juːd/
you would	you'd	/juːd/
(s)he is	(s)he's	/hiːz, ʃiːz/
(s)he has	(s)he's	/hiːz, ʃiːz/
(s)he will	(s)he'll	/hiːl, ʃiːl/
(s)he had	(s)he'd	/hiːd, ʃiːd/
(s)he would	(s)he'd	/hiːd, ʃiːd/
they are	they're	/ðeɪə(r)/ or /ðeə(r)/
they had	they'd	/ðeɪd/
John has	John's	/dʒɒnz/

Auxiliary verb + not

is not	isn't	/ˈɪznt/
are not	aren't	/ɑːnt/
am not	aren't	/ɑːnt/*
cannot	can't	/kɑːnt/
do not	don't	/dəʊnt/
did not	didn't	/ˈdɪdnt/
does not	doesn't	/ˈdʌznt/
will not	won't	/wəʊnt/
would not	wouldn't	/ˈwʊdnt/
should not	shouldn't	/ˈʃʊdnt/
must not	mustn't	/ˈmʌsnt/
has not	hasn't	/ˈhæznt/
have not	haven't	/ˈhævnt/
had not	hadn't	/ˈhædnt/
need not	needn't	/ˈniːdnt/
ought not	oughtn't	/ˈɔːtnt/

13.6 Juncture and Liaison

The term 'juncture' refers to the relationship of a particular sound with its immediately preceding and following sounds. Let us take the case of the words *might rain*. In rapid speech, these may be heard as /maɪt reɪn/ or /maɪ treɪn/. In /maɪt reɪn/, the relationship between /aɪ/ and /t/ is one of *close juncture*, whereas that between /t/ and /r/ is one of *open juncture*. In /maɪ treɪn/, on the other hand, the relationship between /aɪ/ and /t/ is one of *open juncture* and that between /t/

*The contracted form of *am not* is *aren't* /ɑːnt/.

and /r/ is one of *close juncture*. Again, in /maɪt reɪn/, /aɪ/ is shorter in duration than /aɪ/ in /maɪ treɪn/, and /t/ unaspirated as against its aspirated counterpart in /maɪ treɪn/. So if the identity of the words *might rain* is to be maintained as /maɪt reɪn/, then the junctural relationship between /aɪ/ and /t/, and between /t/ and /r/, as described above has to be preserved.

'Liaison', mostly represented in English as a 'linking' /r/ and 'intrusive' /r/, is in a way a special case of juncture. In RP, the letter *r* is usually not pronounced in the word-final position, but it is pronounced to link up two words when the first word ends with the letter *r* (or the letters *re*) and the second begins with a vowel sound. Look at the following examples:

66a My *father is* here. /ˈfɑːðər ɪz/
66b My *sister can* go. /ˈsɪstə kən/

The phoneme /r/ in 66a is called the linking /r/. Following this analogy, many RP speakers use /r/ to link up two words even when the first ends in a vowel sound, and not in the letter *r* or the letters *re*, and the second begins in a vowel sound. Look at these examples:

67 The *idea of* going it alone is frightful. /aɪˈdɪərəv/
68 The *India of* those days. /ˈɪndɪərəv/

The phoneme /r/ in 67 and 68 is called the 'intrusive' /r/ because, not being in the spelling, it literally intrudes.

13.7 Summary

Some words in connected speech are more prominent than others. Such words are said to be accented. Words which are accented are generally *content*, or *lexical*, words. These are nouns, main verbs other than *be*, adjectives, adverbs, the words *yes* and *no*, and demonstrative and interrogative pronouns. On the other hand, words which are not accented are generally *form*, or *grammatical*, words. These are pronouns (other than demonstrative and interrogative), helping verbs, articles, prepositions, and conjunctions.

The rhythm of English is often described as *stress-timed*. This is because accented (or 'stressed') syllables in English utterances tend to occur at approximately equal intervals of time, irrespective of the number of unaccented syllables between any two accented ones. As most of these unaccented syllables constitute form words or parts of form words, it is very difficult to maintain the characteristic rhythm of English unless these form words are pronounced in their *weak forms* when several of them come together between any two accented syllables. The learning of weak forms is therefore extremely necessary. Many non-native speakers of English, who generally use only strong forms of these words in their pronunciation, fail to approximate to the characteristic rhythm of English, thus reducing considerably the level of intelligibility of their pronunciation, especially in relation to native speakers of RP.

The term 'juncture' refers to the relationship between a sound and its immediately preceding and following sounds. The relationship between sounds within a word is called a 'close juncture' and that between sounds across words is called an 'open juncture'. The understanding of this concept is useful in that it helps disambiguate similar-sounding expressions such as *he lies* and *heal eyes*.

EXERCISES

A Listen and Repeat

I Listen to and repeat the teacher's (or recorded) pronunciation of the following groups of words:

1 'round 'table
2 'blue 'shirt
3 'beautiful 'woman
4 'very 'difficult
5 ex'tremely 'nice
6 'hot 'water
7 'quite 'fair
8 'well 'done
9 'badly 'torn
10 'almost de'stroyed
11 'bright 'light
12 'cold 'water
13 'English 'language
14 'too ex'pensive
15 'very 'well

II The accented syllables in the following exercise are spaced in an approximately regular rhythm. Listen to each rhythmic group and repeat it.

(1) 'Shoes /a 'pair of 'shoes / a 'new 'pair of 'shoes / a 'new 'pair of 'black 'shoes / a 'new 'pair of 'black 'canvas 'shoes / a 'brand 'new 'pair of 'black 'canvas 'shoes.

(2) A 'tower / an 'old 'tower / an 'old 'clock 'tower / a 'leaning 'old 'clock 'tower / a 'leaning 'old 'clock 'tower in the 'street / a 'leaning 'old 'clock 'tower at the 'end of the 'street.

III Each of the following 6 exercises has a different pattern of accented and unaccented syllables. Repeat them after the teacher. Remember to pronounce the weak forms of grammatical words exactly like the teacher. The pattern is indicated before each exercise, *I* representing an accented syllable, and *U* an unaccented one.

(i) *I U I*

1 'Try a'gain.
2 'Write it 'down.
3 'Draw a 'line.
4 'Ring me 'up.
5 'Sing a 'song.
6 'That's a 'lie.
7 'Go to 'sleep.
8 'Make the 'tea.
9 'Where's your 'hat?
10 'Jump the 'queue.

(ii) *I U U I*

1 'Give me a 'book.
2 'Give him some 'tea.

3 'Leave it a'lone.
4 'Show me the 'pen.
5 'Come for a 'swim.
6 'Send me the 'car.
7 'Meet him to'day.
8 'Bring me a 'chair.
9 'Where have you 'been?
10 'Kill him at 'once.

(iii) *U I U U U I*

1 He 'wanted me to 'go.
2 I 'promised to be 'good.
3 He 'needn't go to 'school.
4 We 'waited in the 'house.
5 You 'only have to 'say.
6 She 'wasn't on the 'line.
7 She's 'eaten all the 'bread.
8 I 'thanked him once a'gain.
9 We 'ought to take it 'home.
10 We'll 'see them in a 'month.

(iv) *U I U I U I*

1 The 'bus is 'very 'late.
2 We 'practised 'every 'day.
3 He 'didn't 'know the 'house.
4 I 'want to 'do it 'now.
5 The 'table is 'not yet 'laid.
6 She 'goes to 'work by 'train.
7 We 'played a 'game of 'chess.
8 I 'think he'll 'come at 'night.
9 We 'ought to 'know his 'trick.
10 It's 'not an 'easy 'chore.

(v) *U I U I U I U I*

1 I 'think he 'ought to 'come in 'time.
2 It's 'time he 'came to 'take us 'home.
3 He 'used to 'come to 'help us 'here.
4 The 'children 'went to 'bed at 'ten.
5 They 'say they 'have to 'leave at 'six.
6 He 'asked me 'not to 'leave to'day.
7 I'll 'try my 'best to 'pass the 'test.
8 He 'didn't 'want to 'go a'lone.
9 You've 'bought a 'cow to 'feed the 'cat.
10 The 'cat I 'need to 'scare the 'mice.

(vi) *U I U U I U U I U U I*

1 He 'says that he 'wanted to 'come in the 'day.
2 The 'quilt and the 'sheet have been 'put on your 'bed.
3 He 'tied up the 'files and then 'sent them by 'post.

4 It 'isn't the 'first time you've 'come at this 'hour.
5 You 'turn to the 'left at the 'end of the 'street.
6 The 'book you've just 'seen is the 'one that you 'lost.
7 I 'gave him the 'tip for the 'thing he has 'done.
8 We 'ought to be 'happy we 'haven't gone 'there.
9 He 'helped me a 'lot in the 'daily af'fairs.
10 An 'apple a 'day is the 'secret of 'health.

IV The following sentences consist of miscellaneous accentual patterns. Note, as you listen to and repeat them after the teacher, that the accented syllables tend to be fairly regularly spaced out.

1 He 'came 'late to the 'office 'yesterday.
2 I 'think he has for'gotten to 'leave his ad'dress.
3 It's 'very 'kind of you to 'come.
4 'Some people are 'simply 'difficult to 'deal with.
5 'Will you come 'over for a cup of 'tea?
6 I in'vited 'almost 'everybody to my 'son's 'wedding.
7 You can 'send out invi'tations to a 'dinner 'party.
8 'When was the 'steam 'engine in'vented?
9 He's be'come so 'fat that he's been ad'vised to 'diet.
10 The 'hungry 'girl de'voured her 'dinner.

B Recognition

Listen to the teacher's (or recorded) pronunciation of the sentences in the following 4 exercises, and mark the accent:

I

1 Show him out.
2 Put it back.
3 Switch it on.
4 Turn it off.
5 Look it up.
6 Invite them.
7 Stop her.
8 Take one.
9 Eat some.
10 Help him.

II

1 Pass me the salt, please.
2 I must get my hair cut.
3 Give me another one.
4 We asked her to find us a bigger one.
5 Let me help you complete the work.
6 She wants me to buy her some this morning.
7 Give him one if he wants it.

8 He bought himself a new one.
9 Please help yourself.
10 He himself gave it to me.

III

1 We must take them home just now.
2 He should have been taught how to do it.
3 They should have come here earlier.
4 We've been working through the night.
5 It would be better to call in the doctor.
6 We could have written all the letters by eight o'clock.
7 She's been knitting a white pullover.
8 They will be coming along later.
9 I would like to come sometime in the afternoon.
10 It would have been a good idea to have gone for a picnic in this weather.
11 I don't really think he can read it.
12 I shouldn't have gone there at all.
13 He won't be required to report for duty.

IV

1 Where have you put the books?
2 How far is it from here to Delhi?
3 Why can't you come in time?
4 What have you been doing the whole night?
5 How much do you owe him?
6 Have you phoned for the doctor yet?
7 Would you like to go with him?
8 Is it possible to help him now?
9 Did someone meet you at the station?
10 Can anybody tell me where they've gone?

C ***Production***

I In the following sentences the prepositions between the pronouns are more prominent than the pronouns. The teacher should therefore read out the sentences using the strong forms of the prepositions, and the students should produce them after him.

1 Tell it to me.
2 Send it to him.
3 Cut it for me.
4 Sell them to us.
5 Take him to them.
6 Put it on her.
7 He gave it to them.
8 We've stolen it from her.
9 He won't give them to her.
10 I bought them for him yesterday.

II The accent is marked in the following sentences. Say them in such a way that the accented syllables occur at regular time-intervals as far as possible.

1 'Tell him to 'come here as 'soon as 'possible.
2 He 'asked me if I could 'give him 'some 'money.
3 'Tell the other man to 'put all the things on the 'desk.
4 They 'ought to have pro'vided themselves with 'necessaries.
5 'This is 'not the time to be 'asking for a 'raise.
6 We'll 'tell the maid to 'clean it a'gain.
7 I 'don't think it'd be 'possible for him to 'read the 'letter.
8 It was sug'gested that he should ac'cept the 'challenge.
9 You must 'tell all the girls to 'go there and 'search.
10 'Let's 'start as 'early as we 'can.

III Mark the accent in the following sentences and say them in as regular a rhythm as possible, taking care to pronounce the weak forms correctly.

1 It was no trouble at all.
2 This is not the thing I wanted.
3 Would you mind calling me again?
4 I made up my mind to help him.
5 Her courage will carry her through.
6 Rising costs have made it hard to carry on business.
7 It's no business of your to oversee my work.
8 The dog rubbed itself against my legs.
9 The taxi-driver has brought us a long way round.
10 We must give him a good run for his money.

IV Write the following sentences in phonemic transcription, using the weak forms appropriate to the accentuation shown. (Practise saying these sentences as best as you can):

1 'Mary 'ate an 'apple and a 'pear.
2 We were the 'last to ar'rive at the 'gate.
3 'Come for a 'meal to my 'house to'morrow.
4 'How did you 'manage to be 'there in 'time?
5 'Wasn't it ex'tremely 'kind of him?
6 'Who will 'meet him at the 'airport?
7 I'll 'take them all a'way with me.
8 He 'doesn't 'want us to 'see them.
9 'What are you 'telling us a'bout them?
10 There are some 'more 'articles in the 'box.

V We now give some sentences for pronunciation practice. Write them in phonemic transcription, mark the accented syllables, and use the weak forms appropriate to the accentuation. After you have done this, say each of these sentences at least three times.

1 There were two of them.
2 He's never travelled by air.
3 What have they done?

4 It's been a very enjoyable evening for all of us.
5 You must promise to send a telegram on your arrival.
6 What time does the morning train for Kanpur leave?
7 He's not given me a full explanation.
8 She is more beautiful than her mother and sisters.
9 My elder son has decided not to take up engineering as a career.
10 Have you met his daughter before?
11 Give them some if they want it.
12 Read it out as well as you can.
13 Mr Brown is building a garage for her daughter.
14 I've been waiting the best part of an hour.
15 I wish you all the best!
16 It's very difficult to bend a bar of iron.
17 He left nothing but debts behind him.
18 There was an orchard behind the house.
19 The meeting will begin at seven o'clock.
20 His good bearing caused all the children to like him.
21 She beat me at chess.
22 We made an application to the court for an enquiry.
23 All of us want to go.
24 They met at the agreed time.
25 We could not agree how it should be done.

VI Describe the junctural relationship between the sounds in the following pairs of word groups:

1 ice cream; I scream
2 an aim; a name
3 night rate; nitrate
4 peace talks; pea stalks
5 keeps ticking; keep sticking
6 how strained; house trained

VII Study the following sentences and point out where RP speakers will use /r/ as a linking /r/ and where they will use it as an intrusive /r/:

1 The Shah of Persia had to abdicate.
2 The man standing there was the father of Mary.
3 This volume has been brought out in honour of Mr Bhatnagar.
4 The idea is not bad though its author is unpopular.
5 Who would bother about such small things?
6 China and India seem to be coming closer and closer.
7 Russia is caught in a great economic mess.
8 The more I try, the more I get depressed.

14

Assimilation

14.1 Introduction

We have seen that phonemes (see Chapter 6) are minimal sequential contrastive units of sound in the sound system of a language. Although, for the purpose of convenience, an utterance may be analyzed in terms of a sequence of phonemes (or segments), we should not forget that these phonemes are not discrete units neatly joining together to form that utterance. In fact, they are abstractions from a continuous flow of interacting and overlapping sounds. The sounds that actually occur in the flow share some, and in no case all, features with their corresponding phonemes. This is so because these actual occurrences (or realizations) are the sounds which have resulted from various adjustments between neighbouring articulatory postures. Since speech is a continuum and such adjustments are taking place all the time during speech, sounds in the continuum tend to be similar to their neighbouring sounds in one way or other. The process by which sounds adapt to, or become similar to, their neighbours is called 'assimilation'.

14.2 Scope of Assimilatory Changes

Assimilations affect both consonants and vowels. Vowels change only in two ways, which are discussed below.

14.21

First, they are nasalized when they are followed as well as preceded by nasal sounds:

/æ/ is nasalized [æ̃] in *man*.

Second, they are realized as longer sounds when they are followed by a voiced sound than when they are followed by a voiceless sound. And they are realized as still longer sounds when they occur finally in a syllable. Look at these examples:

seat	:	[si · t]	(i)
seed	:	[si : d]	(ii)
see	:	[si⁝]	(iii)

As indicated by the length marks in the transcriptions, the vowel in (iii) is longer than the vowel in (ii), and the vowel in (ii) is longer than the vowel in (i).

14.22

As for assimilations affecting consonants, they are mainly of three types: (a) those involving the place of articulation, (b) those in which the manner of articulation changes, and (c) those involving voice.

14.221 Assimilations involving place of articulation

Under such assimilations, consonants assimilate to the place of articulation of the following consonants. Look at these examples:

(i) /t/ assimilates to /p/ in *that boy* [ðæp bɔɪ]
(ii) /d/ becomes [d̪] in *sad thought* [sæd̪ θɔːt]
(iii) /n/ becomes /ŋ/ in *ten calls* [teŋ kɔːlz]
(iv) /t/ becomes [t̪] in *get these* [get̪ ðiːz]
(v) /s/ becomes /ʃ/ in *this sheet* [ðɪʃ ʃiːt]
(vi) /z/ becomes /ʒ/ in *his years* [hɪʒ jɜːz]
(vii) /l/ becomes [l̪] in *hail them* [heɪl̪ ðəm]
(viii) /m/ becomes [ɱ] in *comfort* [kʌɱfət]

It is clear from the above examples that the alveolar sounds /t, d, n, s, z, l/ are most likely to adapt to their following sounds.

14.222 Assimilations involving manner of articulation

Under such assimilations, consonants change in terms of their manner of articulation. The following examples will illustrate this:

(i) /t/ is laterally released [tᴸ] when it is followed by /l/ as in *bottle, cattle.*
(ii) /r/ becomes a fricative [ɹ̝] in *drab, bad room.*
(iii) /t/ may become /s/ in expressions like *that song.*
(iv) /j/ becomes a fricative [ç] in words like *cute, pupil, human.*
(v) /w/ becomes a fricative [ʍ] after the aspirated /t, k/ as in *quiet, twin.*

14.223 Assimilations involving voice

In such assimilations, consonants assimilate to their preceding or following sounds in terms of voice. Look at these examples:

(i) /n/ is partially devoiced [n̥] in such words as *snow.*
(ii) /r/ is fully devoiced [ɹ̥] when it is preceded by an aspirated /p/, /t/, or /k/ as in *press, try, crow, apprise.*
(iii) /l/ is fully devoiced [l̥] when it is preceded by an aspirated /p/ or /k/ as in *plain, clone, apply, declass, declare.*

14.3 Direction of Assimilatory Changes

In terms of direction, assimilatory adaptations or changes, which affect only consonants, are of two kinds: *regressive* and *progressive*. If a sound changes to become like its following sound, the assimilation is called *regressive* or *anticipatory*. The following examples illustrate this kind of assimilation.

(a) /l/ in *call* becomes dental [l̪] in *call them* under the influence of the dental /ð/ in /ðəm/.

(b) /s/ in *that's* becomes post-alveolar [s̱] in *that's real* under the influence of /r/, which is post-alveolar.

On the contrary, if a sound changes to become like its preceding sound, the assimilation is called *progressive*. The following examples illustrate such assimilation.

(c) /l/ in *play* is devoiced [l̥] under the influence of the preceding aspirated /p/.

(d) /r/ in *through* becomes a partially devoiced tap [ɾ̥] under the influence of the preceding voiceless dental fricative /θ/.

(e) /j/ in *huge* becomes a voiceless palatal fricative [ç] partly under the influence of the preceding /h/.

14.4 Extent of Assimilation

In respect of the degree of assimilatory change involved, which applies to consonants only, assimilations may be usefully classified into two categories: those involving allophonic changes and those involving phonemic changes.

14.41 Assimilations of the Allophonic Kind

Assimilations of the allophonic kind have already been dealt with in some detail (see Chapter 10). In such assimilations, phonemes become similar to their neighbouring phonemes in one or more of their phonetic features. That is to say, they are realized just as different allophones of their respective phonemes and do not change into different phonemes. Some examples are given below.

Within a word

(i) /w/ is devoiced [w̥] when it is preceded by an aspirated [tʰ] or [kʰ] as in *twice, question.*
(ii) /r/ becomes a tap [ɾ] when it occurs between two vowels as in *carry, very.*
(iii) /d/ is realized as a post-alveolar plosive [ḏ] as in *drum, address.*
(iv) /t/ is released laterally [tᴸ] when it is followed by /l/ as in *rattle, kettle, bottle, shuttle.*
(v) /n/ is realized as a dental nasal [n̪] as in *month, ninth.*

At word boundaries

(i) /l/ is devoiced [l̥] when it is preceded by a voiceless plosive as in *at least.*
(ii) /p/ is articulated with the rounded lips when it is followed by /w/ as in *cheap woman, shop window, tape-worm.*
(iii) /d/ is realized as a dental plosive [d̪] before a dental sound as in *add them, said that.*
(iv) /t/ is realized as a post-alveolar plosive [ṯ] if it is followed by /r/ as in *that race.*
(v) /m/ is realized as a labio-dental nasal [ɱ] when it is followed by a word beginning with /f/ or /v/ as in *come forth, same vest.*

14.42 Assimilations of the Phonemic Kind

In such assimilations, phonemes change into other phonemes under the influence of their neighbouring phonemes. (It may however be pointed out here that such changes are not essential for learners to acquire.) Examples of such changes are given below.

Within a word

(i) /n/ sometimes changes into /m/ when it occurs after /p/ as in *happen, open.*
(ii) /s/ sometimes changes to /z/ as in *resources.*

At word boundaries

(i) /d/ in *bad* /bæd/ may change into /t/ in *bad test* /bæt test/.
(ii) /n/ in *one* /wʌn/ may change into /m/ in *one place* /wʌm pleɪs/.
(iii) /s/ in *miss* /mɪs/ may become /ʃ/ in *Miss Shaw* /mɪʃ ʃɔː/.
(iv) /t/ in *that* /ðæt/ may become /k/ in *that course* /ðæk kɔːs/.
(v) /v/ in *of* /əv/ may change into /f/ in *of course* /əf kɔːs/.
(vi) /ɡ/ in *big* /bɪɡ/ may become /k/ in *big cat* /bɪk kæt/.

14.5 Summary

Phonemes are not discrete units of sounds combining sequentially to constitute utterances or continua of speech. In fact, they are abstractions from a continuous flow of interacting and overlapping sounds. The sounds that actually occur in a speech continuum result from various adjustments between neighbouring articulatory postures. As a result of these adjustments, sounds in the continuum tend to be similar to their neighbouring sounds in one way or another. The process by which sounds become similar to their neighbours is called *assimilation.*

Assimilations affect both consonants and vowels. Vowels assimilate in two ways only: They are *nasalized* when they are followed as well as preceded by nasal sounds. Secondly, they are realized as *longer* or *shorter* depending upon whether they are followed by silence or a voiced sound, or a voiceless sound. As for consonants, they assimilate in three ways, that is, in terms of their *place of articulation, manner of articulation,* and *voice.*

In terms of the direction of assimilatory changes, assimilations are generally classified as *regressive* and *progressive.* In the former, the following sound affects its preceding one; in the latter, on the contrary, the preceding sound affects its following one.

Finally, in respect of the degree of changes, assimilations may be divided into two kinds. The first kind comprises assimilations of the *allophonic* kind, in which phonemes change in respect of some of their features but remain the same phonemes. The second kind comprises assimilations of the *phonemic* kind, in which phonemes change into different phonemes.

EXERCISES

I Say whether the following assimilations are regressive or progressive:

1 /t/ becomes [t̪] in *that theory* [ðæt̪ θɪərɪ].
2 /m/ becomes [ɱ] in *comfy* [kʌɱfɪ].
3 /n/ becomes [ŋ] in *ten cards* [teŋ kɑːdz].
4 /n/ becomes [n̪] in *tenth* [ten̪θ].
5 /l/ is devoiced [l̥] in *place* [pʰl̥eɪs].
6 /r/ becomes a fricative [ɹ̝] in *drain* [dɹ̝eɪn].
7 /n/ is partially devoiced [n̥] in *snail* [sn̥eɪl].

II Say whether the following assimilations are of the phonemic kind or the allophonic kind:

1 /t/ in *that* becomes post-alveolar [t̠] in *that room.*
2 /l/ becomes dental [l̪] in words such as *stealth, healthy.*
3 /d/ is laterally released [dᴸ] in *saddle, hurdle, bad luck.*
4 /b/ in *tube* may become /p/ in *tube please.*
5 /d/ in *good* may become /t/ in *good tour.*
6 /s/ changes to /ʃ/ in *this shoe.*
7 /z/ changes to /ʒ/ in *his shawl.*

III Name the changes involved in the following assimilations in terms of the manner of articulation, the place of articulation, and voice in respect of consonants, and in terms of nasalization and length in respect of vowels:

1 /t/ becomes [t̪] in *get those* [get̪ ðəʊz].
2 /m/ becomes [ɱ] in *symphony* [sɪɱfənɪ].
3 /l/ becomes [l̪] in *call them* [kɔːl̪ ðəm].
4 /t/ may become /p/ in *that place* [ðæp pleɪs].
5 /j/ becomes a fricative [ç] in *huge* [hçuːdʒ].
6 /r/ becomes a tap [ɾ] in *three* [θɾiː].
7 /s/ becomes post-alveolar [s̠] in *that's right.*
8 /n/ may change into /m/ in *open.*
9 /uː/ may be realized as [ũː] in *noon* or *moon.*
10 /iː/ is realized as [i.] in *seat*, as [iː] in *seed*, and as [iː] in *see.*

15
Intonation

15.1 Introduction

In Chapter 1, we studied the vibration of the vocal cords and saw that it produces a kind of musical note ('hum'), called *voice*. The vocal cords are capable of vibrating at varying rates. Now, the number of cycles per second (cps) at which they vibrate is called the *frequency of vibration*, which determines the *pitch* of the voice. The higher the frequency, the higher the pitch, and vice versa.

No language in the world is spoken on a monotone (i e on the same musical note) all the time. It is very rarely that we speak with an unvarying pitch. In normal speech, the pitch of our voice goes on changing constantly: now going up, now going down, and sometimes remaining level or steady. Different pitches of the voice combine to form patterns of pitch variation, or *tones*, which together constitute the intonation of a language. The intonation of a language, thus, refers to the patterns of pitch variation, or the tones, it uses in its utterances.

15.2 The Form and Function of Intonation in English

We shall discuss the intonation of English in relation to both its *form* and *function*. Under the form of intonation, we shall study in some detail the nature of pitch variations in English; under the function of intonation, we shall examine how some of these pitch variations are linguistically significant and communicate meaning.

15.21 The Nature of Pitch Variations

The nature of pitch variations will be studied under Tone Group, Tonic Syllable, and Nuclear Tone.

15.211 Tone group

A stretch of speech over which *one pattern of pitch variations*, or *contour* of pitch, extends is called a *tone group* (or a *tone unit*). A tone group may thus consist of one syllable or more than one syllable. A short utterance quite often forms a single tone group, while a longer one is made up of two or more. While speaking, we divide long utterances into small, manageable groups of words, between which we pause. So a tone group may also be defined as a stretch of speech between any two pauses. Very often, punctuation also helps in determining tone groups in a particular utterance, though it is not always a reliable guide. A few examples given below should make the concept of the tone group clear. The tone group boundary is indicated by an oblique sign.

1 Yes.
2 I'll come tomorrow.
3 Why don't you help me?
4 I'm not afraid of them.
5 The door has been opened.
6 I want to finish this work / before he returns.
7 Please do it now / if you have time.
8 If he comes back by tomorrow, / we can manage the show.
9 Do you know / that he is planning to write a book / on the controversial subject of higher education?
10 They have plenty of time, / but we haven't / in spite of the holidays.

Sentences 1-5 consist of one tone group each. There is no pause anywhere between them, and they are all said with one pattern of pitch changes coterminous (that is, beginning and ending) with each tone group. Sentences 6-8 contain two tone groups each and sentences 9 and 10 contain three each, since in all of them we pause at the point indicated by the oblique bar, and each of these word groups separated by the bars forms a compact unit, marked off from the next by a particular intonation pattern. Sentence 8, for example, has two contours of pitch, clearly dividing it into two tone groups:

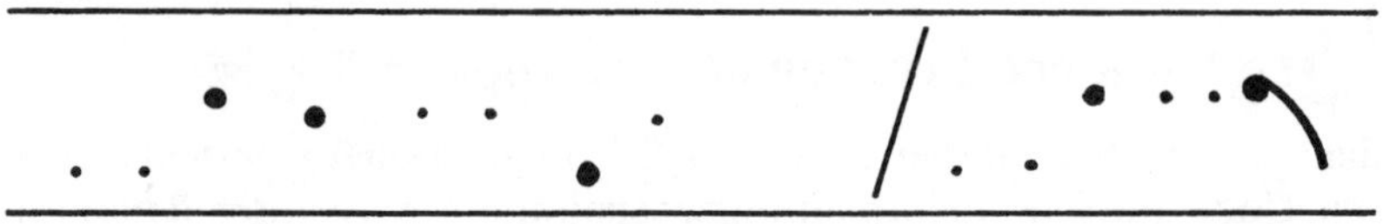

If he 'comes 'back by to'morrow, / we can 'manage the 'show.

15.212 Tonic syllable

Within a tone group comprising more than one syllable, there is one syllable that stands out from amongst the rest of the syllables because it initiates a major change in pitch direction. This kind of syllable is called the *nucleus* of the tone group, or the *tonic syllable*. Let us look at the following sentences.

11 The 'postman 'didn't come '*yes*terday.
12 'Have you 'met my 'brother be'*fore*?

In sentence 11, the syllable *yes-* is more prominent than *post-* and *did-*, and in sentence 12, the syllable *-fore* stands out from *Have*, *met* and *bro-*, because both (i e *yes-* and *-fore*) initiate on themselves a major change in the direction of the already varying pitch. These two syllables are said with moving or *kinetic tones*. The other accented syllables in these two sentences are said with level (unmoving) or *static tones*. In other words, a tonic syllable is one that carries the kinetic tone in the tone group. Incidentally, the kinetic tone is also sometimes called the *nuclear* tone, as its placement determines the location of the nucleus of the tone group.

We know now that each tone group has one tonic syllable, or nucleus, on which a major pitch movement is initiated. It is not arbitrarily, however, that a particular syllable in a tone group is made its nucleus. Generally, the choice (of the nucleus) is determined by the meaning that the speaker wants to convey. Only that syllable is made the nucleus, or carries the nuclear tone, which the speaker may wish to make most prominent. The examples that follow illustrate this (the nucleus being italicized in each case).

13a 'John 'generally 'leaves at 'seven in the '*morn*ing. (*morn-* is the nucleus here. The speaker possibly wants to emphasize that John leaves at seven in the morning, and not in the evening.)

13b 'John 'generally 'leaves at '*se*ven in the 'morning. (*se-* is the nucleus here. The speaker wants to say that John leaves at seven o'clock, and not earlier or later than seven.)

13c 'John 'generally '*leaves* at 'seven in the 'morning. (By placing the nuclear tone on *leaves*, the speaker wants to say that he is talking about John's leaving, and not getting up, etc.)

13d 'John '*gen*erally 'leaves at 'seven in the 'morning. (Here *gen-* is the nucleus. What the speaker wants to convey is that there may be occasions when John fails to leave at seven.)

13e '*John* 'generally 'leaves at 'seven in the 'morning. (*John* is made the nucleus here, because the speaker wants to say this about John, and not Tom or Mary.)

In the above one tone-group utterance, the speaker can make any part of it prominent, depending upon what he intends to say. The tonic syllable in each case is the focus of the information which is being conveyed. As the focus shifts from one syllable to another, a different kind of information is conveyed. It is however not always the case that a particular syllable in a tone group has to be made specially prominent. Sometimes there is no contrast involved, such as we find in sentence 13, and therefore no particular part of the tone group carries 'new' information (or focus of information): the entire tone group carries new information. In such cases, the last important word (or the last accented syllable in the last important word) in the tone group is made the nucleus. Let us look at the following utterances (nucleus italicized):

14 It may 'rain to'*mo*rrow. (*-mo-*, the accented syllable in the last important word, is the nucleus.)

15 I 'can't '*do* it. (*do*, the last important word, is the nucleus.)

16 I 'think it's 'quite '*fair*.

17 In 'spring it 'rains a '*lot*.

18 She 'lunches 'rather '*ear*ly. (*ear-*, the accented syllable in the last important word, is the nucleus.)

19 'Nothing can 'save him '*now*.

20 I don't under'stand it at '*all*.

21 Do you 'want me to '*stay*?

22 'This is 'not the way to 'work for a '*living*. (*liv-*, the accented syllable in *living*, is the nucleus.)

23 I 'doubt if he'll a'gree to '*come*.

15.213 Nuclear tone

The nuclear tone refers to the kinetic tone carried by the tonic syllable, or the nucleus, in a tone group. Unlike static or level tones, it is a major change in pitch direction. An accented syllable in a tone group is said on a level pitch, high or low, but the most prominent syllable in it (i e the nucleus) is said with a changing pitch. This changing pitch, or tone, is of several different kinds, the most important of which are called *fall*, *rise*, *fall-rise*, and *rise-fall*. The *fall* and *rise* can be subdivided into *high fall* and *low fall*, and *high rise* and *low rise*, respectively. These tones, together with the signs with which they are generally marked in a text, and their graphic representations, are given below. The parallel lines between which the nuclear tones are represented circumscribe the normal human pitch range (namely, the upper and lower limits of the human voice):

1. High fall :	the pitch falling from very high to very low.	[ˋ]	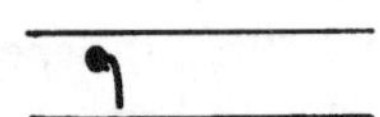
2. Low fall :	the pitch falling from mid to very low.	[ˎ]	
3. High rise :	the pitch rising from (a) mid to high, or (b) low to high.	[ˊ]	
4. Low rise :	the pitch rising from low to mid level, or a little above.	[ˏ]	
5. Fall-rise :	the pitch falling from about mid level to low and then rising to more or less the same level. The fall and rise may be (a) within one syllable, or (b) on different syllables.	[ˇ]	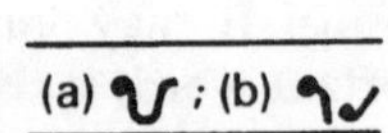
6. Rise-fall :	the pitch rising from low to about mid and then falling to low.	[ˆ]	

While these six nuclear tones should suffice for the purpose of our course, it must be borne in mind that there is considerable variation of pitch movement within each of these nuclear tones. For example, the falling tone has, in practice, variants which cannot be described as just high fall or low fall; the rising tone also has variants which cannot be described simply as high rise and low rise. And then, there are 'compound' tones, such as falling plus low-rising, and rising-falling plus low-rising, which in *form* are combinations of these six nuclear tones.

In the examples given earlier (see section 15.212), we marked the accented syllables with a vertical bar above and in front of them. We can now refine our marking in order to indicate somewhat precisely how a particular tone group is to be said. In the following examples, we shall mark the tonic syllable with one of the above tone signs and the other accented syllables (which are said on a level pitch) with ['] and [ˌ], the first showing a high level and the second a low level pitch. (The student will do well to listen carefully to the teacher's, or model, pronunciation of these sentences.)

24 ˌCan he be 'quite ˏsure?
25 'When do you ˏwant it?
26 'Will you come ˌover for a cup of ˏtea?
27 It 'all 'went ˎwrong.
28 'Put it 'on the ˎdesk.
29 ˌWhy do you ˋwant it?
30 I ˌquite aˋgree with him.
31 ˌHave you ˌbought the ˎtickets?
32 She 'won't be ˏlong.
33 ˌCan you ˊcome?
34 ˌCan he afˇford it?
35 We 'haven't 'much ˇappetite?
36 I'm ˋwaiting.
37 It was ˆhorrid.
38 ˌCan you be ˆsure?

In the sentences given above, we have marked high fall, low fall, high rise, and low rise wherever they occur. However, in the rest of our description, for the sake of simplicity, we shall mark the falling and rising nuclear tones (whether high or low) with [ˋ] and [ˏ] respectively, and the accented syllables (whether said on a high, or low, level pitch) with only ['], with the exception that the level-pitch accented syllables between nuclear syllables, and also after a nuclear syllable, will be marked with [ˌ].

15.214 Structure of the tone group

We have so far studied the nature of pitch variations, or the form of intonation. In order to examine the function of intonation, it will be necessary first to look at the structure of the tone group, that is, the units that constitute it. The first accented syllable (viz the syllable said on a level pitch, high or low) in a tone group, if any, is called the *head*; the tonic syllable is called the *nucleus*; the syllable or syllables occurring between the head and the nucleus, if any, make up the *body*; the syllable or syllables before the head, if any, constitute the *pre-head*; and the syllable or syllables coming after the nucleus, if any, are called the *tail*. For the purpose of illustration, nine tone groups are analysed in Table 2 in terms of their structure.

Table 2 Analysis of Nine Tone Groups in Terms of Their Structure

Serial number	*Pre-head*	*Head*	*Body*	*Nucleus*	*Tail*
1	We	'went	to 'stay with our 'cousins in	\`Lon-	-don.
2	But he's	'not	'really	\`in-	-terested in it.
3		'What	a 'stupid mi-	-\`stake!	
4		'Can	you 'tell me the 'time it	ˏo-	-pens?
5		'Do	sit	ˏdown	
6	I am			ˇwait-	-ing.
7	Do			\`you	ˌlike it?
8				\`Does-	-n't he?
9				\`When?	

It will be clear from this table that the nucleus is the only obligatory unit, all the rest being optional. This means that there cannot be a tone group without the nucleus.

15.22 ***The Function (or Role) of Intonation***

Intonation is not a mere melody (i e pattern or contour) of pitch variations, superadded to an utterance already complete in all respects and ready to yield its full meaning without this addition; it is complementary to it. In other words, it does not play a mere decorative role, but performs a *linguistic function*. It is part of English grammar in very much the same way as tense, or mood, or different types of subordinate clause, which we are accustomed to regarding as parts of grammar, and conveys distinctions of 'meaning' in the same way.

15.221 Grammatical function

In the first place, intonation distinguishes different types of sentence. For example, the difference between the following two sentences, which are grammatically identical, is only one of intonation:

39a He is ar'riving ˋlate. (statement)
39b He is ar'riving ˏlate? (question)

Similarly, the difference between a command and a request is that the former is said with a falling tone and the latter with a rising one as in the following pair of sentences:

40a 'Shut the ˋdoor. (command)
40b 'Shut the ˏdoor. (request)

Secondly, intonation performs this grammatical function in another way too. It is intonation which helps the speaker divide longer utterances into smaller, grammatically relevant word groups (in this case, tone groups), each carrying a different pattern of pitch changes and indicating for the listener whether a particular tone group is a complete or incomplete utterance. The following example will illustrate this:

41 'When you ˏcome here, (incomplete) / I'll 'get you what you ˋwant. (complete)

Thirdly, intonation signals the precise kind of grammatical subordination of a relative clause to its main clause. The relative clause functions as a defining clause if it forms part of the same tone group as its antecedent, whereas it functions as a non-defining clause if it forms a separate tone group. Look at the following pair of sentences:

41a Bill's wife *who lives in Delhi*/has been convicted. (defining clause)
41b Bill's wife, /*who lives in Delhi*/, has been convicted. (non-defining clause)

Here, 41a means that Bill has more than one wife, and the one who lives in Delhi has been convicted. 41b, on the other hand, means that Bill has only one wife.

15.222 Attitudinal function

Intonation is perhaps the chief means by which the speaker conveys his attitudes and emotions. The grammar of an utterance does not reveal in any noticeable way whether the speaker's attitude is one of politeness, assertiveness, incredulity, querulousness, etc. In other words, intonation makes distinctions of 'meaning' (attitudinal nuances) to which grammar most often gives no structural clues. Thus we can say that intonation also performs an attitudinal function. The following pairs of sentences will show how intonation signals the speaker's attitudes and emotions.

42a 'When can you ˋcome?
42b 'When can you ˏcome?
43a He is 'very ˋgood.

43b He is 'very ˇgood.
44a ˋThank you.
44b ˏThank you.
45a He'll ˋfall.
45b He'll ˇfall.

Sentence 42, when said with a falling tone, as in 42a, is a normal question, neither polite nor impolite. When said with a rising tone, on the other hand, as in 42b, it expresses politeness, even deference. As for the second pair, 43a, which is said with a falling tone, is a plain statement, whereas 43b, which is said with a falling-rising tone, expresses reservation on the part of the speaker: it means something like 'but you don't know the other side of the picture'. In sentence 44, "Thank you" expresses a feeling of genuine gratitude, when said with a falling tone (44a), but sounds rather casual, when said with a rising tone (44b). And in 45a, the falling tone indicates that the speaker is uninterested, while in 45b, the falling-rising tone expresses the speaker's concern for *He*. (See also Section 15.4.)

15.223 Accentual function

Intonation performs an accentual function in that it enables the speaker to make any part of his utterance prominent in accordance with the meaning he would convey. As we saw in section 15.212, any part of an utterance can be specially emphasized or focussed by choosing the appropriate nucleus, i e by putting the tonic on the appropriate syllable. In an utterance said in isolation (i e out of context), or for the first time in a certain given context, no particular part of it supplies 'new' information, and therefore it need not be emphasized or focussed. In such cases, the tonic is placed on (the accented syllable of) the last important (or content) word in the tone group. Let us look at the following sentences:

46a X: They 'told me at the ˏstation / that the 'train 'leaves at ˋseven.
46b Y: ˋWho ˌtold you ˌthis?
46c X: The 'man at the enˋquiry ˌoffice ˌtold me.

In sentence 46a, the entire information being 'new', the tonic is placed on the accented syllables of the last important words *station* and *seven* in the two tone groups. In sentence 46b, *Who* carries the tonic and becomes the focus of information: *told* and *this* are (already) 'given'. In sentence 46c, it is *enquiry* which conveys the new information and hence receives accentual prominence. (*man*, *office*, and *told* only refer back to, or repeat, what has already been said.)

It is clear from this short conversation between X and Y that there can be no meaningful communication between them unless they give accentual prominence to (or place the tonic on) the appropriate word or syllable, as they get along. Thus we can say that intonation (i e its accentual function) helps distinguish between the 'new' and the 'given', and thereby enables the speaker to determine the choice of the tonic syllable. In other words, intonation, in its accentual role, conveys 'meaning' in the sense that it helps speakers communicate as it helps X and Y in the above dialogue.

15.224

We can safely conclude from the foregoing sections that intonation is by no means merely ornamental or decorative in value. It is extremely important in that it performs a linguistic function in very much the same way as grammar does. In the organization and communication of meaning, it is complementary to grammar: no sentence, however carefully constructed grammatically, can convey the desired message unless it is said with appropriate intonation. In all the three functions it performs, grammatical, attitudinal, and accentual, it conveys meaning in one sense or another.

15.3 Uses of Tones

We have seen so far that every utterance has one or more than one tone group and every tone group has its own pattern, or contour, of pitch variation. We have also seen that this pattern will depend upon the number of accented syllables in a particular tone group, the location of the tonic syllable in it, and the nature of the change of pitch direction on the tonic syllable. In this section, we shall try to establish a kind of correlation between the various types of sentence (or tone group) and the tones with which they are generally said.

But while listing the types of sentence, which would be said with the falling tone, the rising tone, etc, we shall not take into account the variants of these tones, e.g. high fall, low fall, etc, mentioned in section 15.213. We shall also ignore for the time being the variations of pitch levels that take place in the pre-tonic section (viz up to the tonic syllable) of the tone group. Thus every accented syllable said on a level pitch, high or low, will be marked with ['] (except those occurring between and after nuclear syllables), and the fall, rise, fall-rise, and rise-fall with [`], [ˏ], [ˇ] and [ˆ], respectively.

15.31 Falling Tone

The following types of sentence are generally said with a falling tone:

(i) *Statements which are complete and definite*

He's 'just been pro`moted.
He 'made me 'feel at `ease.
I 'didn't 'do it on `purpose.

(ii) *Wh- questions which are matter-of-fact and intended to be neither polite nor impolite*

'Where are you `going?
How 'long will it 'take you to `come here?
'Why should he 'grudge me my 'first pro`motion?
'Who is `knocking at the ˏdoor?

(iii) *Commands*

'Shut the `window.
'Don't make a `noise.
'Take the 'boy to the `doctor.

(iv) *Invitations*
Come 'over for a cup of `tea.
Why 'don't you 'come and `dine with me?

(v) *Exclamations*
'Good `heavens!
Fan`tastic!
'What a 'fine `weather!
Oh, 'this is 'too `much!
'How `beautiful!

(vi) *Tag-questions forcing the listener to agree with the speaker*
You're `coming to ˌday / `aren't you?
He 'can't `help it / `can he?

15.32 Rising Tone

The rising tone is used with the following tone groups:

(i) *Yes/no type question*
Are you 'leaving for 'Delhi toˏday?
Was he 'present ˏyesterday?

(ii) *Statement intended to be a question*
You 'won't ˏcome?
He 'isn't ˏgoing?
You 'don't 'want to 'lend me the ˏbook?

(iii) *Non-terminal tone group*
If you 'don't come in ˏtime... (I'll `leave).
When'ever she ˏcalls on us... (she 'creates `problems).
Un'less you de'cide to sucˏceed... (you `can't sucˌceed).
I'll inˏform you... (if he `comes).

(iv) *Terminal tone group said as an afterthought*
I'll 'not op`pose him / if you ˏlike.
You're 'going a`way / I supˏpose.

(v) *Request*
'Pass me the 'salt ˏplease.
'Listen to me for a ˏminute.

(vi) *Command intended to sound like a request*
'Close the ˏdoor.
'Don't dis'turb me at ˏodd ˌhours.
'Don't be ˏlate.

(vii) *Wh- question showing politeness, friendliness, warmth, personal interest*
'How is your ˏson?
'What is your ˏname ˌchild?

(viii) *Repetition-question which repeats someone else's question, or wants him to repeat some information*

ˏWhat did I ˌsay?

(It will take me two hours.) ˏHow ˌlong?

15.33 Falling-rising Tone

The following tone groups are generally said with the falling-rising tone:

(i) *Incomplete statement leading to a following tone group*

If you 'don't beˇhave, / (I'll 'punish you seˋverely).

(ii) *Statement intended to be a 'correction' of the information received*

(He has three sons.) He has ˇfour.

(She teaches English.) ˇFrench.

(He can't speak Hindi.) He 'can't 'speak 'Hindi ˋvery ˏwell.

(iii) *Statement intended to be a warning/reproach, or to express concern*

You 'mustn't 'go like ˇthis. (warning)

(I'm going to jump over the wall.) ˇCareful. (concern)

(I want all this money.) You might 'give some to your ˇbrother. (reproach)

(iv) *Imperative meant to be a pleading request*

ˋDon't ˌget on my ˏnerves.

ˋDo atˌtend to his reˏquest.

ˋCome as ˌsoon as you ˏcan.

(v) *Statement which shows a kind of reservation on the part of the speaker*

He's ˇgood. (but I can't trust him)

I can 'do it toˇmorrow. (but not today)

His per'formance 'wasn't ˇbad. (you must admit)

You 'owe him an aˇpology. (you must admit)

I ad'mire your ˇcourage. (I must admit)

15.34 Rising-falling Tone

The following tone groups are said with the rising-falling tone:

(i) *Statement showing enthusiastic agreement*

It was ˆhorrid.

ˆYes.

Of ˆcourse.

(ii) *Question showing suspicion, indignation, incredulity, or mockery*

'What has he been ˆdoing? (suspicious)

'Will you be 'able to ˆdo it? (mocking, suspicious)

'Can you 'finish it by toˆmorrow? (knowing, suspicious)

(iii) *Imperative expressing petulance, haughtiness*

'Go and 'break your ˆhead. (haughty)

'Come and 'face the ˆmusic. (petulant, supercilious)

(iv) *Exclamation expressing sarcasm, irony*

'How ˆgood for you! (sarcasm)

'Good ˆevening. (ironical)
Oh, ˆreally. (sarcasm)

15.4 Tones in Relation to Attitudes

In Section 15.3, we focussed on the grammatical role of intonation rather than on its attitudinal function. In this section, we shall concentrate on how the various pitch patterns, or tones, convey various attitudes and emotions in respect of various types of sentence. However, since attitudes may come into play even in the discussion of the grammatical role of intonation, there may occur, in this section, some overlap with Section 15.3.

Note that the examples given in each subsection bring out attitudinal contrasts.

15.41 Wh-questions

(1) 'Where are you ˋgoing?
'What's your ˋname?
(Falling tone: matter-of-fact enquiries—neither polite nor impolite)

(2) 'Where are you ˏgoing?
'What's your ˏname?
(Rising tone: enquiries showing politeness, warmth, and friendliness)

15.42 Tag-questions

(3) (You're ˋcoming toˌday,) ˋaren't you?
(Falling tone: authoritative, almost forcing the listener to agree)

(4) (You're ˋcoming toˌday,) ˏaren't you?
(Rising tone: seeking the listener's confirmation, but at the same time giving him/her the option to disagree)

15.43 Statements

(5) She's 'very ˋbeautiful.
(Falling tone: a matter-of-fact statement)

(6) She's 'very ˇbeautiful.
(Falling-rising tone: showing certain unstated reservations on the part of the speaker, e.g. '... but, I'm not sure how good she is at her work.')

(7) I 'can't 'lend my 'books to ˋanybody.
(Falling tone: a matter-of-fact statement, meaning: I don't lend my books at all.)

(8) I 'can't 'lend my 'books to ˇanybody.
(Falling-rising tone on *anybody*, meaning: I can possibly lend my books to some special people, but not to all.)

15.44 Commands/Requests

(9) 'Sit ˋdown.
(Falling tone: command)

(10) 'Sit ˏdown.
(Rising tone: request)

15.45 Yes/No Questions

(11) Are you ˋsure?
(Falling tone: demanding an answer)

(12) Are you ˏsure?
(Rising tone: seeking an answer)

(13) Is it ˊpossible?
(high rising tone: expressing surprise)

(14) Is it ˏpossible?
(Low rising tone: normal, matter-of-fact enquiry)

15.46 Greetings

(15) 'Good ˋmorning.
(High falling tone: cheerful, hearty greeting)

(16) ˌGood ˏmorning.
(Rising tone: perfunctory greeting)

Notice that, with the rising tone, while *good morning* is a perfunctory greeting, *good evening* is a cheerful one, especially when *good* is said on a high pitch.

15.47 Saying 'thanks'

(17) ˋThank you.
(Fallling tone: genuine and proper expression of gratitude)

(18) ˏThank you.
(Rising tone: customary and routine thanks)

15.48 Saying 'All right'

(19) 'All ˋright.
(Falling tone: carrying the effect of a threat)

(20) 'All ˏright.
(Rising tone: normal)

15.5 Summary

The pitch of the voice is determined by the frequency (i e number of cycles per second) of vibration of the vocal cords. In normal speech, the pitch of the voice goes on changing all the time. Different pitches of the voice combine to form certain patterns of pitch variation, called *tones*. The intonation of a given language refers to the tones it makes use of in its utterances.

A stretch of speech over which one tone extends is called a *tone group*. A short utterance quite often forms a single tone group, whereas longer utterances may be divided into two or more than two tone groups. Every tone group has one *tonic syllable* (the *nucleus*), which stands out from amongst the rest of the accented syllables in that tone group by initiating on itself a change in pitch direction. A tone group is said to have a falling tone, rising tone, etc, depending upon the kind of change in pitch direction (that is, whether the pitch falls, rises, etc) initiated on its tonic syllable.

Intonation performs a linguistic function, viz it helps convey distinctions of 'meaning'. In its grammatical role, it distinguishes types of sentence; in its attitudinal functions, which cannot quite be separated from its grammatical function, it helps the speaker convey his attitudes and emotions by using appropriate tones; and in its accentual function, it renders any part of a tone group prominent, depending upon what meaning is intended to be conveyed.

The uses of tones, with reference to the grammatical function of intonation mainly (see Section 15.3), are summarized in Fig. 41 in the form of a schematic diagram, which will serve as a general guideline.

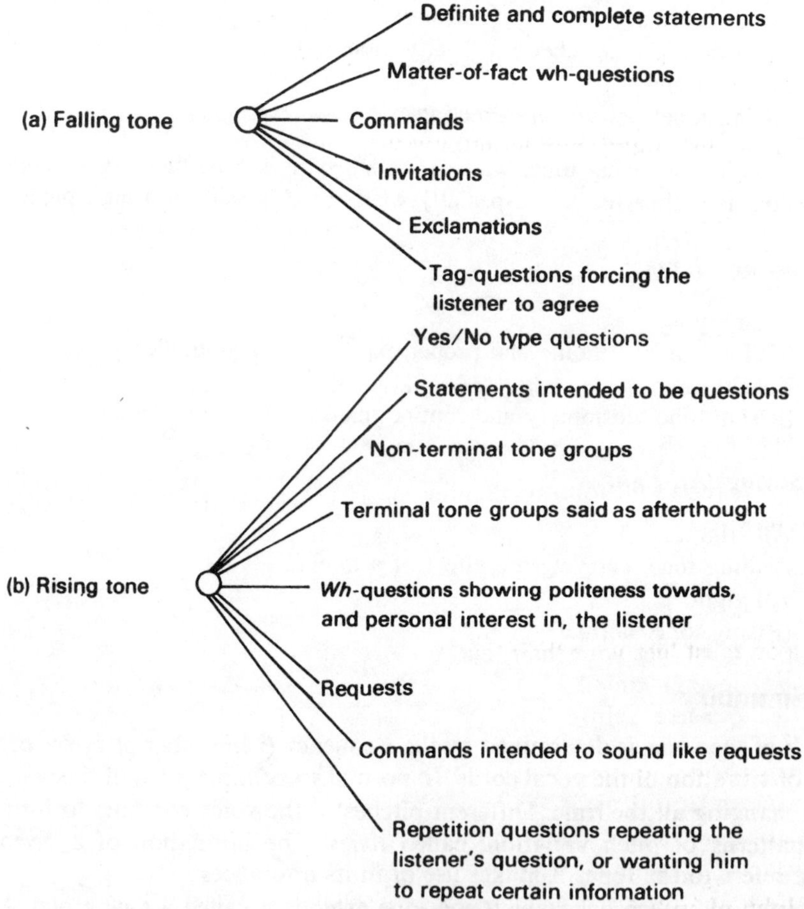

Fig. 41 (*Contd.*)

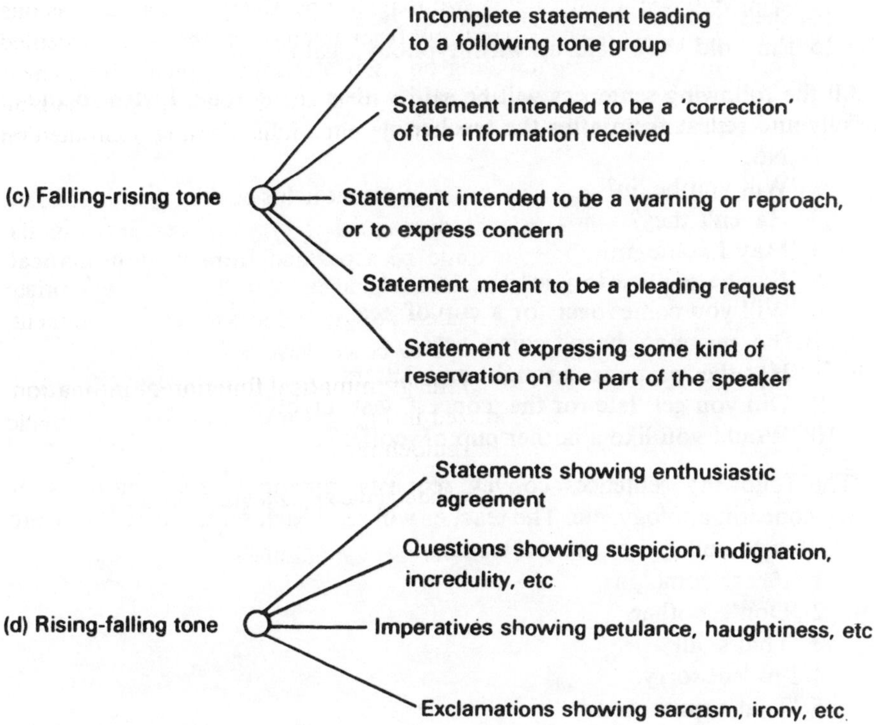

Fig. 41

EXERCISES

A Listen and Repeat

I Listen to and repeat the following sentences. All the sentences will be said with a falling tone.

1 We're `late.
2 I `know.
3 You're `right.
4 You must 'get your `hair ,cut.
5 We 'haven't `time.
6 It 'looks like `rain.
7 'Let's 'go for a little `stroll.
8 'What's the `time?
9 'Where do you `live?
10 'Where does he 'want to `go?
11 'Who would 'like to 'ask for a `ride?
12 'John plays 'cricket every 'Friday `morning.
13 It's been a 'very de'lightful `evening.

14 She's 'reading a most 'interesting ˋbook.
15 I'm 'told she's 'laid up with ˋtyphoid aˌgain.

II All the following sentences will be said with a rising tone. Listen to them carefully and repeat them after the teacher.

1 ˏNo.
2 'Will you be ˏin?
3 ˏHaven't they?
4 'May I come ˏin?
5 'Has he reˏplied to you?
6 'Will you come 'over for a cup of ˏtea?
7 The ˏpostman ˌhasn't come ˌyet?
8 'Has the 'postman 'brought any ˏletters?
9 'Did you get 'late for the ˏconcert ˌlast ˌnight?
10 'Would you like a'nother cup of ˏcoffee?

III The following sentences convey requests, greetings, and emotions of sorrow, concern, apology, etc. The teacher will read each sentence with a rising tone. Listen to and repeat them after him.

1 'Please come ˏin.
2 'Don't ˏbother.
3 'That's ˏall.
4 I'm 'so ˏsorry.
5 'That's quite ˏgood.
6 'Good ˏmorning.
7 'Goodˏbye.
8 It's 'all ˏright.
9 I 'shan't be ˏlong.
10 'Open the ˏwindow.
11 I 'beg your ˏpardon.
12 'Don't lose ˏheart.
13 'Bring me a ˏchair.
14 'Take ˏcare.
15 'Be a ˏsport.

IV The following sentences will be said by the teacher with a falling-rising tone. Repeat them after him.

1 ˇYes.
2 ˇCareful.
3 He's ˇgood.
4 She 'isn't very ˇpretty.
5 This 'isn't ˇyours.
6 She 'said she'd come aˇlone.
7 You're 'going there in the ˇmorning.
8 ˋI will ˏcome.
9 ˋMary came in ˏtime.
10 The ˋcar is ˏgood.

B Recognition

I Listen to the teacher's pronunciation of the sentences in the following exercises and mark the accent and intonation:

(a)

1 John wanted to take it away.
2 He's not happy with him.
3 He's not been coming for many days.
4 I'm sorry I can't come.
5 I'll come as soon as I can.
6 What do you want me to do?
7 Which one?
8 How are you?
9 Who are you going with?
10 Why didn't you come to meet me at the station?

(b)

1 Have they come back?
2 Does it work?
3 You've not been invited?
4 Will you be writing to me about it?
5 Was it your birthday yesterday?
6 You don't like tea in bed?
7 Have you met my father before?
8 Must you insist on an apology from him?
9 What's the time? (polite enquiry)
10 Come over here. (pleasant invitation)
11 Good morning. (friendly greeting)
12 Go and open the window. (request)

II The following sentences will be read with a falling tone, rising tone, falling-rising tone, or rising-falling tone. Listen to them carefully, divide them into tone groups, where necessary, and mark the accent and intonation.

1 No.
2 I've been waiting.
3 Do sit down.
4 Mind how you deal with him.
5 Yes, of course.
6 I'll write to him today, if there's time.
7 That's not the right thing, as far as I know.
8 They haven't done anything, as a matter of fact.
9 Yes.
10 It was terrible.
11 You can be sure?
12 Oh, indeed.
13 Good morning.
14 No, it wasn't.
15 He's a nice man, isn't he?

C Production

I Mark the accent and intonation in the following sentences and practise saying them:

1 Have you decided to accept the post?
2 Is smoking prohibited here?
3 I've never been to Delhi.
4 What have you been doing the whole day?
5 Do you believe he was responsible for it?
6 He can't afford to offend him.
7 I don't think you'll understand my point.
8 It's time we went to bed.
9 He hasn't yet given a satisfactory explanation.
10 Where did you say you were going to stay?
11 I'm sorry I can't quite make out what you're saying.
12 Have they all decided to participate in the seminar?
13 Will you come over for a cup of tea?
14 Which is the platform for the nine o'clock train?
15 It was kind of you to have come.

II Divide the following sentences into tone groups and mark the accent and intonation in each group and practise saying them:

1 He went to the post-office and sent a money order.
2 It's a film for children only, not suitable for adults.
3 First turn right, then left, and then again right.
4 As long as he is here, he will continue to help us.
5 You must be quick if you want to get your shopping done in time.
6 Whenever he has a headache, he takes a cup of strong tea.
7 You'll get late if you can't hurry up.
8 I'll be ready in a minute, if you'll wait.
9 She looks after her husband well, of course.
10 After we've had our lunch, we can sit in the drawing-room and play cards.

III Prepare the following passages for reading by marking tone group boundaries, and the accent and intonation:

(1) He was a difficult child indeed. What had his parents not done to correct him! But the result was anything but satisfactory. He was disobedient and rude, and sometimes even violent. At home he was a terror to his younger brother and sister, who often complained of his cruelty. At school he was a bully of the worst kind. His classmates and his juniors were mortally afraid of him, and his teachers, one and all, complained of his rudeness and even arrogance. The Headmaster, finding himself under great pressure from both his students and colleagues, bundled him out one day, leaving his parents alone to bear the brunt of his madness.

(2)

Tom Well that, honestly, that was a marvellous meal.

Mary	Oh I'm glad you enjoyed it. It was really nice having you over.
Tom	Well I enjoyed it as well.
Mary	How about some more tea?
Tom	Er, yes I'd love some.
Mary	Right, I'll just get some for you.
Tom	No, let me get it for you.
Mary	Oh no, don't bother, I can do it myself.
Tom	Right, OK. Would you mind very much if I smoked?
Mary	Not at all. Where's the ashtray?
Tom	Oh it's over there. I can get it for you.
Mary	Right, OK.
Tom	Do you know I didn't realize you were such a good cook?
Mary	Oh.
Tom	You, you never told me this.
Mary	Well, I just had a few evening classes, that's all.
Tom	But you're a real good cook.
Mary	Thank you . . . . Oh look, would you mind very much if I went out for a few minutes just to make a phone call, it's rather important.
Tom	Yes, you go ahead.
Mary	Thanks, thanks a lot.

16
Conversational Passages for Practice

In Chapter 5, we discussed the use of phonetic transcription and listed a fairly large number of phonetic symbols, and signs and diacritics, which are used in this book. In this chapter, we give a few conversational passages in phonemic transcription. As their primary aim is to give the student some practice in pronunciation, accent and intonation are also marked in them. The passages in ordinary spelling are also given alongside, so that the student may easily refer the transcribed texts back to them, when necessary. The symbols used in these transcriptions, as also throughout the rest of the book, are those of Daniel Jones's *English Pronouncing Dictionary* (14th and 15th editions), which are identical with those of A.S. Hornby's *Oxford Advanced Learner's Dictionary of Current English* (3rd and later editions) and of *Longman Dictionary of Contemporary English* (1986). And while the single oblique bar [/] marks the tone group boundary, the double oblique bar [//] marks the end of the sentence.

Text 1

Mother	Reena, you must have a bath.
Reena	No, I don't need one, mother. I'm not dirty.
Mother	Yes, you are. Look at your arms and legs. They're filthy!
Reena	I ought not to have a bath, mother. I have a bad cold.
Mother	No, you haven't. Don't try to play tricks on me. Go on, have a bath. The water is hot. And wash all your dirty handkerchiefs.
Reena	Can't we give them to a washerman? Did you have to wash your handkerchiefs when you were a girl, mother?
Mother	I had to wash all my clothes. We were poor.
Reena	All right, mother, I'll wash them. But must I go to school today? I can really feel a cold coming on.
Mother	You needn't stay at school the whole day. Come home at lunch time.

Text 2

Neera	Where's the sugar, father?
Father	Sugar? What are you talking about?
Neera	The sugar I sent you the money for?
Father	The money? When did you send me the money?
Neera	Half an hour ago, through the boy you sent here. I gave him a bag, too.
Father	But I didn't send any boy to you.
Neera	What! I gave the money and the bag to a boy—he said you had sent him.
Father	We've been tricked! What did the fellow look like?
Neera	He looked honest enough. I wouldn't have given the money to anyone who looked sly or dirty. And besides, he gave me a slip of paper with our address on it!
Father	He gave us the slip all right.

Text 3

Alick	What's that you're saying, David?
David	The thing I'm speaking about is Love.
James	Do you stand there and say you're in love, David Wylie?
David	Me; what would I do with the thing?
James	I see no necessity for calling it a thing.
David	Oho, has she got you, James?
James	Nobody has got me.
David	They'll catch you yet, lad.
James	They'll never catch me. You've been nearer catched yourself.
Alick	Yes, Kitty Menzies, David.
David	It was a kind of a shave that.

Text 1

Mother	ˇri:nə/jʊ məs 'hæv ə `bɑ:θ//
Reena	`nəʊ/aɪ 'dəʊnt `ni:d wʌn ˌmʌðə//aɪm 'nɒt `dɜ:tɪ//
Mother	'jes jʊ `ɑ://'lʊk ət jɔ:r 'ɑ:mz ən `legz//ðeə `fɪlθɪ//
Reena	aɪ ɔ:t `nɒt tə ˌhæv ə ˌbɑ:θ ˌmʌðə//aɪ hæv ə 'bæd `kəʊld//
Mother	`nəʊ/jʊ `hævnt//'dəʊnt traɪ tə 'pleɪ `trɪks ɒn mɪ//'gəʊ `ɒn/ˆhæv ə ˌbɑ:θ//ðə 'wɔ:təz `hɒt//ən 'wɒʃ 'ɔ:l jɔ: 'dɜ:tɪ `hæŋkətʃɪfs//
Reena	'kɑ:nt wɪ 'gɪv ðəm tʊ ə ˏwɒʃəmən//dɪd ˏju: ˌhæv tə ˌwɒʃ jɔ: ˌhæŋkətʃɪfs/wen jʊ wər ə ˏgɜ:l ˌmʌðə//
Mother	aɪ 'hæd tə 'wɒʃ `ɔ:l maɪ ˏkləʊðz//wɪ wə `pʊə//
Reena	'ɔ:l ˏraɪt ˌmʌðə/aɪl `wɒʃ ðəm//bət 'mʌst aɪ 'gəʊ tə `sku:l təˏdeɪ//aɪ kən 'rɪəlɪ 'fɪ:l ə 'kəʊld kʌmɪŋ `ɒn//
Mother	jʊ 'ni:dnt `steɪ ət ˌsku:l ðə ˌhəʊl ˏdeɪ//kʌm 'həʊm ət 'lʌntʃ `taɪm//

Text 2

Neera	'wɛəz ðə `ʃʊgə ˌfɑ:ðə//
Father	ˏʃʊgə//'wɒt ə jʊ `tɔ:kɪŋ əˌbaʊt//
Neera	ðə 'ʃʊgər aɪ 'sent jʊ ðə `mʌnɪ fɔ://
Father	ðəˏmʌnɪ//ˆwen dɪd jʊ ˌsend mɪ ðə ˌmʌnɪ//
Neera	'hɑ:f ən 'aʊər əˏgəʊ/θru: ðə `bɔɪ jʊ ˌsent ˌhɪə//aɪ 'geɪv ɪm ə `bæg ˌtu://
Father	bət aɪ `dɪdnt send ˏenɪ ˌbɔɪ tə jʊ//
Neera	`wɒt/aɪ 'geɪv ðə'mʌnɪ ən ðə 'bæg tʊ ə `bɔɪ/hɪ 'sed `ju:d ˌsent ɪm//
Father	wi:v bɪn `trɪkt//'wɒt dɪd ðə 'feləʊ `lʊk laɪk//
Neera	hɪ 'lʊkt `ɒnɪst ɪˏnʌf//aɪ 'wʊdnt əv 'gɪvn ðə 'mʌnɪ tʊ ˇenɪwʌn/hʊ 'lʊkt `slaɪ ɔ: ˏdɜ:tɪ//ən bɪˇsaɪdz/hɪ 'geɪv mɪ ə 'slɪp əv 'peɪpə wɪð aʊər ə`dres ɒn ɪt//
Father	hɪ 'geɪv əs ðə `slɪp ɔ:l ˏraɪt//

Text 3

Alick	'wɒts 'ðæt jʊə ˇseɪɪŋ ˌdeɪvɪd//
David	ðə 'θɪŋ aɪm 'spi:kɪŋ əbaʊt ɪz `lʌv//
James	'du: jʊ 'stænd ðeər ən 'seɪ jʊər ɪn ˏlʌv ˌdeɪvɪd ˌwɪlɪ//
David	ˏmi:/'wɒt əd aɪ `du: wɪð ðə ˌθɪŋ//
James	aɪ 'si: 'nəʊ nə'sesɪtɪ fə 'kɔ:lɪŋ ɪt ə ˇθɪŋ//
David	əʊˆhəʊ/həz ʃɪ ˏgɒt jʊ ˌdʒeɪmz//
James	'nəʊbədɪ z ˇgɒt mɪ//
David	ðeɪl 'kætʃ jʊ `jet ˌlæd//
James	ðeɪl `nevə ˌkætʃ mɪ//ˆju:v bɪn ˌnɪərə ˌkætʃt jɔ: ˏself//
Alick	`jes/'kɪtɪ `menzɪz ˌdeɪvɪd//
David	ɪt wəz ə 'kaɪnd əv ə `ʃeɪv ˌðæt//

Alick	It's a curious thing, but a man cannot help winking when he hears that one of his friends has been catched.
David	That's so.

Text 4

Trotter	What a lovely smell of bacon!
Mason	Yes, sir. I reckon there's enough smell of bacon in here to last for dinner.
Trotter	Well, there's nothing like a good fat bacon rasher when you're as empty as I am.
Mason	I'm glad you like it fat, sir.
Trotter	Well, I like a bit o'lean, too.
Mason	There *was* a bit of lean in the middle of yours, sir, but it's kind of shrunk up in the cooking.
Trotter	Bad cooking, that's all. Any porridge?
Mason	Oh, yes, sir. There's porridge.
Trotter	Lumpy, I suppose?
Mason	Yes, sir. Quite nice and lumpy.
Trotter	Well, take the lumps out o'mine.
Mason	And just bring you the gravy, sir? Very good, sir.

Text 5

Chambers	Hm--yes. It's this increasingly low vitality of yours that worries me. No life in you—none... .
Elizabeth	Well, Doctor, if you shut a person up in one room for years on end, you can't very well expect to find her bursting with life and vigour! Why not prescribe something really exciting, for a change.?
Chambers	Exciting, eh?
Elizabeth	A gallop three times round the park every morning—a course of calisthenics—a long sea voyage...
Chambers	How I wish I could, my dear!
Elizabeth	It's funny to think of it now—but you know, Doctor, as a child I was a regular tomboy!
Chambers	Yes, I've heard all about that—and, mentally, you're a tomboy still! To tell you the truth, Miss Elizabeth, I'm always hearing it from your brothers and sister... .
Elizabeth	Oh, please...

Text 6

Mary	And what do you say this novel is called?
John	*The Sleeping Dog.*
Mary	*The Sleeping Dog.* I must remember that. When will you publish it?

Alick	ɪts ə `kjʊərɪəs ˌθɪŋ/bət ə 'mæn 'kænət help ˇwɪŋkɪŋ/wen ɪ 'hɪəz ðət 'wʌn əv ɪz `frendz əz bɪn ˌkætʃt//
David	'ðæts ˏsəʊ//

Text 4

Trotter	'wɒt ə 'lʌvlɪ 'smel əv `beɪkən//
Mason	`jes ˌsɜ://aɪ 'rekən ðəz ɪ'nʌf 'smel əv 'beɪkən ˏɪn hɪə/tə 'lɑ:st fə `dɪnə//
Trotter	ˇwel/ðəz 'nʌθɪŋ laɪk ə 'gʊd 'fæt 'beɪkən ˏræʃə/wen jʊər əz 'emptɪ əz `aɪ æm//
Mason	aɪm 'glæd jʊ 'laɪk ɪt `fæt ˌsɜ://
Trotter	`wel/aɪ 'laɪk ə bɪt ə `lɪ:n ˏtu://
Mason	ðə`wɒz ə bɪt əv 'lɪ:n ɪn ðə ˏmɪdl əv jɔ:z sɜ:/bət ə 'kaɪnd əv 'ʃrʌŋk 'ʌp ɪn ðə `kʊkɪŋ//
Trotter	`bæd ˌkʊkɪŋ/'ðæts `ɔ:l//'enɪ ˏpɒrɪdʒ//
Mason	əʊ `jes ˌsɜ://`ðeəz ˌpɒrɪdʒ//
Trotter	`lʌmpɪ/aɪ səˏpəʊz//
Mason	`jes ˌsɜ://'kwaɪt `naɪs ən ˏlʌmpɪ//
Trotter	`wel/'teɪk ðə 'lʌmps aʊt ə `maɪn//
Mason	ən 'dʒʌst brɪŋ jʊ ðə ˏgreɪvɪ ˌsɜ://'verɪ `gʊd ˌsɜ://

Text 5

Chambers	'hm... `jes//ɪts ðɪs ɪn'kri:sɪŋlɪ 'ləʊ vaɪ`tælɪtɪ əv jɔ:z/ðət `wʌrɪz mɪ//'nəʊ `laɪf ɪn jʊ/`nʌn...//
Elizabeth	`wel ˌdɒktə/ɪf jʊ 'ʃʌt ə pɜ:sn 'ʌp ɪn 'wʌn ˏru:m/fə 'jɜ:z ɒn ˏend/jʊ 'kɑ:nt 'verɪ 'wel ɪksˏpekt/tə 'faɪnd ə `bɜ:stɪŋ wɪð ˌlaɪf ən ˏvɪgə//waɪ 'nɒt prɪs'kraɪb sʌmθɪŋ 'rɪəlɪ ɪk`saɪtɪŋ/fər ə ˏtʃeɪndʒ//
Chambers	ɪkˏsaɪtɪŋ/ˏeɪ//
Elizabeth	ə 'gæləp 'θri: 'taɪmz raʊnd ðə 'pɑ:k 'evrɪ ˏmɔ:nɪŋ/ə 'kɔ:s əv kælɪsˏθenɪks/ə'lɒŋ si: ˏvɔɪɪdʒ...//
Chambers	'haʊ aɪ 'wɪʃ aɪ `kʊd maɪ ˌdɪə//
Elizabeth	ɪts `fʌnɪ tə ˌθɪŋk əv ɪt ˏnaʊ/bət jʊ ˏnəʊ ˌdɒktə/'æz ə ˏtʃaɪld/aɪ wəz ə 'regjʊlə `tɒmbɔɪ//
Chambers	`jes/aɪv 'hɜ:d 'ɔ:l əbaʊt `ðæt/ən ˇmentəlɪ/jʊər ə 'tɒmbɔɪ `stɪl//tə 'tel jʊ ðə ˏtru:θ mɪs ɪˌlɪzəbəθ/aɪm 'ɔ:lwɪz 'hɪərɪŋ ɪt frəm jɔ: 'brʌðəz ən `sɪstəz//
Elizabeth	'əʊ ˏpli:z...//

Text 6

Mary	ən 'wɒt də jʊ 'seɪ ðɪs 'nɒvəlz `kɔ:ld//
John	ðə 'sli:pɪŋ `dɒg//
Mary	ðə 'sli:pɪŋ ˏdɒg//aɪ məs rɪ`membə ˌðæt//'wenl jʊ `pʌblɪʃ ɪt//

John	We'll send you a copy. If you're here when it comes out, I'll give you a ring about it.
Mary	Oh, of course you're in the city office now.
John	Yes, I am. Though I still come up here as often as I can.
Mary	You know you people make such an intimate little group that you confuse me. I can't make out who's here and who's in the city office.
Freda	It's very simple. It's so arranged now that the married ones—my brother Gordon and Betty and Robert and I are here—and the single ones, John and Stanton, are in the city office.
John	And come back here every time there's the smallest excuse. Only I haven't the luck to have as many excuses as Charles Stanton has. But I do my best.
Mary	I'm sure you do. So would I.

Text 7

Dulcimer	Trump!
Trump	Yes, sir!
Dulcimer	The rooms look very naked!
Trump	I didn't get any fresh flowers, sir.
Dulcimer	And why didn't you get any fresh flowers?
Trump	You haven't used the ones from Silver Gates, sir. The gardener sent them up this morning.
Dulcimer	Why didn't you tell me sooner? I'm terribly overdressed for doing flowers.
Trump	Shall I get you an apron, sir?
Dulcimer	No. I don't think I'll have an apron.
Trump	Could you trust me to arrange them?
Dulcimer	What flowers has Paget sent?
Trump	Tulips, sir! ... And irises and a rose or two.
Dulcimer	I don't think I could trust you with a tulip.
Trump	Perhaps not, sir.
Dulcimer	I'll do them. Get me that little table and my gloves.
Trump	Very good, sir.

Text 8

Crespin	Does your Highness speak English?
Raja	Oh, yes a little. (As a matter of fact he speaks it irreproachably.)
Crespin	Then I have to apologize for our landing uninvited in your territory.
Raja	Uninvited, but, I assure you, not unwelcome.
Crespin	We are given to understand that this is the State of Hoon.
Raja	The Kingdom of Hoon, Major—if I rightly read the symbols on your cuff.

John	wi:l 'send jʊ ə `kɒpɪ//ɪf jʊə 'hɪə wen ɪt 'kʌmz ˏaʊt/aɪl 'gɪv jʊ ə `rɪŋ əˌbaʊt ɪt//
Mary	`əʊ/əv 'kɔ:s jʊər ɪn ðə ˏsɪtɪ ˌɒfɪs ˌnaʊ//
John	'jes aɪ`æm//'ðəʊ aɪ 'stɪl kʌm 'ʌp ˏhɪə/ əz 'ɒfn əz aɪ `kæn//
Mary	jʊ ˏnəʊ/jʊ 'pi:pl meɪk 'sʌtʃ ən 'ɪntɪmət 'lɪtl ˏgru:p/ðət jʊ kən`fju:z mɪ//aɪ 'kɑ:nt meɪk 'aʊt `hu:z ˏhɪər/ən 'hu:z ɪn ðə `sɪtɪ ˌɒfɪs//
Freda	ɪts 'verɪ `sɪmpl/ɪts 'səʊ əˏreɪndʒd ˌnaʊ/ðət ðəˏmærɪd wʌnz/maɪ 'brʌðə ˏgɔ:dn/ən ˏbetɪ/ən 'rɒbət ənd ˏaɪ/ə ˏhɪə/ən ðə ˏsɪŋgl wʌnz/'dʒɒn ən ˏstæntən/ər ɪn ðə `sɪtɪ ˌɒfɪs//
John	ən 'kʌm ˏbæk ˌhɪə/'evrɪ 'taɪm ðəz ðə 'smɔ:lɪst ɪk`skju:s//'əʊnlɪ aɪ 'hævnt ðə 'lʌk tə 'hæv əz ˏmenɪ ɪkˌskju:sɪz/əz 'tʃɑ:lz `stæntən ˌhæz//bət aɪ 'du: maɪ `best//
Mary	aɪm `ʃʊə jʊ ˌdu://'səʊ wəd `aɪ//

Text 7

Dulcimer	ˇtrʌmp//
Trump	`jes ˌsɜ://
Dulcimer	ðə 'ru:mz lʊk 'verɪ `neɪkɪd//
Trump	aɪ 'dɪdnt get 'enɪ 'freʃ `flaʊəz ˏsɜ://
Dulcimer	ən ˏwaɪ ˌdɪdnt jʊ ˌget ˌenɪ ˌfreʃ ˌflaʊəz//
Trump	jʊ `hævnt ˌju:zd ðə wʌnz frəm ˌsɪlvə ˏgeɪts ˌsɜ:// ðə 'gɑ:dnə 'sent ðəm 'ʌp 'ðɪs `mɔ:nɪŋ//
Dulcimer	'waɪ 'dɪdnt jʊ 'tel mɪ `su:nə//aɪm 'terəblɪ ˏəʊvədrest/fə 'du:ɪŋ ˇflaʊəz //
Trump	'ʃæl aɪ 'get jʊ ən ˏeɪprən ˌsɜ://
Dulcimer	`nəʊ//aɪ 'dəʊnt θɪŋk aɪl 'hæv ən `eɪprən
Trump	'kʊd jʊ 'trʌst mɪ tʊ əˏreɪndʒ ðəm//
Dulcimer	`wɒt ˌflaʊəz əz ˌpædʒɪt ˌsent//
Trump	`tju:lɪps ˌsɜ://ənd ˏaɪərɪsɪz/ənd ə 'rəʊz ə `tu://
Dulcimer	aɪ 'dəʊnt θɪŋk aɪ kəd 'trʌst jʊ wɪð ə ˇtju:lɪp//
Trump	pə'hæps `nɒt ˌsɜ://
Dulcimer	`aɪl ˌdu: ðəm//'get mɪ 'ðæt 'lɪtl ˏteɪbl/ən maɪ `glʌvz//
Trump	'verɪ `gʊd ˌsɜ://

Text 8

Crespin	'dʌz jɔ: 'haɪnɪs 'spi:k ˏɪŋglɪʃ//
Raja	əʊ `jes/ə `lɪtl//
Crespin	'ðen aɪ hæv tʊ əˌpɒlədʒaɪz/ fər aʊə 'lændɪŋ ʌnɪn'vaɪtɪd ɪn jɔ: `terɪtrɪ//
Raja	ʌnɪn ˇvaɪtɪd/bət aɪ ə'ʃʊə jʊ 'nɒt ʌn`welkəm//
Crespin	wɪ ə 'gɪvn tʊ ʌndəˏstænd/ðət 'ðɪs ɪz ðə 'steɪt əv `hu:n//
Raja	ðə kɪŋdəm əv 'hu:n 'meɪdʒə/ɪf aɪ 'raɪtlɪ 'rɪ:d ðə 'sɪmblz ɒn jɔ: ˏkʌf//

Crespin	Major Crespin. Permit me to introduce my wife—
Raja	I am delighted, Madam, to welcome you to my secluded dominions. You are the first lady of your nation I have had the honour of receiving.
Lucilla	Your Highness is very kind.
Crespin	And this is Dr. Basil Traherne, whose aeroplane—or what is left of it—you see.
Raja	Doctor Traherne? The Doctor Traherne whose name I have so often seen in the newspapers?
Traherne	The newspapers make too much of my work. It is very incomplete.
Raja	But you are an aviator as well?
Traherne	Only as an amateur.
Raja	I presume it is some misadventure that has carried you so far into the wilds of the Himalayas?
Traherne	Yes—we got lost in the clouds... .

Text 9

Mrs. Honey	Do permit me to look at your work one moment, my dear Rose.
Rose	With pleasure, Mrs. Honey.
Mrs. Honey	Very pretty indeed. Nothing could be in better taste than these Berlin wool patterns.
Rose	I got the design from the *Englishwoman's Domestic Magazine*. It's to be one of three cushions for father's study.
Mrs. Honey	I had an idea of doing the same sort of thing for my husband, after we moved into the new house here, three years ago. But then, when he died, I hadn't the heart to go on. So I'm crocheting lace now, instead, for Gertrude's trousseau. Will you have some more coffee?
Rose	No, thank you.
Mrs. Honey	Just a drop. Gertrude, pour out—Now where has Gertrude disappeared to?
Rose	She left the room some moments ago.
Mrs. Honey	Even between dinner and coffee she must be off.
Rose	But why?
Mrs. Honey	Do I know, my dear? Just managing the house and managing it, and managing it. Upon my word, Gertrude performs the duties of the place as if it were the foundry and she were John. My son and daughter are so alike.
Rose (enthusiastically)	One's as splendid as the other.

Text 10

Arnold	My dear, I've been hunting for you everywhere. What *have* you been doing?

Crespin	'meɪdʒə `krespɪn//pə'mɪt mɪ tʊ ɪntrə'dju:s maɪ 'waɪf ——/
Raja	aɪm dɪˏlaɪtɪd ˌmædəm/tə 'welkəm jʊ tə maɪ sɪ'klu:dɪd də`mɪnɪənz//jʊ ə ðə 'fɜ:st 'leɪdɪ əv jɔ: ˏneɪʃn/aɪv 'hæd ðɪ 'ɒnər əv rɪ`sɪ:vɪŋ//
Lucila	jɔ: 'haɪnɪs ɪz 'verɪ `kaɪnd//
Crespin	ən 'ðɪs ɪz dɒktə 'bæzɪl trəˏhɜ:n/hu:z ˏeərəpleɪn/ɔ: 'wɒts ˏleft əv ɪt/jʊ `si://
Raja	'dɒktə trəˏhɜ:n/ ðə 'dɒktə trəˏhɜ:n/hu:z 'neɪm aɪv səʊ 'ɒfn 'si:n ɪn ðə ˏnju:speɪpəz//
Traherne	ðə `nju:speɪpəz ˌmeɪk tu: ˏmʌtʃ əv maɪ ˌwɜ:k//ɪts 'verɪ ɪnkəmp`li:t//
Raja	bət jʊər ən ˏeɪvɪeɪtər əz ˌwel//
Traherne	'əʊnlɪ əz ən ˇæmətə//
Raja	aɪ prɪˏzju:m/ɪts sʌm mɪsədˏventʃə/ðəts 'kærɪd jʊ 'səʊ ˏfɑ:/ɪntə ðə 'waɪldz əv ðə hɪməˏleɪəz . . . /
Traherne	`jes/wɪ gɒt 'lɒst ɪn ðə ˏklaʊdz . . . /

Text 9

Mrs. Honey	'du: pəˏmɪt mɪ/tə 'lʊk ət jɔ: 'wɜ:k wʌn ˏməʊmənt maɪ ˌdɪə ˌrəʊz//
Rose	wɪð `pleʒə mɪsɪz ˌhʌnɪ//
Mrs. Honey	'verɪ `prɪtɪ ɪnˌdi:d// 'nʌθɪŋ kəd bɪ ɪn 'betə ˏteɪst/ðən 'ði:z bɜ:'lɪn wʊl `pætənz//
Rose	aɪ 'gɒt ðə dɪˏzaɪn/frəm ðɪ 'ɪŋglɪʃwʊmənz də'mestɪk mægə`zi:n//ɪts tə bɪ 'wʌn əv 'θri: ˏkʊʃnz/fə 'fɑ:ðəz `stʌdɪ//
Mrs. Honey	aɪ 'hæd ən aɪˏdɪə/əv 'du:ɪŋ ðə 'seɪm sɔ:t əv 'θɪŋ fə maɪ ˏhʌzbənd/ aftə wɪ ˏmu:vd ɪntə ðə ˌnju: ˌhaʊs hɪə/'θri: 'jɜ:z ə`gəʊ//bət ˏðen/wen ɪ ˏdaɪd/aɪ 'hædnt ðə 'hɑ:t tə 'gəʊ `ɒn//'səʊ aɪm 'krəʊʃeɪɪŋ ˏleɪs ˌnaʊ ɪnˌsted/fə 'gɜ:tru:dz `tru:səʊ//'wɪl jʊ 'hæv səm 'mɔ: ˏkɑfɪ//
Rose	'nəʊ `θæŋk jʊ//
Mrs. Honey	'dʒʌst ə ˏdrɒp/ ˇgɜ:tru:d/'pɔ:r `aʊt/ 'naʊ 'weəz gɜ:tru:d dɪsə`pɪəd tu://
Rose	ʃɪ 'left ðə 'ru:m 'sʌm `məʊmənts əˏgəʊ//
Mrs. Honey	'i:vn bɪtwi:n 'dɪnər ən ˏkɒfɪ/ʃɪ mʌst bɪ `ɒf//
Rose	bət `waɪ//
Mrs. Honey	'du: aɪ ˏnəʊ maɪ ˌdɪə//'dʒʌst `mænɪdʒɪŋ ðə ˌhaʊs/ən `mænɪdʒɪŋ ɪt/ən `mænɪdʒɪŋ ɪt//ə'pɒn maɪ ˏwɜ:d/'gɜ:tru:d pə'fɔ:mz ðə dju:tɪz əv ðə ˌpleɪs/əz ɪf `ɪt wə ðə ˏfaʊndrɪ/ən ˏʃɪ/wə `dʒɒn//maɪ 'sʌn ən 'dɔ:tər ə 'səʊ ə`laɪk//
Rose	'wʌnz əz `splendɪd əz ðɪ ˌʌðə//

Text 10

Arnold	maɪ ˇdɪə/aɪv bɪn 'hʌntɪŋ fə jʊ `evrɪweə//wɒt 'hæv jʊ bɪn `du:ɪŋ//

Elizabeth	Nothing! I've been standing on my head.
Arnold	My father's here.
Elizabeth (startled)	Where?
Arnold	At the cottage. He arrived last night.
Elizabeth	Damn!
Arnold (good-humouredly)	I wish you wouldn't say that, Elizabeth.
Elizabeth	If you're not going to say "Damn" when a thing is damnable, when are you going to say "Damn"?
Arnold	I should have thought you could say, "Oh, bother!" or something like that.
Elizabeth	But that wouldn't express my sentiments. Besides, at that speech day when you were giving away the prizes, you said there were no synonyms in the English language.
Ana (smiling)	Oh, Elizabeth! It's very unfair to expect a politician to live in private up to the statements he makes in public.
Arnold	I'm always willing to stand by anything I've said. There *are* no synonyms in the English language.
Elizabeth	In that case I shall be regretfully forced to continue to say "Damn" whenever I feel like it.

Text 11

Edith	It's too big, the Atlantic, isn't it?
Edward	Far too big.
Edith	And too deep.
Edward	Much, much too deep.
Edith	I don't care a bit, do you?
Edward	Not a scrap.
Edith	Wouldn't it be awful if a magician came to us and said: "Unless you count accurately every single fish in the Atlantic you die tonight?"
Edward	We should die tonight.
Edith	How much would you mind—dying, I mean?
Edward	I don't know really—a good deal, I expect.
Edith	I don't believe I should mind so very much now. You see, we could never in our whole lives be happier than we are now, could we?
Edward	Darling, there *are* different sorts of happiness.
Edith	This is the best sort.
Edward (kissing her)	Sweetheart!
Edith	Don't darling, we don't want any more of the stewards to know we're on our honeymoon.
Edward	Why not? It gives them so much vicarious pleasure.

Elizabeth ˋnʌθɪŋ//aɪv bɪn 'stændɪŋ ɒn maɪ ˋhed//
Arnold maɪ 'fɑːðəz ˋhɪə//
Elizabeth ˋweə//
Arnold ət ðə ˋkɒtɪdʒ//hɪ ə'raɪvd 'lɑːst ˋnaɪt//
Elizabeth ˋdæm
Arnold aɪ 'wɪʃ jʊ 'wʊdnt seɪ ˇðæt ɪˌlɪzəbəθ//
Elizabeth ɪf jʊə 'nɒt gəʊɪŋ tə 'seɪ ˏdæm/wen ə θɪŋ ˋɪz ˏdæmnəbl/ˋwen ə jʊ ˌgəʊɪŋ tə ˌseɪ ˌdæm//
Arnold aɪ ʃəd əv 'θɔːt jʊ kəd ˏseɪ/'əʊ ˏbɒðə/ɔː ˋsʌmθɪŋ laɪk ˌðæt//
Elizabeth bət ˋðæt ˌwʊdnt ɪkˌspres maɪ ˏsentɪmənts//bɪˇsaɪdz/ət 'ðæt 'spiːtʃ ˏdeɪ/wen jʊ wə 'gɪvɪŋ ə'weɪ ðə ˏpraɪzɪz/jʊ 'sed ðə wə 'nəʊ ˋsɪnənɪmz ɪn ðɪ 'ɪŋglɪʃ ˏlæŋgwɪdʒ//
Ana 'əʊ ɪˋlɪzəbəθ/ɪts 'verɪ ʌn'feə tʊ ɪk'spekt ə pɒlɪˏtɪʃn/tə ˋlɪv ɪn ˏpraɪvɪt/'ʌptə ðə ˋsteɪtmənts hɪ ˌmeɪks ɪn ˏpʌblɪk//
Arnold aɪm 'ɔːlwɪz ˏwɪlɪŋ/tə 'stænd baɪ 'enɪθɪŋ aɪv ˋsed//ðər ˋɑː ˌnəʊ ˌsɪnənɪmz ɪn ðɪ ˌɪŋglɪʃ ˌlæŋgwɪdʒ//
Elizabeth ɪn ˋðæt ˏkeɪs/aɪ ʃəl bɪ rɪ'gretflɪ ˏfɔːst/tə kən'tɪnjuː tə 'seɪ ˏdæm/wen'evər aɪ ˋfɪːl laɪk ɪt//

Text 11

Edith ɪts 'tuː ˋbɪg/ðɪ ətˋlæntɪk/ˋɪznt ɪt//
Edward ˋfɑː ˌtuː ˌbɪg//
Edith ən 'tuː ˇdiːp//
Edward 'mʌtʃ ˋmʌtʃ ˌtuː ˏdiːp//
Edith aɪ 'dəʊnt keər ə ˋbɪt/də ˏjuː//
Edward 'nɒt ə ˋskræp//
Edith 'wʊdnt ɪt bɪ ˏɔːfl/ɪf ə mə'dʒɪʃn 'keɪm tʊ əs ən ˏsed/ən'les jʊ 'kaʊnt ˏækjʊrɪtlɪ//'evrɪ 'sɪŋgl 'fɪʃ ɪn ðɪ ətˏlæntɪk/jʊ ˋdaɪ təˌnaɪt//
Edward wɪ ˋʃʊd daɪ təˌnaɪt//
Edith haʊ 'mʌtʃ wəd jʊ ˋmaɪnd/ˋdaɪɪŋ aɪ ˏmiːn//
Edward aɪ 'dəʊnt ˋnəʊ ˌrɪəlɪ/ə 'gʊd ˋdɪːl/aɪ ɪkˏspekt//
Edith aɪ 'dəʊnt bɪˏlɪːv/aɪ ʃəd 'maɪnd 'səʊ verɪ ˋmʌtʃˏnaʊ//jʊ ˏsiː/wɪ kəd 'nevər ɪn aʊə 'həʊl 'laɪvz bɪ ˏhæpɪə/ðən wɪ ə ˋnaʊ/ˋkʊd wɪ//
Edward ˇdɑːlɪŋ/ðər ˋɑː ˌdɪfrənt ˌsɔːts əv ˏhæpɪnɪs/
Edith ˋðɪs ɪz ðə ˌbest ˌsɔːt//
Edward ˋswiːthɑːt//
Edith ˏdəʊnt ˌdɑːlɪŋ/wɪ 'dəʊnt wɒnt 'enɪ 'mɔːrəv ðə 'stjuːədz tə ˏnəʊ/wɪə ɒn aʊə ˋhʌnɪmuːn
Edward waɪ ˋnɑt/ɪt 'gɪvz ðəm səʊ 'mʌtʃ vaɪ'keərɪəs ˇpleʒə//

Edith	Are all honeymoons like this?
Edward (firmly)	Exactly
Edith	Oh, Edward—that's rather disheartening, isn't it? I do so want this to be unique.
Edward	It is, for us.

Edith	ər 'ɔːl 'hʌnɪmuːnz laɪk ˏðɪs//
Edward	ɪgˋzæktlɪ//
Edith	ˋəʊ ˌedwəd/'ðæts 'rɑːðə dɪsˋhɑːtnɪŋ/ˋɪznt ɪt//aɪ 'duː 'səʊ wɒnt 'ðɪs tə bɪ juː ˋnɪːk//
Edward	ɪt ˋɪz/fər ˏʌs//

Bibliography

The books intended for required reading are asterisked.

Abercrombie, David. "RP and local accent". *Studies in Phonetics and Linguistics*. Oxford: Oxford University Press, 1965.

*Abercrombie, David. *Elements of General Phonetics*. Edinburgh: Edinburgh University Press, 1967.

Adams, C. *English Speech Rhythm and Foreign Learner.* The Hague: Mouton, 1979.

Arnold, G.F. *Stress in English Words*. Amsterdam: North Holland, 1957.

Arnold, G.F. and A.C. Gimson. *English Pronunciation Practice*. London: University of London Press, 1967.

*Arnold, G.F. and Olive M. Tooley. *Say It with Rhythm*. Book 1. London: Longman, 1973.

Baker, A. *Introducing English Pronunciation*. Cambridge: Cambridge University Press, 1982.

*Balasubramanian, T. *A Textbook of English Phonetics for Indian Students*. New Delhi: Macmillan, 1981.

*Ball, W.J. *Steps to Fluency in Spoken English* (Pupils' Book). London: Longmans and Green and Co., 1968.

*Bansal, R.K. and J.B. Harrison. *Spoken English for India*. Madras: Orient Longman, 1983.

Borden, Gloria J. and Katherine S. Harris. *Speech Science Primer: Physiology, Acoustics and Perception of Speech*. London: Williams and Wilkins, 1980.

Brazil, D., M. Coulthard, and C. Johns. *Discourse Intonation and Language Teaching*. London: Longman, 1980.

Central Institute of English and Foreign Languages. *Exercises in Spoken English*. Parts I, II and III. Delhi: Oxford University Press, 1974.

*Christophersen, P. *An English Phonetics Course*. London: Longman, 1956.

Couper-Kuhlen, Elizabeth. *An Introduction to English Prosody.* London: Edward Arnold, 1986.

Crystal, D. and D. Davy. *Advanced Conversational English*. London: Longman, 1975.

Fudge, E C. (Ed.). *Phonology*. Harmondsworth: Penguin Books, 1973.

Fudge, E.C. *English Word Stress*. London: George Allen and Unwin, 1984.

Gimson, A.C. *A Practical Course in English Pronunciation.* London: Edward Arnold, 1975.

Gimson, A.C. and S.M. Ramsaran. *An English Pronunciation Companion.* Oxford: Oxford University Press, 1982.

*Gimson, A.C. *An Introduction to the Pronunciation of English.* 4th ed. London: Edward Arnold, 1989.

Gimson's Pronunciation of English. 5th ed. Revised by Allen Cruttenden. London: Edward Arnold, 1994.

Halliday, M.A.K. *A Course in Spoken English.* Oxford: Oxford University Press, 1966.

Hardcastle, William J. and John Laver (Eds.). *The Handbook of Phonetic Sciences.* Oxford: Blackwell, 1997.

Hill, L.A. *Drills and Tests in English Sounds.* London: Longman, 1961.

Hornby, A.S. *Oxford Advanced Learner's Dictionary of Current English.* 3rd ed. New Delhi: Oxford University Press, 1981.

Hornby, A.S. *Oxford Advanced Learner's Dictionary of Current English.* 5th ed. New Delhi: Oxford University Press, 1996.

Hughes, Arthur and Peter Trudgill. *English Accents and Dialects.* 2nd ed. London: Edward Arnold, 1987. (First published, 1979).

International Phonetic Association. *Principles of the International Phonetic Association.* Rev. ed. London: 1949.

Jones, Daniel. *The Pronunciation of English.* 8th ed. Cambridge: Cambridge University Press, 1956.

Jones, Daniel. *An Outline of English Phonetics.* 9th ed. Cambridge: Cambridge University Press, 1975.

Jones, Daniel. *English Pronouncing Dictionary.* 14th ed. Revised by A.C. Gimson. London: ELBS and Dent, 1984.

Jones, Daniel. *English Pronouncing Dictionary.* 15th ed. Peter Roach, et al. (Eds.). Cambridge: Cambridge University Press, 1997.

Jones, W.E. and John Laver (Eds.). *Phonetics in Linguistics.* London: Longman, 1973.

Kingdon, R. *English Intonation Practice.* London: Longman, 1958.

Kingdon, R. *The Groundwork of English Intonation.* London: Longman, 1958.

Kingdon, R. *The Groundwork of English Stress.* London: Longman, 1958.

Ladefoged, Peter. *A Course in Phonetics.* 2nd ed. New York: Harcourt Brace Jovanovich, 1982.

Laver, John. *Principles of Phonetics.* Cambridge: Cambridge University Press, 1994.

Mortimer, C. *Weak Forms.* Cambridge: Cambridge University Press, 1978.

Munro Mackenzie, M.D. *Modern English Pronunciation Practice*. London: Longman, 1978.

O'Connor, J.D. *Stress, Rhythm and Intonation*. New Delhi: Orient Longman, 1958.

O'Connor, J.D. *Phonetics*. Harmondsworth: Penguin Books, 1973.

*O'Connor, J.D. *Better English Pronunciation*. 3rd ed. Cambridge: Cambridge University Press, 1980.

O'Connor, J.D. and G.F. Arnold. *The Intonation of Colloquial English*. 2nd ed. London: Longman, 1973.

Pike, K.L. *Phonetics*. Michigan: University of Michigan Press, 1943.

Poldauf, Ivan. *English Word Stress—A Theory of Word Stress Patterns in English*. Oxford: Pergamon Press, 1984.

Pring, J.T. *Colloquial English Pronunciation*. London: Longman, 1959.

*Roach, Peter, *English Phonetics and Phonology*. Cambridge: Cambridge University Press, 1983.

*Sasikumar, V. and P.V. Dhamija. *Spoken English—A Self-learning Guide to Conversation Practice*. New Delhi: Tata McGraw-Hill, 1993.

*Sethi, J. and D.V. Jindal. *A Handbook of Pronunciation of English Words*. New Delhi: Prentice-Hall of India, 1993.

Stetson, R.H. *Motor Phonetics*. 2nd ed. Amsterdam: North Holland, 1951.

Tibbitts, E.L. *Practice Material for the English Sounds*. Cambridge: Heffer, 1963.

Wells, J.C. *Accents of English*. 3 Vols. Cambridge: Cambridge University Press, 1982.

Index